C. R. Webster's *From the Cradle to the Cyclone Fence* is a well written, frank, eye opener to the carnage wreaked by substance abuse in her family. If you have dealt first hand with drug or alcohol abuse in your family then *From the Cradle to the Cyclone Fence* will certainly strike a raw chord with you. If you haven't, it will make you kiss your family and thank the Good Lord for sparing you from this horrific war zone.

—R. Groves, stewardship team,
Independent Bible Church

C. R.'s compelling story leads you through years of the nightmare darkness that engulfs a family when fighting to save a child from his world of addiction. It is a heart wrenching story of a mother struggling desperately to hold onto her family, her faith, and her sanity. There is hope in God, the rock that holds in the midst of life's worse storms. *From the Cradle to the Cyclone Fence* is a must read for anyone who has been forced down this path.

—B. Evans, MITI leader for ten years,
member of Long View Baptist Church

What a captivating read. Every step of the way, I felt locked in on the emotions as they poured out of the heart and onto paper. As someone who has endured the same pains, the same lies and the same ugly deceits takes me back to the great healing power that just awaits those who are bound. How difficult it is to know the truth, to have experienced that truth, only to see loved ones ignore that truth. But, God is patient and his heart for Randy to break free from the hellish lifestyle that he has had and that many others experience is just a prayer away.

All along *From the Cradle to the Cyclone Fence* you'll experience a wide variety of truths as this story of a broken family treads ahead in life, searching for the many miracles that bring freedom. It's a quest

for answers that shows glimpses of hope, only to fall back away to greater spiraling depths. C. R. unpacks the truth in the end that hope lies within God alone when we reach the point of letting go.

I would invite you to read *From the Cradle to the Cyclone Fence,* see within which character you find yourself and prayerfully reach the ending conclusion—that we all need God and that he will patiently wait!

—D. Dent, pastor of recovery, Independent Bible Church

C. R. took me back through the hell I traveled with my daughter, as I also fought the demons of spiritual warfare. In my gut-wrenching screams to God, I finally realized that I was powerless and I had to let her go. The poem "Cradled" written by C. R. explains it best; she was just a gift to me and I had to give her back. I am blessed today that she is clean.

—C. Young, forensic nurse

FROM THE CRADLE TO THE CYCLONE FENCE

FROM THE CRADLE TO THE CYCLONE FENCE

C.R. WEBSTER

TATE PUBLISHING & Enterprises

Published by Tate Publishing & Enterprises, LLC
127 E. Trade Center Terrace | Mustang, Oklahoma 73064 USA
1.888.361.9473 | www.tatepublishing.com

Tate Publishing is committed to excellence in the publishing industry. The company reflects the philosophy established by the founders, based on Psalm 68:11,
"The Lord gave the word and great was the company of those who published it."

Book design copyright © 2009 by Tate Publishing, LLC. All rights reserved.
Cover design by Blake Brasor
Interior design by Lindsay B. Behrens

Published in the United States of America

ISBN: 978-1-61566-510-5
1. Biography & Autobiography / Personal Memoirs
2. Psychology / Psychopathology / Addiction
09.11.09

CRADLED

Finely crafted, predestined, meticulously designed
Toiled and labored from the touch of the Potter's hand.
A small treasure with no imperfection to her eye,
Cradled in her arms and sheltered from the shifting sand.
Entrusted in her care, the task of molding the clay,
Too soon the darkness loomed to threaten the binding tie.
A fingering crack in the clay, seen only by her.
To patch the flaw, too tiresome, the mending of a lie.
A raging storm cast shadows on the fading calm,
The sorrowing Potter had sent the gift as a loan.
The clay could not be mended; the hot sun's rays beat down.
No shade from the smoldering heat, her prayer a moan.
Still clinging to her possession, the time growing nigh,
The Potter would be returning, his gift to recall.
She knew the bloodless war, non-relenting, had won,
Reclaiming her gift, powerless to prevent the fall
Mending the crack, the Potter began his tedious work
Never to return, he slowly concealed the defect.
He cradled the gift gently under his loving wing.
On her knees, she saw him, and the work he did perfect.

By C. R. Webster

To the parents of:
Scott
Darren
Erin
and
Sam

There was an empty room in the house where a battle was lost in a bloodless war. There were memories burned in the minds of those who loved and lost. These memories would soothe the soul, lasting a lifetime. Memories cannot be taken away.

To my son Randy

Look for the narrow path, which is the way to life and peace; that path is the hardest to travel. Take someone with you to help. He will not forsake you. Do not forget that the man in this book no longer exists. There is a new man that has taken his place. As you travel on the narrow road, take with you the gifts that God gave you: wit, charm, intelligence and good looks. You will need them. Keep looking for the light.

ACKNOWLEDGMENTS

Thank you, Tate Publishing, for believing in my ability to write, but also for believing the message in this book will be a help to parents whose child is trapped in the world of substance abuse. The coming together of this book is a dream I have had all my life.

A special thanks to my mother and aunt, who always believed that I would eventually have a book published. I did it, Mov!

Thank you, Robin, for your encouragement and for holding me accountable to finish what I started, even when my computer woes were escalating.

Thank you, Tim, for taking the time to help me with my writing and for your patience with my computer illiteracy. You remain an inspiration to me, my constant one.

My dear family, a special thanks for allowing me to share our story with the public, by letting the secrets out of the house. We pray that this book will offer comfort to other families in knowing they are not alone.

Thank God, for helping me through this crisis with my sanity still intact, such as it is!

I want to thank "Brad" for teaching me all that strange computer stuff, like highlighting, drag, cut and paste, etc. I thank you for your patience.

The last special thank you is to "Randy," my other computer whiz, but an even bigger thank you for supplying me with the material for this book. Without you, there would have been nothing to write.

TABLE OF CONTENTS

FOREWORD

For those who have traveled the road of pain in parenting, such as the turmoil of a wayward child, the inner struggle with being a parent of a wayward child, the stress upon the marriage of a wayward child, and the effects of alcohol and drugs in the overall scheme of this path, you will find this book a blessing. You will see yourself at times, whether spoken or contemplated. You will see the torturous agony of souls misdirected. You will see the inner heart like few can express. You will see, graphically displayed, the child's own personal struggle to get free from the bondage of addiction. This book is real, but it ends with hope.

C. R. has allowed us into her life, her thoughts, her struggles, and her own personal hell. You will see firsthand that these issues are life and what life can sometimes throw at you. You will also see the author's personal quest for God as she attempts to discern his will in the midst of unspeakable pain. This book is the real deal.

They say that experience is the best teacher. I would say that wisdom gained through the experiences of others is the better teacher. Let this book teach you about life, pain, parenting, marriage, and God, and let their experiences be a help to you on your quest for God. If you can move more to the path of knowing God and growing to fall more in love with him on your journey and this book can be a help, then you have in your hands a treasure. Be sure to stay with it all the way to the end. You will laugh, cry, get angry, and maybe even disagree. But hopefully when you have finished, you will have become the better person because you have journeyed through life with C. R. May this family's pain and ordeal be a challenge to you to choose carefully and wisely and become a family united to combat the evils of the day. A house divided cannot stand. A house centered on Jesus Christ has great potential. Choose you this day who you will serve.

My challenge would be to read this book, and then read God's Word as he shares intimately his desire to have a personal relationship with you. May that also become a reality in your quest for God.

—Dr. H. Wallace Webster

There was a bloodless war, a secret war, in the house. There were invisible wounds inflicted by bullets of verbal combat. The battles were intense. There was an ambush on the family in the house as they were attacked with silent weapons by a dark world of deception and destruction. It was a spiritual war.

This book was written about that war, the one that everyone in the house tried to keep a secret. But the secret was much too massive to hide. The dark world of substance abuse exploded in the house, attacking just one member of the family while the others were sleeping, unprepared. But the others felt the shock with destruction leaving deep scars.

There was one that suffered the most, the one caught in the trap, the one in the spider's web. He was confused, being blinded by the lies in his own head. He was suspended between the good and bad worlds. He was captive in an ugly world that sought to destroy him.

What happened to him during this time? Did his responses to the curves in his life make him more vulnerable to seek refuge in all the wrong things? There were warning signs flashing all over my house. I missed them. Stay alert so that you won't make the same mistake.

Visiting your child behind the cyclone fence is easier than visiting him at the graveside and seeing the empty room that can never be filled. A child is safe behind the cyclone fence, the iron-gate with barbed wires. There they could think and come to themselves, as the prodigal son did. At least there was hope. Without hope, there is nothing.

As parents, our only hope is in the cross. There is hope and there is light. The burden I was carrying became heavy as I stumbled with my care to the cross. I couldn't hold him up much longer, but I couldn't seem to put him down. He couldn't walk alone. He had fallen and so had I. I was so close to the cross that I could feel the presence of something I had never seen. I had to believe that there was relief at the cross.

Then I saw it—the shadow of the cross surrounded by a bright light. I fell down to my knees as the strength left my body. I couldn't go on any farther. With tears in my eyes, I looked down at my broken son. I put him down because there was nothing else I could do for him. He had to finish the course without me. I had to leave him at the foot of the cross!

But I didn't leave him. I tried to, but I couldn't. I reached down and picked him up in my arms. I turned my back on the cross and headed home.

In order to protect my family, friends and those who shared their stories with me, I have changed the names, events, places, and characters out of respect for everyone's privacy. We are not in this war alone.

There were only two sounds in my home, the sporadic yelling and the deafening silence. I never knew which one I hated the most. Was it the ugly words of anger that had viciously attacked our souls, or was it the chilly silence in the air when no one was talking? But there was a war in my house. Someone would lose the battle when they gave up the fight. Someone had to lose. To the victor, what would remain? What would be left of the house? Who would be living in it?

Thump. Thump. Thump.

I heard the familiar thumping of the basketball outside on the concrete court, making soft echoing sounds as I watched my son's lonely game, or maybe I could hear my own heart beating from uncontrollable anxiety. There was stillness in the air, a false sense of calm that added a mystery to the storm that just left my living room.

As I glanced out of the window, I couldn't help noticing the leaves that were falling like snowflakes. The scene was breathtaking. At any other time, I would have been impressed, but not at that moment. My attention was on my son; my heart was heavy.

Where had the time gone? It seemed like yesterday when I cradled him, my first born, in my uncertain arms. I was so full of doubt when I gazed into his dark eyes. He looked at me. We were locked into one another's gaze. We were unaware of the adventure ahead of us that would someday, all too soon, erupt into an emotional roller coaster with heights and depths unperceivable.

I felt an ache in my heart as I watched his idle game. I wanted to be near him, to hold him, but I knew that he was too angry, and besides I could not deal with the probable rejection. He was trying to find his way in a difficult world where I had no place. I felt isolated from him, wanting to bridge the gap, yet not knowing where to begin.

I looked out at the sky for a fleeting moment, taking in the beauty of the fall day—no clouds, no wind, a still calm. It reminded me of a saying the waterman on the Eastern Shore had for moments when the Chesapeake Bay was perfectly still to the naked eye. They called it "slick cam," when you could see for miles and the water looked like glass.

There was no evidence of the storm in the house that left us both angry—a storm created by betrayal and lies.

Tears ran down my face as I recalled the angry words spoken. I had invaded his privacy, and he had lied. We were both guilty.

Now the storm had passed, leaving an eerie stillness in the house.

I saw him stop shooting the basketball and then turn to come inside. Hastily, I moved away from the window, pretending to be busy cleaning the magazine rack. I avoided eye contact, still anticipating the anger to be lingering in the air.

"Mom, do you wanna play a game of HORSE?" he had asked uncertainly as he stood in the doorway.

I looked at him, my handsome son. How typical of him, my child with a big heart. He was my impulsive one, who liked to live for the moment, worrying about the consequences later.

"Sure," I quickly answered. For this time that he had invited me into a small corner of his world, I would be thankful. I would go to his small world cherishing the moments. What did it matter if the exercise killed me? I would die smiling. He had asked because he was bored. I had consented because I just wanted to be near him.

The game was predictable, since he was an excellent basketball player, and me, well, I was just getting older. What did a forty-six-year-old mother and her teenage son have in common on a concrete court besides the same blood type?

I stood on the court looking at him. I must love him especially when he seemed to need it the least. I knew that he was still angry with me for eavesdropping on his phone conversations. I felt so guilty, yet I couldn't stop myself. I was afraid for him, didn't he see that? His choice of friends was not good. He always defended them, but I knew the truth because I had heard it on the phone.

I had gotten a warning a few months earlier that should have caused me to fear for Randy, but I had chosen to ignore it. One evening my husband, Jeff, told me Randy was "high." I got angry, very angry. I ought to know if my fourteen-year-old son was on drugs. I should have seen it first; after all, I looked all the time for just that one thing. It was a threat; it was powerful, and sadly, Jeff had been right. But I could overcome it if I had to. In the next months to follow, I had tried, but the battle was too big for me to handle alone. I didn't know it at the time, but the battle would rage for years.

I called the parents of the boys in the secretive circle. I stirred all sorts of hornet's nests. I got all kinds of comments, disturbing me greatly. Most of the parents just hung up on me. Only one mom actually listened. The others drilled me, wanting to know how I knew all the things that I shared with them, but I refused to confess that I had a tape recorder attached to the phones in my own home. I had heard it all. No one listened to me, except one mom. She was different than the others. Pat didn't need proof, not asking to hear the tapes.

I called at least five sets of parents telling them that our kids were smoking pot; their responses alarmed me. Here were a few:

"Boys will be boys."

"I smoked pot when I was their age."

"It could be worse."

"It's only pot."

I felt isolated and threatened. Hello people, these kids were only fourteen years old. This was serious stuff. Shouldn't we be doing something to keep our children away from the invasion of the dark world? What if they were doing other stuff like hanging, also called "Flatline," "Space Monkey," and "Suffocation Roulette?" This was mind altering as well, being a fun game at sleepovers for kids as young as age eight. The game was life-threatening!

I was on a crusade, but no one wanted to join my forces. If one woman could get prayer out of the public schools, surely a band of parents could achieve so much more. I needed allies. Together we could keep our children safe. We could call each other joining in the bloodless war, but no, they didn't want to know. They didn't want to hear it. Only one parent in the circle of friends knew about the dark world. Pat feared it, having bravely faced the battle alone. She was a single mom, but she did what she had to do.

I admired her strength. Pat called the police when her own son took her car without her permission. She watched as the police handcuffed him in her own home, taking him to the place beyond the cyclone fence.

"I hate you. I hate you!" were his words echoing from behind his closed bedroom door as the school bus passed our house without him. He had finished the eighth grade with summer at an end. His buddies were on the school bus heading to high school. He would not be joining them. The reality of being yanked out of public school was too much for him to bear. It was no longer an idle threat. It was another desperate effort of mine to keep him safe. He was so angry with me. He didn't understand.

His grades were dangerously slipping, and the principal had called several times. There were school fights, gangs, and things were just not right. I knew that something had to be done. I made the hard decision to take him out of his little world away from the distractions.

I said to myself, "Yes, I know you hate me. But that's okay; I don't even like me today. Someday you will understand. I hope it will be soon." My fragile relationship with Randy had taken a beating. We were both knocked down. There was damage, plenty of it, with words exchanged that I would take to my grave. Words cannot be taken back, not ever. They get loose in the mind, resurfacing whenever they want. They never leave the injured alone.

He allowed me three practice shots smiling at me when I missed all three. I smiled in return, nodding that I was ready—no conversation, just a game!

He threw the ball to me, allowing me to shoot first. I seized the opportunity to toss my favorite eight-foot shot, *swish.* Yeah, I still had some game. Now it was his turn. He did the same thing. It was an easy shot for him.

He knew that the farther away from the hoop he got, the better became his chances of winning. My days of launching a basketball half court were gone with the wind. I wondered how I ever managed to shoot so far away.

We were both concentrating on the game. No talking. No yelling. No anger. No chill, just peace and quiet on an outside basketball court.

He paused, looked at me, and grinned, probably because I was more competition than he expected me to be. When he smiled at me, I felt my heart soften as the anger was slowly beginning to fade.

I wanted to say that I was sorry, not for invading his privacy, because I did what I had to do, but for the angry words that lingered in the air like smoke swirling around in my mind until my temples ached. The harsh words left pain behind long after there was no sound. The guilt was tremendous for me. Why had I stooped to such trickery with the tape recorder? I knew that one day he would find out my secret, yet I was desperate enough to risk our relationship. I had tried to save him from his own self. I had failed miserably.

I feared that I had tipped his canoe, leaving him upside down to fight the strong current. I could not save him. How I had tried! He was struggling, but only he could pull himself out of the raging waters. He was too near the dark world. I was so afraid for him.

He was winning the game—H-O-R to my H. We had eye contact as we admired the skill of each other. I could feel him softening; perhaps he was sorry, or was that just my imagination? He probably thought I'd never find out, but there were harsh words that lingered in the air.

There was no anger now, just two people playing a game, a game that would soon reveal a winner.

I knew who the winner would be, but I had to give the game my best effort. I would have to hang in there trying hopelessly to win. I would stay on the court as long as he would have me there, precious moments lost in time.

There were so many things I wanted to say to him, but I was afraid to break the spell of temporary peace. Perhaps I had said too much already. There was nothing left to say. Time was on our side. One day, he would come to himself understanding how much I loved him. One day he would know that there were times a mother did what she had to do to protect her child from the dark world.

The trust was gone. Our relationship was struggling. I didn't know how to clear the air. I didn't know why his friends made me feel uneasy. It was just a mother's intuition, something I couldn't explain, but I had been right. He was making bad choices. The harder I tried to steer him in another direction, the harder he seemed to ignore my warnings. It made no sense to me.

I was tired of searching his room, tired of doubting him, tired of worrying about him. I was even more tired of finding things that caused more concern. He was certainly in trouble. Didn't he see that?

The game intensified with H-O-R-S on me. I only had H-O on him. Every shot counted now; I had to concentrate. I had to make the game last, for all too soon it would be over. The treasured time would be gone. There may not be another moment for a long time, maybe never again.

My shots soon became air balls. I knew that I was getting too old for the game of basketball, but I still gave my last effort as I lost the game. I was aching and sweaty. I tossed the ball to my son.

He smiled at me saying, "You're pretty good for a girl."

I returned his smile and said, "I've had my day. I was good, once."

He replied, "You're still good, Mom!"

We stood facing one another for a brief moment. I searched deep into his eyes, trying to look into his very soul as if I could find my little boy there. But he was not a little boy.

I wondered if he knew that I was sorry for my role in the betrayal. I didn't say anything. I didn't want to break the spell.

I turned, walking back into our home. The game was over, the special time to be close to my son had ended. The moment would be cherished, tucked away in my heart forever.

The house was quiet. I was just a worried mother, and he was a child who wanted to do his own thing. Tomorrow would be a new day. I had to prepare for the possibility that a huge storm could come back in my own home. The storm was a battle that was capable of exploding anytime. I had to be looking for the dark clouds. I had to be more alert to the warnings.

I felt so alone. The storms were already so mighty. Where was the shelter? I had to find the way to safety so I could carry Randy there!

THE DARK WORLD

The sun streamed through the many hazy windows, beckoning one's soul to search beyond the locked doors. The drapes were hanging at odd angles. The carpet smelled of being old and used. The chairs revealed their age, bearing tiny slits in the upholstery. Why should this have bothered me? This wasn't a five star hotel.

The large room, void of merriment or luxury, contained about sixteen nameless people from all walks of life. We were lacking a common bond, except one. We were a sad collection of young and old, black and white. We were strangers thrown together for the same reason. We all had a need to be in that room.

I brought some extra clothes and toiletries, leaving them at the front desk as they were carefully searched. I cringed at the very thought of such an invasion of privacy, as if I was being violated somehow. I watched in shock as the staff member tediously went through Randy's personal belongings, even looking in the inside lining of the baseball caps. What in the name of heaven did they expect to find there? For crying out loud, surely parents didn't try to smuggle drugs into a drug rehab? Wouldn't that be kind of pointless?

I could not see my son, Randy, until we attended the required meeting to inform us about the dark world of addictions. Hadn't I been living in the dark world already? What good would come of my being a part of that sad little group? Everyone was sad. It was so depressing. I knew that I must be dreaming. Soon, I would wake

up and get out of bed. I would just have to wait out the tormenting dream that just never seemed to end. What would be the point
of talking or hearing other sad stories? What difference did it made
anyway? It was just a dream.

I sat stiffly on the worn out chair staring straight ahead at the
speaker, a ghost of a man lacking in personality, but having a strong
message to send. He was there for a reason, to lecture on addiction
with it's devastation on the family. He was probably not as old as he
looked, but as he revealed his past with his addiction problems, it
was clear that he had been in a war, a war that he had created all by
himself. He had suffered losses; it was written all over his pale face.
There was sadness in his eyes.

We had all been bruised and battered by various addictions of
someone close to us. No one really understood the penetrating fingers
of addiction that were capable of tearing down the walls of an entire
house.

I didn't want to be in that room. I kept asking myself why I was
there. I felt as if I was attending a bad-parenting support group. We
would probably have to form small groups, socialize together, and
share how horrible our parenting skills had become.

I glanced curiously around the room. A man sitting two rows
ahead of me caught my attention. His hair was white, curly, and
mashed down with a faded baseball hat. He was different from the
others in the room; he was alone. He was older, maybe wiser, but like
the others, he looked tired. Why was he there? I couldn't believe that
I was there. It must not be a dream after all.

I turned my attention back to the speaker as he slowly paced
in front of his captive audience. He was enlightening us as to the
way society encourages addictions. As he spoke, he walked directly
in front of the old man with the hat. The old man sat motionless. I
thought he may have fallen asleep. I was getting a little sleepy myself
from nights of weariness.

Finally, the time came for questions. I watched as the shaky hand of the old man was raised. I listened as he spoke of his nephew's addiction problem. I heard him tell how he had visited halfway houses in hope of finding the right one. But was there such a thing, the right one? What difference did right make? Only his nephew could decide that. He was there for his nephew, not a son. He was committed, tired, and his voice cracked as he spoke of the ten year emotional roller coaster with his nephew. He made me cry. I felt his pain.

I was awed by his obvious love and devotion for a child that was not his own. I wondered why the nephew's parents were not in the room. Maybe they had kicked their son out, maybe they had given up on him, and who could blame them? The war was exhausting with no end in sight.

Why was the uncle there alone? I didn't want to be there either! It would be years later before I witnessed firsthand the love of an uncle for his nephew.

My attention went back to the speaker as he continued to explain how addictions affected the lives of everyone in the family, the entire house. He called addiction a family disease. My house was badly shaken, the foundation was cracking, and I felt powerless against the dark world. The dark world was bigger than anything I had ever come up against. It was mighty and torturous.

But the uncle had not retreated. He had never given up on his nephew. Maybe I was there to learn how an old man still had love and patience. Maybe I was there to understand the sacrifice of an old man for a boy who had lost his way!

I wondered where my love and patience had been. These virtues had been replaced by anger and intolerance. I didn't feel like being nice. I was hurting and sulking. I was having a pity party all for myself.

I had been fighting the dark world alone for four years now. Jeff had managed to detach, so good for him. God had not helped me, even though I had asked him everyday. He had the power; why didn't he answer me? I felt so helpless most of the time. I was running out of tricks and plans to save Randy, who didn't even know that he needed saving. I was a run-a-way train, totally out of control.

I had stooped to all sorts of crazy schemes, even worn a disguise at a carnival, so I could spy on Randy. I got an eyeful. I saw him walking along with a group of rough looking kids puffing on a cigarette. Come to think of it, he looked rough too, like one of them. How odd! The friends were not the real threat, not at all. This was about choices and just saying "yes" to drugs. Randy had chosen. I had wasted valuable time getting angry with the wrong people. They were not the issue, but the dark world that filled my child with lies; the world that gave Randy relief from his pain. He liked that world, more than anything else.

He wasn't getting anywhere in the dark world. He couldn't seem to find the light. He was a prisoner, a captive in a lonely place. Now he was in rehab. Was this the light? Was this the way? Would he learn from this, never to return to the lifestyle of illusions again?

The speaker liked to hear himself talk, but he knew his business. He was describing me, the enabler, so clearly that I wondered if he and I had met in another life. I was more alert now. The lecture was getting a little more interesting.

He continued by describing the addict. Wouldn't you know it that was me as well? I was addicted to potato chips and chocolate. I knew that I could never give them up because they were my choice. No one would tell me what to eat or not to eat. I would decide to quit on my own, when it suited me to quit!

But this was not about addictions to chips and chocolates. This was about substance abuse, mind-altering drugs, and the power of the dark world.

I wanted to get up and leave. I already felt that I was failing as I mother. Why did I need to be in that little, drab room? The twelve steps were just too late. How could those steps change anything?

The speaker kept interrupting my thoughts. I was bothered by this since I really didn't want to be there. I heard the word *detachment*. I hated the sound of that word. Mothers didn't detach. I couldn't see that happening. My every thought was consumed by the choices Randy was making. I was so afraid for him. Wouldn't detachment mean that I didn't care anymore? Well, it seemed like that to me anyway.

I felt some anger toward the speaker, but I knew he was right. My life had become unmanageable because I had allowed it to be. I had exhausted all my energies fretting over Randy, and what had come of it? Nothing! Everyday the storm had raged with more arguing. I wished that I could just shut up since I got on my own nerves. All my lectures fell on deaf ears.

I was a broken record, saying the same old stuff over and over, the warnings, the threats. Why? He was not listening. Would he listen in this twenty-eight-day program? I doubted his sincerity about being there. I believed Randy came to the rehab as a quick way out of a bad situation when he took something of value that belonged to me. He had lied, again. Did he even know the truth?

Maybe he would listen if I wrote him a letter from my heart. Would he even read it? After all, good mothers didn't have sons in drug rehab. Good mothers had focused kids who lived on the right side of the law. Good mothers had respectful kids who adored their parents, didn't they? So, I was not a good mother. I had beaten myself up for years with that thought in my head. Now I was losing Randy. I was going crazy with desperation to save his life.

Dear Randy,

Somehow I have failed you since you are a lost sheep. I cannot find you anywhere. Are you adrift on the high seas? Do you see the lighthouse yet? The rocks are all around you. You must come to the light. Do you see the light?

Oh, if I could raise you all over again, a second chance, a fresh start with you being my little baby boy. I can see you as my little baby. I can feel you cradled in my arms, smelling the baby shampoo on your dark hair.

But I will not get a second chance. I had one chance to do it right, but I have failed. What would I do differently if given a second chance? I do not know, but surely there must be something.

I did what I thought was the right thing to do. I did my best, but I cannot rescue you. You do not want to be saved, not yet. I know. I see it in your eyes!

This is a bad dream, and I will wake up soon. You will be my little boy who plays with trucks in the sandbox. I will hear you make the motor sounds of the trucks over and over. I will kneel down beside you to play with you, making motor sounds too.

I can see your impish smile with your shiny, dark eyes, concealing what is really going on in your head.

I will search for the little boy deep inside you, for he is there. I will never stop looking until I find you again. I cannot give up the search.

Love, Mom

I looked forward to Sundays, so I could visit Randy. By the second visit, I could tell that he hated the program, for all too soon, he tried to found a way out of there. I got the phone call from the staff telling me that Randy was suicidal. They added that he came to their infirmary many times wanting some type of medication. They stated that he was "drug-seeking." I wondered why they felt like sharing that revelation. Didn't this type of behavior happen in a drug rehab? Wasn't drug-seeking behavior the reason for a drug rehab? They ended the conversation by telling me that they were not "equipped with the proper staff to care for individuals who were suicidal." They were sending him to a crisis center.

I asked to speak with Randy on the phone. He was threatening to run out on the highway in front of traffic. His monotone voice sounded strange to me. Panic gripped my soul. What if he did? I agreed to have them send him to a place where he could receive professional help.

I visited Randy at the crisis center, but wondered if he had made up the suicide story just to get out of the rehab since he was coming up with all sorts of excuses to get out of the center as well. He tried all his lines with me; he didn't really belong there, he didn't like the staff, he heard patients yelling at night, and he couldn't sleep. He had a long list of complaints. He wanted to come home. He kept telling me that he was "going to flip out." I wondered what earthly good he thought that would do? So I asked him if he planned to be put in an isolation room, which would add days to his visit there. I had hoped that the possible threat of more days would be enough for him to stay calm.

Randy was clever, and I couldn't help but think that he was wasting a great talent. He could argue a case relentlessly. He had the gift of charisma with persuasive language. He had been born with these talents. I was familiar with all of them.

How strange that no one seemed to notice his ability to manipu-
late to get his way. I wondered why they couldn't see right through
him. They were professionals. They saw such behavior all the time.
How hard could it be?

But I had no control. He would be released when they said so.
Apparently, there was a lengthy evaluation that needed to be done in
order to have a treatment plan. The process took around five days.

Even though he hated it there, he was stuck fast. He had created
his present situation. He would just have to wait to be released.

I drove home when the sadness of Randy's situation came down
on me like a huge mountain that I could not lift. I carried the load of
his fragile mental health on my shoulders. Randy had been raised by
two parents that loved and cared about him. What had gone wrong?
None of this made any sense to me. This was all just a bad dream.
Any time now I would just wake up, and it would all be over. I hoped
it would be soon. I was tired.

THE ROCKS

The rain pelted the windshield as the dreariness of the moment took a painful stab at my aching soul. Deep in thought, I was oblivious to the dampness created by the cold rain, captivated by the scene before my eyes.

The barbed wires were twisted in all directions on the very top of the iron fence, the cyclone fence that encircled the square building. Iron bars were in front of the windows of the structure that was devoid of warmth standing parallel to the courthouse. There was an eerie quiet, and quite deceivingly, the building appeared to be vacant.

Beaming high above the street of official buildings, strategically located perhaps, was a white steeple of an old church. I could barely see the hazy light seeping through the stain-glassed windows.

What a weird place for a church, I thought. The church was old, having been the first building on that street in a time when blueprints for local offices were but a dream.

Maybe someone thought the church would serve as a reminder of something. Maybe it did! After all, I was there, sitting and thinking, entranced by the beauty of the old church, but it was night, and I couldn't see the light. The fog, like a soft blanket, was lowering down over the street, masking the dim lights on the street poles. Yet, I saw the lone figure. The slim body and familiar droop of his shoulders gave away his identity. The young man was waiting for his ride as he stood out in the rain in front of the cyclone fence of the detention center.

No one else was on the street, but why would anyone be standing outside on this dreary night? He was alone. The rain had slowed me down, causing me to be a little late. I wondered if he felt isolated out there. Did he feel anything these days? I wondered if he thought of how he got himself into this mess or if he noticed the church with the towering steeple, resembling a lighthouse beaming safety to ships too near the rocks.

I knew that he was dangerously too near the rocks, but he didn't seem to sense the alarm. The rocks were capable of beating his body, wearing him down. They would destroy him, yet he had no fear. He was invincible!

Standing in the rain, all alone, the figure appeared to be oblivious to the damp night. The figure was becoming a stranger to me. Randy was no longer a boy, but he was far from being a man.

Didn't he see the lighthouse waiting ever so patiently to get him safely to the shore? I must wait for him to heed the warning of the rocks. Time was endless. Where was the light to chase away the darkness?

Pulling up to the curb where he stood, he recognized our van and quickly got inside; then the deafening silence. I couldn't think of a thing to say. I couldn't ask how the AA meeting was since I knew that he hated going to them. The meetings were for "old losers," men who had lost their homes and families, men who had really "messed up their lives," not for young guys "who liked to party," like him. All those "losers" were his age once upon a time with cars, homes, jobs, and a life. They lost it all as a result of substance abuse. He couldn't see that picture. I knew there was no need to say it all again.

As I pulled away, I glanced in the rear view mirror, seeing the cyclone fence shining in the rain. I could barely see the dreary building that was enclosed by the fence. For some reason, the sight behind me caused new fear to grip my heart. What if Randy didn't shape up being sent behind the cyclone fence? That's where he was heading; was that where he wanted to go? Did he want to see the world from an inmate van, picking up paper along the highway? I was praying that he would never see the inside of that building, but I sensed the worst was yet to come. The thought was too painful to bear tonight. He would wake up soon!

The rain and the fog made the drive home painfully slower than usual. I kept thinking about the rocks and the clouds of fog that were masking the danger in his life. Randy didn't see them, but they were surely there. I wanted to lift him over them, protect him from them, and try to remove the rocks. I had tried single-handedly to get rid of the "friends," but each time a new friend took the old one's place. There was always a replacement, one even worse than the one before. These were the rocks, too heavy to move.

I had tried so many times to warn him about the rocks with their razor sharp edge looming in the darkness, waiting for him. Didn't he see them? I wanted him to look hard and to expect them to be there. The rocks had been planted along his path to cause him to lose his way. How could I make him see the danger that was threatening his very existence?

He could not avoid the rocks alone, no one could. Sometimes they couldn't be moved. They would cut into his soul, leaving him bleeding. He already had wounds that left unattended would fester, spreading throughout his body like an infection. The rocks would destroy him. Why couldn't he see that?

I wanted to help him to get around the rocks and to tell him about the path to take to avoid them for the rocks were becoming boulders, too mighty and too big for him. They would overpower him, wearing him down until he was no more, until his soul could not take the load. He mustn't take the short path of temporary relief!

The relief he sought was all part of the master plan to destroy his being. When would he seek the only one that could really help him?

I thought for years that I was that someone; after all, I was his mother. I was carrying a huge load of guilty feelings, feelings of bad parenting with regrets. Maybe something I said, something I did, or something I shouldn't have said. No second chance. This was it.

Mother bears protect their cubs to keep them safe, but he was not a little cub anymore. At that time, he was nineteen years old. He could have chosen between right and wrong, to not drink and drive. This was his first offense. The judgment was a mere slap on the wrist compared to what was coming down the road. His decisions were paving his future, not taking him to the next level. They were not guiding him down the path of success. He was caught in a web of self-destruction. I felt that I could not bear to watch his rapid descent much longer.

How had it come to this? Randy had always been a challenge from the first day he was born. He had entered the world screaming and demanding. Little had changed over the years. Each year brought a new set of challenges. He could wear down a saint. I used to think that he stayed awake at night planning new schemes to drive me bananas the next day. We had battled repeatedly.

Early in his teen years, I had even sought the help of a counselor, who told me to pick the battles. Ironically, Randy got to talk to the counselor first. God only knows what he must have said because the counselor was all ready for my little visit, which was brief. I wondered if the counselor even had children or worse yet, she probably had per-fect children that she raised by the book. This counselor had probably written a book on how to do it right!

I thought to myself, *Okay, going to bed, taking a bath, turning off the TV, what clothes to wear, doing homework,* these were the battles.

Everyday he didn't relent; he wanted it his way. Then the big battles had come; the questionable friends were just the beginning. I wondered why he couldn't ask me a question that I could say yes to, you know, just say yes. It wasn't that I didn't want to say yes, it was that all the questions had answers that were definite no's.

"No, you can't spend the night there; I don't know him or his parents."

"No, you can't go out roaming the neighborhood with nothing to do at night."

"No, you can't buy that CD of filthy lyrics."

"No, you can't have that T-shirt of mushrooms and marijuana plants hidden all over it."

And so the battles seemed to intensify with each passing day.

The second visit to the counselor was very much like the first. This time I was prepared for the counselor. I had a scenario to present to her, a battle you might say. I began to tell her the story of walking into the kitchen finding Randy with his new friend making Orange Julius drinks. I watched as they were about to put in the fourth cup of sugar. At that point, I stopped them, asking them just what were they doing for crying out loud? Randy commented, "The sugar makes me think faster!"

I waited for the counselor to evaluate that situation. Her reply was so simple. She smiled saying, "Pick your battles; it was only sugar, not alcohol." Didn't she see that they wanted a little buzz? It was a bad sign! I worried that alcohol was just a few months away. "Huffing" common household cleaner and consuming massive dosages of DXM, the ingredient in some over-the-counter cough medicines, both resulting in hallucinations, was right around the corner. Huffing equipment could be purchased at specialty stores. Were these battles?

I decided that seeing this counselor was not for me. How could she relate to a real mother when she probably fed her own kids two bowls of ice cream for breakfast on a school day? This was not going to work.

Randy was playing his music on the radio, too loud as usual, but for once I was glad for I feared that he would hear my thoughts. I was screaming inside. I was afraid to cry, knowing I might not be able to stop. I wanted to shake some sense into his stubborn head, but how would that help? A shake would not be enough and neither would my screams because he did not hear and he did not feel.

He refused to see the rocks, but would he believe me when I told him that they were still there? I wanted him to be looking into the darkness to see the rocks that were waiting for him.

If he saw them, he must not face them alone. They were bigger than he could possibly imagine. He must ask someone to guide him around them. If he asked for help, it would come to him and nothing would get in the way that could not be moved.

I prayed every night to God to send an angel of protection to watch over him, to go wherever he went, and to protect him when he was still unaware of his need. The angel was not afraid of the dark or the looming rocks. The angel would be on a mission to protect him by keeping harm away from him. If Randy was very still, he would feel the presence surrounding him. The angel was the light to guide him in the dark.

"This sucks," he finally broke the silence as we neared home. I wanted to ask what exactly sucked. I knew what he meant, having to be driven all over the place by a parent. Why was he angry with me? It wasn't my idea of a fun way to spend the evening. If he had just said no to drugs and alcohol, there wouldn't be any reason for the drug testing or AA's, but he hadn't said no.

Another battle, a big one, a tug of war with him, was that he played down the usage of "pot," but why shouldn't he? That's what everyone else had done. All the talks about "pot" being a gateway for other drugs were wasted words. He had it under control.

The war had just begun.

After weeks of drug testing, I was so relieved that all the urine tests were negative that I let down my guard, stopping the endless searching of his room. One day, I got that nagging feeling in the pit of my stomach, that same feeling that warned me that something was just not right. I hated that feeling. I fought it for days, but it overcame me sending me wandering into his room to search again.

The first drawer that I opened had a bottle of red liquid that was a "wash out" of body toxins. The receipt was in the bag, so I called the place where he bought this strange stuff. The young man that answered the phone told me a bunch of ridiculous things about toxins being in our bodies and that this substance could wash them away.

I got angry with the young man, asking him point blank, "You mean that this stuff will give someone a negative urine test when it washed out the marijuana?"

He laughed and said, "Well, it could be used for that!"

I kept drilling him on what toxins needed to be washed out, but he kept telling me the same thing, "toxins."

Then I got even angrier. I asked him, "Is this stuff legal?" He told me it was sold in all the health stores and was legal. He never even got defensive when I threatened to expose his store by writing the newspaper.

How was this stuff helping kids stay clean? It was just a huge cover-up. I hated all the forces that seemed to be coming out against me. Where was the help?

The war was so one-sided. I was doomed to lose. I couldn't fight all these forces alone. It just couldn't be done.

But I refused to give up the fight, even with all odds against me. I would still fight with all my strength.

THE CYCLONE FENCE

The courtroom was quiet. Everyone seemed to be focused on the judge. The lawyers were having whispered conversations with their clients. No one knew what was coming as they awaited the decision of the man behind the huge desk, the man in control of their client's destiny.

Three DUI cases came before the judge as he seemed to be tiring of these people who just didn't get it. There were sad parents in the courtroom, staring at the backs of their sons. I was no different from them as I sat staring at my son's back. I wondered what Randy was thinking, if he sensed the dreaded decision about to come. I wondered if he was prepared, but how could he be since I was not?

The judge decided to acknowledge one set of parents. They stood together with solemn faces. Did he ask them to stand in their proud moment like they were receiving an honorary award at high school graduation, or did he just want to see what bad parents looked like? Well, he saw us, looking at us for a brief moment. What was there to see? Just battered parents who did the best they could, but it wasn't enough to prevent this day of reckoning.

Then Randy's case was called. This was his second DUI; there would be hell to pay, no slap on the wrist this time. Randy had played with fire, and he would be burned. He walked alongside his lawyer. I sat in the back of the courtroom, staring at their backs, but I could see the judge, and he frightened me. He was so serious. He did not want any delays on any of the cases.

The judge seemed like a fair man. He carefully selected his words before he passed his sentence. For some unknown reason, he thanked the attorney for a fine job. He thanked me for being there in his court. Should I say, no problem judge, it was a pleasure? I thought not. I had many other places where I would prefer to be, like in the dentist chair getting a root canal without Novocain.

I was alone that day in that huge courtroom, except for a bunch of strangers. Jeff's job necessitated him to be out of town. I was in such a selfish state that I allowed that reason to anger me. I wanted Jeff with me that day for support, but there was none. He was not emotionally connected to me anyway. What difference would it have made?

The judge asked me if I wanted to say anything, but what could I say? If I had known what was coming, maybe I could have said something worth hearing. I muttered a few words that drug rehabs had been tried before and that Randy had became suicidal each time. Then the facilities would tell me that they didn't treat dual diagnosis patients, which was depression and drugs.

The judge agreed with me that Randy had suicidal tendencies, making some logical sense to the judge why Randy was driving one hundred miles per hour with an alcohol level just barely over the limit. The judge felt that Randy was a risk on the highway. The judge let me know that he had an obligation to the community to keep the highway safe from drivers like Randy. I never got the chance to tell the judge that Jeff and I had put a club on our son's car months ago or that he had been in college for two weeks now, or that he seemed to be trying to get his life in order. The judge heard all he wanted to hear. He dismissed me along with the other useless parents.

At last, the sentence. The judge thought that sixty days of inpatient rehab would be more beneficial than jail. He added, "The county is going to pay for it." The court liaison, who represented the drug rehab, told the judge that a bed was available. You would think that I would have sensed that something was just not right. I watched my son hang his head and put his hands behind his back as the handcuffs were placed by a police officer. I watched in disbelief. Randy was being taken to the detention center. He couldn't even come home with me while he waited for a bed in the rehab. Surely this was a bad movie. Someone should push the stop button now before anything else bad happened!

Were handcuffs necessary to go to a rehab? What in the name of heaven was going on? I sat as if in a trance as the tears slid down my face. This was it, life behind the cyclone fence. I tried hard to pull myself together, thinking that Randy would be in jail for a short while because he would be going to the rehab soon where he would get some help for his addictions.

Someone knew that the rehab was a figment of the imagination. It was just a place of make believe that was dreamed up by someone. Even the judge thought it was real. The judge was trying to do Randy a favor. It sounded good and looked good on paper, but that's all!

The court liaison patiently answered my questions, telling me that the process took a few days, which still did not help me to understand the reason for Randy to go to jail first. He also assured me that Randy would get his medications and that the jail was fully aware of this need. He was an inmate now, just like 1,300 others. Some of these men had committed violent crimes. But there are no big crimes or little crimes behind the cyclone fence, just like there are no big sins or little sins. Consequences come just the same to everyone.

The court liaison knew that it took thirty to sixty days. He had a secret that no one in the courtroom knew, not even the judge, not even the lady who did the drug evaluation. The only one that knew was the court liaison man.

It seemed that there was a make-believe drug rehab, a place I came to nickname the "Garden." The name sort of speaks for itself, a place of beautiful flowers, and a garden with a strong iron gate that lets no one in. There was a very fine, lengthy process to get in the facility. One could get an audience with the president of the U.S. much sooner.

There was a long list of must haves, such as a TB test, a criminal background check, (How hard could that be? One is in jail, and they need to check for past crimes? Okay!), and then the medical clearance from the detention center. Then of course, there was the wait for funding from the county, which must have been imaginary money that was grown from a seed that took sixty days to bloom.

After a week, I wrote the judge to inform him that Randy was still in jail and not in the rehab. This created a response from the jail, who wrote a beautiful letter about how they were handling things according to protocol. Could this get more frustrating?

Let's make this easy. Jeff and I offered to pay for the rehab. Now that should expedite things a little! No, the jail had to medically clear the inmate. Then the fun part; the jail had to wait for clearance from the rehab. The last frustration to come was this; there were many candidates ahead of him, who have been waiting for some time already. And wait they would because this place was not penetrable; it just didn't exist.

I called first to the detention center, then to the "Garden," but it just wasn't going to happen. It took me some time, but after awhile I caught on, I got it. After days of calling the detention center concerning the antidepressants and anxiety medications Randy had been on and was not receiving, I soon learned that no one gave a flying fig. This was a jail. The employees that answered my calls talked to me as if I were a second class citizen, whatever that is. They were abrupt with an attitude of annoyance. My calls were not returned. The medications were not given. What if he withdrew from the anxiety medications and had a seizure? Who would be responsible then? Was anyone listening to me?

I decided to take Randy's medicine in to the medical department in the original bottle. After waiting one hour for the stone-faced nurse, she took the bottle, telling me she would call the doctor. Of course she didn't say which day this would happen, and I am pretty sure that she had more important things to do.

Jeff called the detention center and spoke to the medical department, indicating to them that they were liable for whatever happened to Randy if he had a seizure from withdrawal. But God took care of that situation. God had to intervene for us. Randy's blood pressure started to rise. We never knew how high and no one called, but the jail decided to give him Librium. I was going to have to be satisfied with that since this was as good as it was going to get as far as medicines were concerned. They monitored his blood pressure daily, waiting for a better reading to stop the Librium.

As usual, I called my brother Tom, who was also our pastor, begging him to go visit Randy. I didn't need to beg Tom since he had already planned to go see our son. But Tom got a little surprise when he arrived at the jail on a regular visiting day for a "spiritual" visitation. The jail attendant asked, "Where are your credentials?" Apparently not only are the inmates liars but so are the people who visit. What pastor totes along his college credentials? Tom's personal business card with his church and his name printed as the pastor just was not good enough.

Tom didn't look like a pastor. He wasn't wearing a dark suit or a white collar. He had on a golf shirt and casual pants. Tom had the most innocent, saintly face imaginable. How could anyone not believe him?

Tom was turned away. He had driven forty-five minutes and no visit, but he was far from giving up. He went to the church office, took down his college seminary degree certificate that was in a frame, and went right back to present it to the guard. This allowed him in to see Randy.

To complicate matters further, someone told Randy that if he did jail time and worked, he would get out sooner. He thought for a few seconds, decided that sixty days of rehab was a pain in the butt, and chose the quick path. I didn't even know that it was an option, but he knew. The "Garden" was not going to happen, not now, not ever!

What else was there to be said? No one else to call, no one to come to the rescue, just the deafening silence in the house. The dark room was empty, the fan was still, but the night light was shining in the dark. I reached down and turned it off, standing in the darkness.

I stood alone in his room looking at the empty bed. I remembered my baby well, but who was this grown person now? Who had he become? He was a twenty-three-old, angry stranger. With whom was he angry?

He was convinced that I loved his brother, Brad, more, yet Randy was the one that I cried for in the still of the night, the one I worried about, and the one that consumed my thoughts day and night. He didn't know my panic when he didn't come home at night. I was always afraid that one day he wouldn't come home. The fear gripped my heart as I prayed to God to watch over him, yet I worried. Oh, he was loved, more than he knew, more than he could ever understand. Someday, he would know when he came to himself as the prodigal son did!

I would be waiting for him to wake up and to learn that the love I have for him was bigger than life itself. I would be waiting for him with open arms. I would be watching. I would see him when he was yet a great way off in the distance. I would run to him, having compassion on him. I would fall on his neck and kiss him.

But it wouldn't be today. There was still too much anger in the house, too much pain in the hearts, too many bad scenes, and too much yelling. The wounds were fresh and needed time to heal. If not, they would reopen with festering until all the body parts would be consumed by its fire. The wounds needed attention. They needed time. What else was there but time?

So Randy had time to think now. I had the same. He thought of getting back home to his comfortable life. I wondered if I was only prolonging his poor attempts of normalcy by letting him come back. Where was the repentance speech? Was there one? I thought that there should be, yet in the quiet of the house, I didn't hear it. No speech. No, "I'm sorry."

Maybe a letter would come today, a letter of regrets; maybe it would come tomorrow. I would wait, and while I waited I would be watching for him to come home.

I sat in the crowded room staring at the metal detector as two green hands illuminated on the frame alternating with two red hands. There was an annoying buzzing sound as people walked in passing through, just like a lighted bug zapper. The guards arriving on duty had to pass through the frame. Some of the guards were females and the others were huge men. I felt intimidated and insecure. I sat there wondering how it all came to this, from the cradle to the cyclone fence.

I glanced around at the people patiently waiting their thirty-minute visit that would take place behind two locked doors. The guards ushered the visitors in and out to a huge room that was protected on two sides by heavy glass and one side with concrete. There was no physical contact with the inmates. The guards did not smile; no one did.

I got to sit down in a small booth with only glass in front of me with a ring less, black phone, my only connection to my son. Finally I saw Randy walk in wearing a blue jumpsuit with other young men dressed all alike. He sat down and picked up the phone.

My heart was pounding, and I prayed that I wouldn't cry. I mustn't let the river of swelling emotion take over now. I feared losing control. This was not the time for tears. There was only thirty minutes to talk, just thirty minutes in a week. There was so much to say and so much left unsaid.

I was screaming inside for having to visit this place, for having to prove my identity to visit, for having to lock my purse up before passing through the annoying metal frame, and for not being able to touch my child. He was still angry. I could see it on his face.

He was counting the days that he would be back home to visit his friends, his beloved friends that hadn't even called to check on him or visit him. He would learn who his true friends were; maybe he needed new ones.

I listened as Randy complained about his everyday needs being ignored, of not being able to brush his teeth for a week, of going to bed hungry, about his roommate snoring, and not being able to sleep. I listened. I hoped he hated it as much as I did. I hoped he hated being miserable so that when he came home, he would change his lifestyle and his friends to start fresh.

I hoped and prayed that he said good-bye to alcohol, his last friend, the one thing that consoled him in the still of the night. Alcohol was the killer of thoughts and pain, the one thing that prevented him from thinking too much. He had spent many hours numbing his every thought. What could be so painful that he couldn't deal with it? What tasted so good that even jail wasn't a threat? He had lost so much already, college, his license to drive, and now his tenuous relationship with his girlfriend.

His friend alcohol had striped him of his dignity. His happy times in bars late at night had been replaced by sad times behind bars, but he was only thinking of drinking again. He believed that he had it under control. He didn't get it.

I told him that he was welcome back when he gave up his friend alcohol, but he got angry. He was not willing to give up his solace. Would he lose his home too? Would he choose alcohol?

The ride home was long with the depression looming over my head. The sadness was there, trying to suck the breath out of my body. I wondered how parents, who had lost a child, coped. How did they live in the same house with the empty room of memories? The thought brought chills to my spine. I must think of something else. I must think that Randy was safe where he was from the harm of alcohol or drugs. He was safe from his loser friends. They didn't get it either.

The evening sun was setting. I couldn't bear the darkness from his empty room. I walked in to turn on the nightlight. Pausing at the door, I saw his deodorant and cologne on his bureau. I reached over picking up the cologne to smell the fragrance. The tears were flowing unnoticed down my cheeks. I couldn't seem to put down the cologne. I had a tight grip on it as if I were trying to make a statement to someone. My fist was clenched around the bottle as I talked aloud to the darkness.

"I will not give up Randy without a fight," I found myself muttering. I didn't know who I was fighting, but there was a war going on, and I would not lose the fight. I would not give up, not yet.

THE HOMECOMING

Time was moving as slowly for me as if I was a child waiting for Christmas Day to come, but this wasn't Christmas Day. I was far from being a child, but I still watched the clock in anticipation. Soon, Randy would be returning home. He had been released from the cyclone fence. His home waited for him. His room was clean, smelling fresh with clean linens. No dirty clothes on the floor, no clutter, an orderly room.

I walked aimlessly down the hall to his room, not only to get another look at the good housecleaning job that I had done, but to listen to the silence.

All loose papers were in folders. All notes and letters were in boxes. All the baseball caps were neatly arranged. The bag of empty Vodka bottles had been pitched, along with cigarette lighters and anything else that looked out of place.

The closet had all the hangers going in the same direction. What was the purpose of that? I didn't really know. I paused for a moment. This didn't look like his room at all. Deep inside me I knew that he would hate all my hard work. He would not see it as cleaning, but as an invasion of his privacy again.

He would not smell the detergent softeners that left the room smelling like the mountains. He would get annoyed that I had dared to venture into his domain, his room of darkness and depression, the place where he hid his friend alcohol, his liquid pain relief that took his mind off of everything.

The many heated conversations about his drinking problems were a waste of energy. He was old enough to drink. All his friends drank. We told him that no alcohol would be allowed in the house, but I feared all that would come of that rule would be to make him more careful to hide it better than before.

Randy had spoken with determination in his voice all those weeks of the sentence time. I knew that he would not stop. He loved the numbness he felt from drinking. Drinking had a hold on him, filling him with lies, making him believe that he needed alcohol to be sociable and congenial. He had lost all confidence in himself, doubting his good looks. His mind was overflowing with lies from the enemy that were very convincing, sending him into the dark world of no hope.

I felt uneasy standing alone in his room. He had shown no signs of remorse or wanting to change his life. There was no letter from him, no regrets, nothing. I was fighting my own mountains of depression. I was fighting hard not to listen to the lies in my mind, the ones that told me what a bad mother I was. I sat down on his bed, touching his bedspread. Then I felt an overwhelming need to get on my knees bedside his bed.

Kneeling down, I laid my head on his bed when my body began to crumble, as if it was falling apart at the seams. I cried for Randy, muttering sobs to God to keep him safe when he came home. I mostly cried because the words came out in chopped syllables, almost like jargon. If anyone else had been in that room, they would not have understood my words, but God knew. God knew my aching heart had taken a blow. Only God could give me peace.

I knelt for what seemed like a long time. I planned to stay there until I felt peace, but I felt nothing more than anxiety. When was God going to listen to me? Today Randy was coming home. What would the house be like? Would it go back to the sporadic yelling, alternating with the deafening silence? How long could this go on? How much more could I take? I was falling apart. I was struggling to hold on as the unraveling took its painful time. I was weak, today of all days, when I needed to be strong.

I glanced at the baby blue wristband on my left arm, reciting the words to myself, "And now these three remain; faith, hope and love. But the greatest of these is love" (1 Corinthians 13:13, NIV). How I came to receive the band or bracelet was more like a dream, but I remembered every detail.

On the last visit to the cyclone fence, I sat next to another mom on small metal stools as we waited for our sons to come to the ring less phone. I glanced over to the mother, who looked tired and pale. Then I noticed the baby blue wristband on her left arm.

"What a beautiful shade of blue! That's my favorite color," I had exclaimed, as I admired it with curiosity. The other woman told me that her pastor had given it to her. Then she recited the words. Both of us had tears in our eyes as we looked at one another with a knowing look of a mother who was in pain, whose son was locked up, a look of empathy for one another.

The mother began to share a short version of her struggles with her son and his addictions. She went to see her pastor for help and guidance for her son. The pastor told her that she was killing her son by allowing him to stay in her home and abuse his body like he was doing everyday. She had gotten the strength to pack him up, sending him out in the rain. She told me that she knew that if she didn't do something, she would lose her son. She cried as her car pulled away leaving him on the curb in the pouring rain. She told me that one day, he would come to himself, like the prodigal son, and he would be back. She had a look of peace, and she smiled.

She then took the baby blue wristband off, handing it to me and telling me, "Please, take this. You need it now. This is what I was supposed to do with the band today. This is why we are here at this moment." We looked into one another's eyes for a moment only because our sons had appeared at the window for visitation.

Just thinking of that moment seemed more like a dream. Was the lady an angel? What was she trying to say? But I knew what the message meant. I glanced at the wristband. I knew what I might have to do.

I got up, going to the bathroom to inspect the damage to my makeup from rivers of crying washing away all the black mascara. I didn't want Randy to see me this way, all weepy and weak of heart. I had to pull it together. Time was ticking. I hurriedly reapplied the makeup, totally covering the dark circles under my eyes, concealing sleepless nights and days of worry. My hands were shaking with my insides jumping. There was a real threat of losing my self-control. I felt some kind of doom was over my head, like a dark cloud before a storm. When would it all go away?

Jeff went that morning to pick him up from the detention center. At 10:00 a.m., I heard the side door open, and I walked into the kitchen to see Randy. I stood back a moment to take in the vision of him being in the house once again. He had lost weight. But I could only focus on his face as I looked into his eyes, trying to make a mental picture of how clear they were. He had survived forty days without any drug of any kind. When had I last seen him look so normal?

I walked slowly to him, but he made no move toward me, yet I kept getting closer to him. I had to touch him, to hug him again. Would he back away? I wondered as the fear of rejection nagged at my heart.

I put my arms around his neck to hug him; he didn't resist, but he didn't return the hug. I looked at him and said, "Welcome home." But he didn't answer. He walked down to his room. I could hear his muttering comments about my playing detective while he was gone. Then he went downstairs on his computer, probably to let all his loser friends know that he was home.

He was not impressed with the rules of no drinking, totally unscathed that a violation of this in our home would mean he would have to leave. Was it a real threat or not? I doubted it; he had heard the same old threats before, and where was he? Back home in his comfort zone. Something had to change.

Maybe living beyond the cyclone fence had taught him a valuable lesson. Who in their right mind would want to go back there to the world of non-caring employees and criminals of all types that would fight at a drop of a hat? It scared me just to think of such a place and to think that he had been there, too. Randy was becoming like a freight train, spinning down a track going in one direction to nowhere. I had to stop that blasted train since God was not listening and there was no one else that I could look to for support.

Talking to others was useless. The conversations always ended the same—go to a counselor! For some reason, I didn't want to go. I knew why I was upset and what could make it all better. I didn't need to spend hours on a couch, spilling out my guts about stuff the counselor had heard a million times before. It was an expensive waste of time. No, I was going to bottle up all the bad feelings inside me and seal the bottle as tightly as I could. I would deal with them later, when I felt like dealing with them.

There was tension in our house. I felt it again like walking on eggs. I could hear him on the phone making plans to go out with his loser friend, the one who never even visited him. I begged Randy not to go, not today, his first day home. But he had an agenda. His plans were no secret to me.

I stood at the window, watching him get into his friend's car and kept looking until the car was out of sight. Just like that, he had decided to go down the wrong road. He hadn't been home one hour before he was making plans to go out and do what? I didn't want to think about what he was doing, but I knew. It felt like a knife in my chest. He had made his choice.

I finally went to bed to toss and turn for hours. At 3:00 a.m., I got up looking out of my bedroom door to see if he had come back home, but his door was open. I felt the same pain of worry. Was he alive? Was there an accident? Would he be home again? This was torture, and I couldn't help myself. I knew that he hadn't come home because he was drinking at his friend's house. His first night back! For weeks all he spoke of was sleeping in his own bed, but he had chosen not to come home. He was with his friend alcohol, and that was first place in his mind. He cared for no one else!

I sat in the dark in the living room, feeling as if the blood had drained from my body. The weight of the worry was threatening my sanity. I knew that I had to get a grip on myself. But at that moment, I didn't care. I understood how someone could pick up a bottle of alcohol to totally forget their pain. I felt like doing the same thing. I had thought of it many times before, but I was so worried about having a drinking problem that I refused to taste it. I knew that once I felt the relaxation, I would want more, fearing it would dominate my life.

I wanted relief from the pain, the pain of feeling like a failure, the pain of my suffering marriage that had taken a severe blow from the arguments about how to deal with Randy. I thought that if we made him leave our home, he would soon come to his senses to return repentant and clean. Jeff thought Randy would die if we made him leave. We argued our cases back and forth. I knew that Randy would surely die if we didn't do something drastic soon. I was afraid that one day I would knock on our son's closed bedroom door and there would be no answer. It was all so overwhelming; I couldn't bear to think of it all at once. It was a mountain, too high, too steep, too rugged, and much too painful.

Sitting in the dark alone, I felt as if someone had died. There was a hole in my heart that was robbing me of any joy. The ache was big; I was losing my son. I was losing the fight.

I felt anger creeping into my heart, the fear of losing him forever, and the nagging anxiety over his lack of desire to change. I found myself fantasizing about his homecoming, the one I had prayed for that existed only in my mind.

I would greet him at the door. We would embrace one another as we cried. He would look into my eyes, telling me how sorry he was for everything and that he was going to try to change. He would ask for my help. I would do anything to help him, but the homecoming didn't happen that way; there was no remorse, no letter.

Why should there have been one since he didn't seem to be sorry? There was a chip on his shoulder, making me angry again. What in the name of heaven would it take for him to see that his life was passing him by, dumping him in a ditch?

Where would I get the strength to pack him up and send him away? Why did it have to be this way? I didn't want him to go away. I wanted him to change his life, start over again.

Finally I went back to bed, but sleep would not come. I kept listening for the side door to open.

It wasn't until late that afternoon that he decided to come home. He looked like he had been awake all night with his eyes half shut. How I hated that look! I was angry again that he hadn't even bothered to call to say that he wasn't coming home. Was that too much to ask? Why must he torment the people that loved him the most? What was in it for him?

I greeted him at the door with more angry words swelling up in my throat. He was irresponsible, not caring who he worried. I glared at him before turning away, saying words that I would lie in bed at night and regret.

I knew that he had a new plan, to drink outside the home, but I knew that sooner or later I would find the empty bottles in our home.

I was getting ready to leave for work when Randy walked into the kitchen. He reached into his backpack bringing out a folded yellow piece of paper. He walked up to me and handed the paper to me, saying, "I wrote you something. It's just stupid, but here." Then he walked away.

I was afraid to read it before working my shift at the hospital. What if it was an angry letter? What if he hates me and tells me so? I left for work with the note in my pocket. I would read it when I got home, when it was quiet and no one would disturb me. The letter had come. It had come!

I worked my busy twelve-hour shift with the letter in my pocket. Periodically I touched it, just to make sure that it was still safe. Somehow I knew that the letter would melt away my anger, but I wanted to wait until I got home that night, so that I could savor every word. I wondered if the shift was ever going to end.

The long, tortuous ride home was forty-five minutes of time to think and to imagine what Randy had written to me. He had written it while he was behind the cyclone fence. He had been home two days before he gave it to me. I wondered why he waited. Maybe the content of the letter was not what I expected. I tried to focus on driving, but my mind was going nuts with anxiety. What if I had an accident before I got to read it? How horrible that would be! He would never know that I read it or not. I slowed down a little and tried to relax the racing of my heart.

The moon was full, and the sky was light. What if a deer ran in front of my car? I needed to slow down, but I had a letter to read.

Finally, I was home. With my heart pounding, I ran into the house to sit down at the table to read his letter. Immediately, I recognized his handwriting. With trembling hands I started to read the contents.

The familiar "Dear Mom" was my first sign that the letter was the one that I had prayed for; this was it. Silently I thanked God. God had heard my prayers.

Dear Mom,

Well technically it's Friday here, the day before I get out. It's 3:00 a.m. and I can't sleep. Big surprise here. I've been doing nothing but thinking for the past forty days here. It's like I've gone over every single event in my life five times. It hasn't been fun. I've gotten to think about mostly the bad stuff, it clouds my mind big time.

All the bad stuff that I've done always comes first, followed by all the bad stuff that I couldn't control comes next. It's never fun. Mainly tonight after this whole girlfriend thing and it being my last day makes it hard to sleep. But I had a thought tonight: I am many things. I've been given many labels over my two decades here on earth. They consist of smart, funny, good-looking, a drug addict and a drunk. I think I covered the whole spectrum there. But I forgot the *one* label that has remained steadfast throughout my entire life, including today. Above all those things I am, without a doubt, a momma's boy. Oh yes, it's true, without a doubt.

Mom, we have had our arguments and I have said things that are going to tear me up for years and years, but you are my girl. I mean it. I'm not sure what's going to come of this girlfriend thing, but I'm 95 percent sure that she is ignoring you. Now it's one thing to trash me, I deserve it, but no one ever does my mom wrong. Ever.

It's sad, I had to come to jail to tell you this, but I mean it. Okay, I'm not going to let this letter get too mushy, because I haven't teared up in about a month and I don't want to start now. I love you, Mom, with a love that no one will ever be able to comprehend. I'll see you soon.

Love, Randy

I read the letter over before I tucked it away in my Bible with the other keepsakes. The letter had come. Maybe now we could start a renewed relationship.

He had referred to his relationship with his girlfriend, Jessica, being uncertain. I knew that was true. I had e-mailed her at college almost every day to give her the messages Randy has asked me to send. At first she answered right away, then the replies became farther apart. Then he had complained that she hadn't sent him a letter a day as she had promised and that he had only gotten a total of four letters. I feared the worst. Then his girlfriend stopped answering my e-mails. What did it all mean? It couldn't be good.

At least now that he was home, he could do his own communicating. I hated being in the middle of it all. It was all so frustrating. I imagined his life of mere existence, waiting for e-mail replies that had to be received on his computer at his home to be read by his mother while he was in jail. I worried how he was going to respond to the likelihood of a dissolving relationship.

The next day I got up early, still thinking about the letter. I wanted to tell Randy how much it meant to me, but every time I thought about the letter, I cried. I knew how he hated it when I got emotional, but somehow I had to get the strength to talk to him.

When he got up that morning, I told myself that today I would tell him. But when I tried to talk to him, I just couldn't bring myself to fit the letter into the conversation. It was as if some force was stopping me from doing what I needed to do.

Silently I prayed for the strength, waiting for the moment when the timing would be just right. He was walking into the living room when I jumped up to stand in front of him. Before he could resist me, I quickly reached up, putting my arms tightly around his shoulders.

With an unsteady voice, I said, "You'll never know how much that letter meant to me. I will treasure it forever." Then my voice started to crack. I knew that I couldn't say anymore without the tears.

I released my embrace looking at him. Then I saw it, a little smile, just like the smiles I saw when he was just a little boy. But wasn't he still a little boy?

As he walked away from me, I wondered why I hadn't realized that Randy still needed to feel that I loved him. He had always pushed me away from him, not wanting my kisses and hugs. I had allowed him to withdraw, thinking that he didn't need that attention from me. After all, he was a man now. But today, just a few minutes ago, I saw that he still needed me. I became aware that I needed him, too.

There were rivers of combat that came between us, but we still loved each other. There were mountains of angry words, but we still loved each other. There were dark clouds of angry feelings from both sides, but we still loved each other.

I had allowed anger to control my feelings, smothering them so badly that I didn't even know what my true feelings were anymore. Allowing anger to take control was eating me up inside. Fear was taking over my mind and soul, leaving me with a dreaded emptiness. I lived with the fear of losing my son.

What if God took him away? What if God decided that I had messed up as a mother and didn't deserve my own child that he had given me twenty-three years ago? The thoughts were depressing, but kids died everyday, drugs and alcohol took lives, young and old. It was reality. What if I lost him?

My mind was spinning out of control. I knew that I had to ask God for help and stop trying to save my own child alone. I was losing the war. I had to turn Randy over to God. If I did this, I could stand in the gap for my child. There was nothing else left to do. I had to do it.

That same day, I got a letter from my lifelong friend Mary, who had lost her only sister, Erin, the year before. Her young life had been tortured by depression and drugs. But Mary knew that she was no longer in pain. She held on to that truth.

Mary lived three hours away. We infrequently talked on the phone over a period of twenty-some years; neither of us ever mentioned drugs. It was a secret as we struggled to hide our pain from one another. After the death of Erin, the pain had surfaced. We both needed to talk. It was time to let it all go and look to one another for support.

Mary had taken the time to send me a letter with a verse and a poem. Mary had no idea that it was the same verse that I had had on my refrigerator for three years now on a yellowed index card.

"Be not afraid or dismayed by reason of this great multitude; for the battle is not yours, but God's…ye shall not need to fight in this battle" (2 Chronicles 20:15–17, KJV). I then noticed the beautiful poem:

Standing in the Gap

I'll stand in the gap for my son.
I'll stand 'till the victory's won.
This one thing I know
That you love him so,
And your work with my child is not done.
I'll stand in the gap every day
And there I will fervently pray;
And, Lord, just one favor,
Don't let me waver
If things get quite rough, which they may.
I'll never give up on that boy.
Nor will you, for you promised him joy.
For I know it was true
When he said "yes" to you,
Though the enemy seeks to destroy.
I'll not quit as I intercede,
For you are his Savior, indeed!

Though it may take years,
I give you my fears,
As I trust every moment I plead.
And so in the gap I will stand,
Heeding your every command
With help from above,
I unconditionally love,
And soon he will reach for your hand.

By Shirley Pope Waite

I read the poem over again and wondered about the author. What had she suffered? How long had she waited for her son to reach for God's hand? I felt the pain for her. We had something in common. We saw the power of the enemy "as a roaring lion…seeking whom he may devour" (1 Peter 5:8, KJV). Our sons were in jeopardy. How long had the author stood in the gap? How long could anyone stand in the gap, just waiting and waiting, hoping and praying?

It was a test of one's faith to see if a mother really thought that God would overpower the evil one, the dark world. God could just say the word and everything would be all right. Why didn't he? Why did he wait?

I fastened the club on Randy's car. I liked to hear the click of the locked club that represented safety to me by giving me power. With the club on his car, he would be safe. Jeff and I decided that our son could use the car during the day in search of a job, but no night driving.

But Randy was too clever for that weak rule. He asked to use the car to meet his friend for lunch one Saturday afternoon. The lunch somehow got extended until nighttime. He called around 8:00 p.m., saying that he wouldn't be home. I offered to pick him up, but he refused. Then he just hung up the phone. I stood listening to the irritating dial tone.

I couldn't sleep that night, expecting the police to call or knock on the door. I just knew that he was dead. Why did he have to push the rules all the time? Didn't he see that I was just trying to keep him safe?

The next day, he called from a motel. He was proud of himself for not driving impaired. He finally came home that day around 5:00 p.m. with no apology for the worry he had caused. No concern that he had broken the car rules. He felt he was very responsible by not driving impaired and that he and his friend had stayed in a motel. I wondered how they got there! Somebody drove the car. It opened clouds of anxiety with more worry about his safety behind the wheel of a car.

In the week that followed, I didn't like the way he looked. I couldn't put my finger on it, but a mother just knows. Randy was under the influence of something. He saw a new doctor, who prescribed new medications that Jeff locked in the safe in order to give Randy only what was ordered. Yet, Randy seemed impaired. Was it his eyes? Weren't they glassy? Was it his stride? Wasn't he off balance? What was it?

I knew that he and Jessica had broken off their relationship. He never did well with such things. His coping skills were nowhere when he needed them. He had sought relief from the pain.

Click went the club. I didn't know what he was doing, but I knew he wasn't driving. Even though he bitterly denied my accusations, I felt that I was right.

He tried on many occasions using all sorts of excuses to get the club off the car. One afternoon, he wanted to go on a job interview. He did appear to be normal to me, so I went out to his car and just sat in the driver's seat staring at the club. I sat there for a short time, not listening to my inner self telling me to leave the club, as it was, tight and secure. But I unlocked the club.

He returned at 11:00 p.m. with a tale of a "fender-bender" that turned out to be a repair worth the same amount as the car. He had rear-ended someone.

So God took his car since I didn't have the ability to listen to my own inner voice. I didn't have any control over my own son. I was not a good parent, so God had to help me out a little. The car was gone, just like that.

While I stood in the gap for my son, God had taken control. He had answered my prayer to keep Randy safe. Now he was safe; stuck in the house, no car, no job, and depressed. I knew how he felt because I felt the same way.

Now the dilemma was whether the car should be repaired or not. Should he drive? But once again, the decision was taken out of my control. The MVA sent a letter for a hearing relating to the same DUI Randy had gotten in the spring. He would have to go before a judge stating why he should not have his license revoked for a year. *Wow,* I thought, *a sixty-day sentence from the court that sent him to jail for forty days and now this.* The news depressed Randy even more.

The deafening silence returned. He retreated to his room, his place of seclusion, his refuge from the real world.

I wanted to make everything all right for him, but I couldn't. His situation was spinning out of control and so was mine. Would I ever wake up from this repetitive nightmare? Was this bad dream ever going to end?

No drinking! I wondered just how long that rule would last. Randy was very clever as he had carefully hidden the empty bottles, but there had been little clues that only a mother would notice, tiny little clues.

Several nights when I got home in the early hours of the morning, I noticed the kitchen was a mess. Someone had been fixing a messy snack that had spilled on the floor and into the ice cube tray. The microwave was blinking. The lights were still on downstairs. I had seen those signs before. I knew what they meant.

When I asked Randy about the mess in the kitchen, he bitterly denied that he was drinking in the house. I knew that he would deny it. I tried to talk to Jeff about it, but he didn't want to know. He didn't look for empty bottles of Vodka. He didn't search Randy's room. Life was easier for him this way. I felt isolated with no one to help me. I had gotten weary of talking to God about it. If God wanted me to find the alcohol, he would direct my feet right to it. But that hadn't happened. Somehow, I still knew.

Finding alcohol meant that Randy had to leave our home. We had agreed on that rule. Finding alcohol was going to cause a major upset. It was going to be tormenting and painful for everyone. I didn't want to find it either. I was afraid to look, of what I would find and then afraid of what I would have to do.

Now that the car was gone, his friends had gotten tired of driving him around. I knew that if he drank, it would be right in the house, under my nose. But maybe it wouldn't come to that; maybe he would decide not to drink. I was getting to the point where I didn't want to know either. I wanted the easy way out, too. But I knew that I would be the one who would find it. I was always the one. Why should that change now?

One night, I got home from work an hour earlier than usual. Randy was still up, meeting me in the kitchen. He was talkative and sweet. He told me that he had a long nap that afternoon and he was going downstairs to watch TV, but he had come up just to say "goodnight." He turned and walked away. Randy had just tossed a smoke screen to throw me off the path, but I knew.

Quietly, I walked downstairs. I didn't know why. I felt as if my feet were sending me down to the lion's den. *In the name of heaven, feet please, don't go down there* were the words that I was muttering to myself. I hoped that I would find him sitting there as he said he would be, just watching TV. He glanced up at me when I entered the family room. I looked into his eyes, I knew. I walked around the side of his chair finding the hidden Vodka and coke.

I hadn't wanted to see it, but it was there. I stared at him in disbelief, saying, "You just made a bad choice!"

Randy became defensive and angry, yelling loudly that he wasn't hurting anybody. As I turned away, I looked over my shoulder, yelling, "What makes you think that your drinking affects only you?" There was no need for conversation; the words were aimless syllables that just floated to the ceiling to crash to the floor. With a heavy heart, I went upstairs to go to bed for another sleepless night.

I lay in bed thinking of him drinking again. He wasn't even being secretive; on the contrary, he was being bold, daring someone to enforce a rule on him. There was nothing unusual about his actions; he never cared about consequences. When he was a young child, the disciplines became so frequent that I had to write them on the calendar, just to remember when one disciplinary action started and when one ended. Many of the offenses happened repeatedly. He didn't really care. If he felt like doing something, he did, and if he felt like saying something, he did.

I vividly recall an incident one day when Randy was three years old. He hid his nine-month-old brother, Brad, who was in a baby walker. I remember the panic, asking him where Brad was, but he "didn't know." I ran to the basement steps, expecting my baby to be at the bottom, but he wasn't there. I looked everywhere!

I rushed into Randy's room. I stood still for just a moment when I heard a sucking sound coming from the closet. I opened the door. There in the dark was Brad, sitting in his little walker, looking confused, but contentedly sucking on his pacifier. What was the point of Randy hiding his brother? I tried to dismiss it from my mind, but I always wondered.

Finally I drifted off to sleep.

I got up early to talk to Jeff before he went to work, but as soon as I started to tell him about the alcohol, he stopped me short by telling me that he didn't want to hear that "stuff" before he went to work. He told me, "I am sick of talking about Randy. That's all you ever talk about!" I wondered when a good time to talk would be. It wasn't after work for sure, and it wasn't before bedtime. Perhaps I should make an appointment with him to pick a time that suited him more. I was alone.

What about the rule? Wasn't our son supposed to be tossed out of the house? It wasn't even discussed. I knew it wasn't going to happen.

It was an empty threat, that's all it was, from two weak parents who just didn't get it.

I had seen enough. I wasn't going to watch Randy slowly kill himself. Since he was staying, then I would just have to leave. Then I wouldn't see it anymore. I wouldn't watch the torture of my child destroying his mind and body. I would go on with my life.

Leaving was more than a notion. What about my other son? Brad would not understand it at all if I left the house. He was away at college, away from the stress of the house. He didn't know that I was dying inside or that my mind may snap if I didn't find release. How could I make him understand if I left? Would he forgive me?

The summer before college began for Brad, I talked to him about my leaving. I started with this, "I am just walking out. I can't handle anymore!" I was not prepared for his reactions. He responded badly to the news by telling me, "Mom, that's the easy way out."

Then he looked me in the eyes, asking, "How can you do this to me before I go away to college? Walking out, now?"

I pleaded with him, "Come with me."

He shook his head, "Dad needs me." I doubted that sincerely, but the guilt was wearing heavy on me at that time, so I had stayed. Three years had passed taking a toll on my mind. I was hanging by a thread.

Brad felt the tension all these years, but he had kept silent. He didn't want to stir up any more strife. He didn't talk, but I knew how he felt because I was the younger sibling who had a brother that drank. I remembered the battles with my parents and my brother Dan. It was almost too painful to recall. I could still see the anger on my dad's face, a man who hated the sound of the word *alcohol.* I could still hear my mother crying long into the night. It was as if someone had died.

My father would lock the doors when Dan went out for the evening. Then Dad would sit up waiting for my brother to return. He would wait late into the night and early morning until Dan tried to open the door. Dad would look into my brother's eyes to see if he had been drinking. If Dan were drunk, my dad would not let him in the house.

One night, somehow Dan managed to get into the house and had been drinking. I heard a commotion on the steps to the upstairs bedrooms. Dan's bedroom was across from mine. Dan was trying to go to bed. Dad was wrestling with him on the steps to throw him out of the house. There was anger in our house in those days. I was just a teenager and didn't understand any of it.

The memory brought back pain. My parents were blown away by Dan's rebellion, but my parents were strong. They stuck together as if they were one. When Dan was eighteen, they made him leave. Just like that! He had disobeyed the rules, and he was gone out of their lives, out of their sight into the night.

They stood in the gap for him for many years, until one day he came home. I found out many years later that making him leave caused as much pain as imaginable. My parents lay in bed at night, holding each other and crying.

Dan now gives his testimony of how his daughter saw him drunk, just the thought of it made him sick to death of alcohol. He said good-bye to his old friend in the bottle, starting a different life. No drug rehab, no AA's, no sponsor, just God. He was forty-two years old at that time. He now speaks to youth about his addiction and is presently a principal in a Christian school. He is a product of two parents that stood in the gap.

So I understood some of what Brad was going through. I knew. I had lived it for years. Sometimes I wondered if I was confusing the old pain with the new pain. Maybe some of my anger was from years ago, just surfacing now. Having Randy at risk of making alcohol his ruination was bringing back some bad times for me.

Was I going to repeat what had happened to my mother during those times, almost having a nervous break down? My mother had spent many hours in her room for months fighting the depression with God's help coming to realize that her other three children needed her. So she gave Dan over to God, putting him in God's care. God did not let my praying parents down. God molded Dan into the man he is today.

It took years, tears, praying, and more praying, but God heard the prayers. He had heard, and he had answered. God did not give up on my brother. Not only was Dan a new man, but God was able to use Dan as a witness to share a powerful testimony.

What if my parents had given up on my brother? What if they had stopped praying for him? They never lost hope for their son. They knew that one day he would come to himself, and he did. His testimony brings tears to the eyes of those who listen. It gives hope. There are no lost causes.

The story of my brother did not raise my spirits. I felt alone. I was losing the war.

The trip to the psychiatrist office was quiet. Randy sat on the passenger side listening to music. His depression had been so apparent. His room had old clothes lying all over the place. The sheets and mattress pad were off the bed. Shoes were everywhere. Papers were scattered. He hadn't showered in days. He was so quiet.

I sat in the waiting room while he went in to see this new doctor. Thanks to that ridiculous HIPAA law, it was all so confidential. But I knew what the visit was all about; Randy wanted something for anxiety, like loads of Xanax the last doctor gave him. I could have benefited from some myself. He wanted something for the pain in his shoulder.

My mind kept wandering back over the years, trying to make some sense of Randy's preoccupation with drugs. The old sports injury was a good excuse for pain medicine. It seemed to me that this was his justifiable need for narcotics. He had been introduced to narcotics early in his life at age fourteen. He broke his arm while surfing. The lower arm bones were totally detached. He was in a cast for months. I never doubted that it hurt.

Then the impacted wisdom teeth and the eventual extraction of them, more pain. One injury seemed to lead to another. Then he broke the same bones in his arm again while wrestling with a friend in our backyard. More cursed pain, always around increasing the need for pain medication.

He had gotten to the point where pain pills became the object of his well-being. He thought that he needed them. They made him "feel good." I tried to tell him that people got addicted to pain medicine for similar reasons, but he always had everything "under control," and I was just "stupid and knew nothing about opiates."

One day, Randy ran out of pain pills early and was denied refills. He tried every angle in the world to get more. Finally, in desperation, he told the doctor's office that someone broke into his room stealing them from him. They told him to file a police report, which he tried to do. But it backfired in his face.

The police officer called me at home to verify his story of the theft. It wasn't so much that he had filed a false police report, but the lies he told and who he accused. The officer read the report of the accusation: "My brother or one of his friends ripped the medicine cabinet off the wall and stole my pain medication." I was horrified at the lie, but even more so that he had stooped to falsely accusing his own brother just to get pain pills. Needless to say, I did not back up his story, which made me a witness for the prosecution. What a desperate act!

After getting off the phone with the officer, Jeff and I sat at the kitchen table in disbelief. We were both ready to pack his bags to send him on his way, but for some reason we had a compelling urge to try to help him. After all, what he had done was irrational. Maybe he would agree to go to drug rehab.

When Randy returned from the police barracks, we were waiting for him. We sat down with him to talk to him. He was cornered, and he knew it. But was he repentant? Was he sorry? I cried as I talked to him, asking him if he realized how low that accusation was, to bring his brother into the whole mess.

The reality of his addiction was apparent to us, but was it to him? We convinced him to go to a twenty-eight day program. I think that he saw it as a way out of a little predicament.

He had been there twenty-two days, not once had he discussed his alcohol use. He had more than one powerful addiction problem. It was a little secret. I wondered what the purpose of the rehab had been. He didn't really want rehab. He had just played the role, putting in the time. He had conned us.

Jeff, Brad, and I went in for the last meeting of the rehab. The counselor asked Randy to tell her what happened at home to prompt him coming to rehab. He thought of a few reasons that he must have rehearsed, but the counselor didn't buy any of it.

Then Jeff decided to tell the counselor about the false police report. For some reason, we never shared with Brad what Randy had done. I had hoped that it would be a secret, tucked away in the jar, but the truth came out as I looked at the shock on Brad's face. Oh, why hadn't we told him so he could be prepared? I wondered how he was even processing the situation. I would never forget the look in his eyes that day.

What was happening to my family? It was an attack, big and powerful enough to shatter the walls forever. It was spiritual warfare.

The day of discharge from the twenty-eight day rehab had arrived. Randy's eyes were sparkling brown, he looked rested, he appeared happy to see me and to get home. But he minimized his alcohol use almost convincing me of this. I knew better. I knew that he replaced one addictive form for another form, but he always had something to take his mind away from the real world.

Now, here I was, in the waiting room of a new psychiatrist's office, while Randy went behind closed doors to convince another doctor of his needs. But this doctor was a surprise because he asked me to come in. I felt elated that I was included in the picture. After a few brief questions from the psychiatrist, it seemed to me that Randy had left out a few details such as the DUI that sent him to jail. More to the point, he had lied.

How was I to know he had left out these things? I was asked to come in by the psychiatrist. I didn't barge my way or ask to come in. It had happened. After the questioning, the doctor changed his course of action, asking that the medicines he prescribed be given to Randy on a daily basis and that the medicines were to be in my care. He would only treat Randy if he agreed to drug testing. Wow! I loved this guy.

We left the doctor's office in silence as I drove Randy to the lab for the drug testing. He was so angry that he refused to get out of the car. Then he told me that he couldn't urinate, so I drove him to McDonalds ordering a large coke. We sat in a booth across from one another with the anger so massive I wondered if other people knew what was going on between the two of us. But how could they? Even I didn't know. What harm could a drug test do? I just wanted to help him.

We went back to the lab as he muttered all kinds of threats, just like a little child who was denied candy before dinner. Finally the ordeal was over. We sat in the car on the short ride home. No one spoke. There was no need for conversation. He was angry with me for interfering with his medications, even though I had been invited into his life. I wanted him to get the help he needed; that was all I ever wanted. But once again, my efforts were believed to be schemes of mine just to make Randy "miserable." More anger over another misconstrued intention. I thought that he wanted to see the psychiatrist to get some help for his anxiety and depression, but he had his own agenda with his own idea of what would make him feel better. He didn't want controlled medication by his parents. He wanted the control. Well, that just wasn't going to happen.

Randy didn't give up very easily. After another week, he told me that he had made another appointment with his psychiatrist to discuss his "meds." He was trying to get some old medications and try the pain medicine scene. I felt helpless again, but then I remembered that the doctor told me to call him for any concerns. I decided to write the doctor a letter telling him about my son mixing alcohol with his medications and his long history of strong alcohol consumption. I hated to have to write it, but surely the doctor could see when a patient was manipulating him. I was a mother begging for someone to help my child.

I sat in the car (per Randy's request) while he saw the original doctor who had ordered the drug testing. When he came out, I saw the anger all over his face. The doctor told Randy about my letter, making him furious with me again. (I guess the HIPAA didn't protect the mother.) Why did everything I try to do to help my son cause me to fall flat on my face, a total backfire? Could he be angrier with me than he was right now? I doubted that. He sat silently the whole ride home.

The deafening silence was back!

THE SPORADIC YELLING

There was anger in the house traveling like lint from one to another. Sometimes, the anger seemed to come from out of the blue, but maybe it never really left. It just sat in the back of ones' mind, just waiting for an opportune time to jump on the tongue so angry words were released in the air for the world to hear. It jumped from one person in the house to another, being satisfied when everyone had been under its attack. Anger was vicious when it bounced around.

The anger was threatening to crack the walls of the house with repetitive chiseling until the foundation of the house started to crumble. Everyone was angry about the same thing, but no one would admit what the real reason was because this would involve confronting the source of the anger. The anger became a secret that was locked in a jar. Everyone stepped around it to avoid the pain. It was easier that way. What was ignored may go away, but it wouldn't be confronted so as to avoid the explosion that would rock the house and cause the walls to fall down.

I was leery of the anger inside me. I was afraid to let it out for fear that I would lose control by starting some insane yelling. It might feel good to let it all out and to say what I was thinking. How dumb would that be since no one was listening?

So the anger sat festering as I exploded over minor infractions, such as unfilled ice cubes trays left on the sink. I was shocked over how nutty I got over the trays, wondering where in the world all that venom came from for crying out loud? But I knew where it came from, and I knew why I was angry. It was an anger of confusion.

Randy left a note that he wanted to get up to go to church with me. *How sweet,* I thought, but I wondered if he had been out late that night. I thought I heard a commotion at 5:00 a.m. Was he just coming home then? If he had been drinking, what shape would he be in?

I knocked on his door, but he didn't answer. Jeff and I got ready for church. Just before we left, Randy came out of his room. What a sight he was! He had been out all night for sure. His eyes were droopy, and he reeked of alcohol. He appeared to me to be drunk at 9:00 a.m.

I hated that look as much as I hated the odor. His room was starting to smell the same way. It was as if Satan lived in there. Satan, that's who I had so much anger for in my heart. He had been given the power to enter my home, stirring up all kinds of havoc. Satan had done a nice job. I hoped he got tired of trying to destroy my child, moving on to another great prize. But Satan wasn't satisfied with just the destruction of one child; he wanted the whole family, the whole house. He wanted to turn us all against one another with anger over all the wrong reasons.

There was a lot of blame in the house. Whose fault was it anyway? Who got the credit for the way Randy looked this morning, all disheveled, looking as if he may fall asleep any minute? I never knew the pain that Randy was having. It was a deep secret.

I could see his reflection in the mirror on the side of the car as we traveled to church. His speech was slurred at times; he was a mess. Why had he wanted to go church anyway? It couldn't have been for sausage biscuits on the way. There must have been another reason.

As we sat in church, I watched him as his head bobbed back while his mouth flew open. It was a disgusting sight. I wondered if anyone else noticed. Who could miss it? The alcohol smell was all around him, in church no less. It wasn't like he was listening to the sermon; on the contrary, he was dozing seeming quite at peace with himself.

I nudged Jeff to look over at Randy. Then the bouncing around anger started. Jeff reached over to touch Randy's arm, who was shocked back into the real world. Randy got angry with his father that he was disturbed since he was "praying." Jeff got angry with me for drawing his attention to what I thought was a slumber party. I got angry with him for actually believing that Randy was praying.

What a perfect time for yelling, but no, this was church. People don't have yelling sprees while the pastor was preaching. So the anger sat in the closed jar, waiting to emerge and surprise everyone.

I kept looking at Randy as he sat with his eyes shut through the whole sermon, looking all relaxed and out of place on a church pew. He should have been in a bed, behind a closed door, where no one could see him. That's where he should have stayed! Then the secret would be safe, no one would know that he drank, but there was no hiding it today.

The nice lady sitting behind us knew. She knew that Randy was under the influence, probably because she had seen it before. At the greeting time, she zeroed in on him, getting close to him. The lady and I looked at one another. There was pain in our hearts. The lady gave a knowing look as we embraced. She didn't need an explanation about my slumbering son. She had been there before.

During the two minute greeting time, the lady, with tears in her eyes, confided in me that her own son was in jail, asking me to pray for him. Jail, the cyclone fence, oh I knew it all too well. I could feel the lady's pain.

I didn't mind praying for her son, but I wondered what good it would do. My prayers certainly weren't helping my own son. Just look at him. I felt like forcing coffee down his throat or throwing a bucket of ice water in his face. That would wake him up for sure. But Randy needed to really wake up to get his life back on track.

I felt the angry feelings trying to bolt from the jar. I mustn't let them loose. The angry words were in my mind, forcing their way to my tongue. I couldn't concentrate on the sermon; I just couldn't. Why did it have to be like this?

Jeff and I were angry with each other instead of the real problem, who sat slumbering beside us both. What was the sense in that? He was an alcoholic!

The ride home was chilling; one could cut the tension with a knife. Occasionally Jeff asked Randy a question in between his head nodding. Obviously, Jeff was not angry with Randy at all. He had a way of not letting our son bother him. I interpreted that way as bailing out, leaving all the worry to me. How could I stop the runaway train my son was on alone?

I was starting to think that Randy liked the fast train, the train of no fear, the train going nowhere. He didn't care that the whole house was affected by his choices. He didn't care that his parents lived everyday with the dread that he may die. He didn't care that substance abuse had a hold on his mind and he was just stumbling along waiting for nothing.

Two days later, Randy asked for a ride to an interview that was taking place the next day. Of course, he needed a ride since his car was still a work in progress with the insurance company. It wasn't that I minded taking him; it was the area where the job was—fifty minutes from home. How did he expect to get to work? Who was going to put in almost four hours of driving? The gas alone would be enough of an issue. But Randy never seemed to think of the sensibility of his choices.

The morning of the interview, he was still sleeping. His appointment was at 1:00 p.m., but at 11:45, he was still in bed. Finally, I knocked on his door asking him if he planned on going. He mumbled something, got up, went to the refrigerator for a snack and sat down at 12:00 noon to eat while watching TV, as if he had all the time in the world.

I was getting a little annoyed; the lid of the jar was getting very loose. I was still angry about Sunday morning and now this. At the very least, he could try to get to the interview on time. The noise in the house started to escalate. I yelled at him, "Get ready for crying out loud. I have to stop to put gas in car, and you will be late!" He had some directions, but was vague as to where the interview was supposed to be, seemingly quite carefree about the whole deal.

The trip turned out to be just short of an hour. I kept lecturing myself to just let it go, he would be late, but I wanted him to work. He needed to do something besides sleep all day. I wanted him to become independent of me because we resented the situation that we were in right now. He hated to be driven places by his mom, again, and I hated the way he kept including me in his messed up situations.

Why didn't he find a job closer to home? But no, this was even in another state. What was the point of all this? Was he just making a job effort to get me off his back?

Then we got into another argument about him wanting to see another doctor about his shoulder. He had already seen two doctors last month. What was the purpose? Then he told me that he needed pain pills because his shoulder hurt all the time. That was it, of course, pain killers.

The lid was off the jar. The lectures started pouring out as if he hadn't heard them all before. My heart was pounding, and my head started to hurt with the same old scene playing again. Even his scribbled directions made me angry. I liked lookout points, distance estimations, not just three street names. How would we know if we passed the place? I hadn't even gotten gas. I was always on edge if I had to listen to that annoying beep from the gas tank light on the dash as the needle dropped toward *E.*

When we got to the destination, I waited in the car forty-five minutes. This was as nutty as could be. I felt anxious with all the sporadic yelling that had just happened. I tried all sorts of things to settle myself down, but nothing seemed to work. When was he going to have his own life and do something positive? Was it ever going to happen?

Finally, I saw Randy coming toward the car. He got in, and instantly I could see the look of despair on his face.

He spoke solemnly, "I'll never get this job. I can't believe how I have screwed up my life!" That was the first time I had ever heard him say anything that remotely sounded like he was in the real world. It caused an ache in my heart to watch him suffer. I wanted to say something to make him feel better, but what could I say? He was starting to feel the rejection caused by bad choices. There would always be some kind of hell to pay.

He sat with his face away from me. I knew that he didn't want to talk, yet I felt that maybe he needed me to encourage him. I said, "People have done worse things with their lives, and they have started over. You can too. Maybe someone in church can give you a chance." He didn't answer me. I knew what he was thinking. He had been in jail, and every time the interviewers did a background check, his would be hazy.

The whole ride home he sat with his eyes shut, not sleeping, just trying to blot out the world. I wondered if he was getting more depressed. He looked so sad that I felt like crying too.

The phone rang. The insurance company was calling. Randy answered it and came running upstairs to tell us that the insurance company decided to fix the car. He was elated. Then some bouncing around anger went flying out of somewhere where it had been hiding for a few days. I told him that he didn't pay his insurance or his car payment, was not working, and couldn't even put gas in his own car.

He automatically transformed into a two-year-old by screaming, "The car is mine!" I yelled, "You have to work to afford to drive."

He replied, "I need a car to find a job!" The anger went from one to the other. Jeff was in on the conversation, but the only one who was yelling was the man-toddler.

The yelling from the toddler got out of hand. I asked him to please go downstairs. But he was not about to go down without a fight, trying to get his father on his side by saying all kinds of nutty stuff about me. Oh yeah, the lid was off the jar completely now. Reluctantly, Randy left the room.

Then the anger, which was still floating around, started to bounce off me then to Jeff and back again. Why were we fighting with each other? He told me that all we talked about was Randy. As if I hadn't heard that line before. Oh yeah, we were getting close to the bone now.

I knew that the conversation may as well be over. What was the point in arguing anymore about Randy? It was always the same type of conversation. I wanted to let our son reach rock bottom so he could start his life over, and Jeff wanted to pick up the pieces so Randy didn't have to hit rock bottom. No one was going to win this one. Why did we have to disagree so horribly? Didn't we both want the same thing?

I was in the war alone. I felt it more than ever. Deep down inside me, I knew that I had to seek help. I decided that I would call the counselor next week, that I would lie on the couch, spill out my guts, and do the little homework assignments that were supposed to make me feel better. I would open the lid of the jar to let all the feelings jump out, blasting the walls. Yeah, I would, tomorrow.

Maybe!

THE TIME BOMB

Those feelings, loosely sealed in the jar, had begun to seep out, ever so slowly. They had some strange familiarity about them. It was as if I had felt this same old stuff—anger, fear, all of it—in another time, in another place. The pain did not seem fresh, but felt as if it had been suspended in the air like a fog cloud waiting to hit the ground. The cloud had been swirling for some time now, lurking around in my mind, just waiting to be felt anew.

How in the name of heaven can prescription drugs be so easily obtained? I knew that Randy was on some kind of medication because I knew my child. He seemed too relaxed, too happy, and too confident. He looked like he had just gotten up from a long nap with drooping eyelids and a stupid look on his face. I hated that look!

As usual, I confronted him. He admitted that he had gotten some "benzos" and "opiates," but he had it under control. These were his legal "scripts." How could it be so easy? How could a doctor be so easy to trick? Randy didn't even have any money. Who helped him get this stuff? Why wonder about it? What could be done? I felt like going on a wild search throwing them all away, all the legal scripts in the trash. What good would it do? He would find a way to get more. He always did.

Of one thing I was certain, Randy would not drive his car. *Slam, click,* the club was on to stay. He had chosen his "scripts," so he had chosen not to drive. The arguing was insane. He once again tried his old line that if he didn't have a car, he couldn't find a job. I offered to take him to any interviews, but he refused. He wanted to drive himself.

Randy's lack of maturity brought back memories of his childhood, when bicycle helmets were required to ride a bicycle. As a matter of fact, it was a law. We bought a bike helmet for him, which he flatly refused to wear. So a power struggle was showing its ugly face. When we told him that he couldn't ride the bike without it, he chose not to ride his bike at all. With eleven-year-old defiance, he told me that helmets were not cool. I tried to tell him that brain injuries weren't cool either, but he never got on the bike again. The bike just sat in the garage and rusted. Maybe that was the beginning of his rebellious thinking. He was in his own little war; winning each battle was crucial to him.

His tantrums in the past had always worked for him. Sooner or later one parent or the other caved in, but not this time. He had come up against a huge wall with neither parent budging.

Now he was a man. Soon he would have the MVA hearing, facing the possibility of losing his driver's license for a whole year. He didn't seem too worried; no on the contrary, he was quite the slug.

It had been years since I thought about anyone who acted like an uncaring slug. That someone was a boy I fell in love with at age sixteen. I was infatuated with him at the time, even though we had little in common. I was the straight and narrow. He was the wild and crazy. For some strange reason, this contrast had drawn me to him. There were rumors of drug use, but I knew that they were lies. Even if they were true, he would quit for me.

I dated him for five years. One night, quite hastily, we ran off and got married against the advice of my parents. That was some thirty-five years ago, when marijuana and alcohol took a sweep over the youth in the country in a time when everyone blamed it on the

Vietnam War. The whole country was in turmoil. The protestors of the war were all over the place.

Those days were still fresh on my mind, as if it were yesterday. He grew long hair, which was the hippy look. Several times I thought that I smelled something strange in the car. But he always had an excuse, a story, and I believed him. The marriage, rooted on lies, was a joke from the beginning and lasted only eighteen months.

My mother tried to warn me, but I didn't listen. All the warnings fell on deaf ears. I was a girl in love who couldn't see the forest for the trees. Everyone knew about the drugs, but I didn't want to believe it. Besides, I would change him.

Then one day, I found the evidence, a variety of pills, mostly "downers." I felt so betrayed and helpless. I was living in the delusion that he would change for me. If he loved me, he would. I tried. I cried, but he didn't care. He had no conscience. He was numb from his drugs, unfeeling. He showed no emotion and felt no moral obligation to the marriage.

He didn't think twice about running out on me with an old acquaintance of his, but I had caught them together. He was careless. One night while I was working late, he and his girlfriend were in our bed. I had walked in on them. The scene before me was like a knife stabbing me in the heart.

I never had the courage to actually go into my own bedroom to see them. Her car in our driveway at 2:00 a.m. was all I needed to see. I cried like someone in mourning.

He had chosen who he really wanted—his drug life and his girlfriend with all his numb feelings. It was like a dream, or rather a nightmare, so unreal. I walked out of the marriage, such as it was, a joint piece of paper. The rejection was unbearable.

I wanted to rid myself of every memory of him, so in the divorce settlement, I took back my maiden name. It was closure, but I was far from ridding myself of the pain.

I became physically ill, losing weight that I could not spare, and then mentally ill. My life became meaningless. I felt that death would be sweet peace. I went to work or stayed in my room back at my parent's home, day after day. Sometimes, several nights would pass and I wouldn't sleep at all. I was exhausted and was wasting away, ever so slowly. Everyone noticed, especially my mother.

My mother had prayed for me, unceasingly. One day, my mother came to my room, telling me how worried she was about me. I cried, but told my mother, "I don't care about living anymore!"

She looked into my eyes speaking softly to me, "If you won't try to get better for yourself, will you do it for me?" My mother reached for me, holding me like a little child. I felt a love like no other and a peace that I hadn't felt for months as the sobs shook my body.

There were no lectures from my mother. There were no lectures of how: "I tried to warn you, but you wouldn't listen," or "I tried to spare you this pain!" My mother knew that I was in a crisis, maybe because my mother recognized my fragile state of mind. She knew all about an emotional crisis. One never forgets!

With the words of my mother on my heart and the strength of an almighty God, the wounds started to heal. I recovered. It was all behind me, or so I thought, but for some reason, it flashed before me now. Why now? It was as if the old wound had reopened as I watched Randy drift through life, day after day. All of his friends were reminders of those days years ago, even my own son was a reminder of a time I thought I had pushed into the back of my mind forever. After all, life was full of learning experiences, and I had learned the hard way. I had suffered.

I had even thought that my life was my own and no one else was affected by it, but learning that lesson was the hardest of all. I had learned how painful it was to see my mother cry. No one should ever make his or her mom cry. Those tears are drops of pain, leaving stains.

That was years ago, but I could still see the pain in my mother's face. I hadn't thought of that look until I saw my reflection in the mirror. It was the same look of anguish and fear that I remembered in my mother's eyes—the look of a mother that may lose a child. The greatest fear for any mother is the fear of losing a child. I feared it everyday. There was no peace, as I feared the worst was yet to come. What if Randy died? What if I lost him forever? To never look into his beautiful, dark eyes again, to never hear him scream at the TV while his favorite basketball team was losing, to never be near him, or to never touch him again. The thoughts were too sorrowful to even think about, too much pain and darkness.

Where was my faith? Yes, where was it? Didn't God know about my pain? How much more would I have to endure? I didn't have the faith that my mother had, and I knew it. What if I had a complete breakdown, ending my thinking and feeling altogether? It had happened to people before; it happened to my mother many years ago.

I had only a sketchy remembrance of my mother's physical illness since I was just six years old at the time. I heard her coughing. I can still see my mother lying on the sofa, ill. One day, my mother's friend came to visit, or so I thought. She told me that she was taking my mother to the doctor, but she didn't bring her back. I stood at the window waiting and watching for hours that day.

My mother was too ill to care for her little children, so my grandmother moved us to her house for the weekends. There were times when my great aunt came to stay in our little house for short times on the weekdays to help out my dad, who was trying to work to support us.

Tuberculosis was having a vengeance on bodies back in the fifties. The treatment was harsh. My mother was taken to a brick sanitarium located in the woods with iron bars at the windows where she was treated with injections of Streptomycin. For the next nine months, my two brothers and I could only wave to her from the parking lot.

I remembered how friendly the squirrels were. I loved to watch them scamper all over the place. They would come right up to my hand, take a peanut, and run back to their tree homes. The squirrels had a great life, no worries; they just played and played.

Her times behind the doors of the sanitarium were hard for my mother. She missed her children, not being able to cuddle and kiss us. The depression sneaked upon my mother as a thief in the night. Before long, she went into a protective shell. She just stopped feeling. It was just too much for her to bear. My mother shut down. She stopped talking or caring for herself. She was almost catatonic.

The doctor told my grandparents that they had to take my mother home before she lost her mind, which they did. For many months, she still didn't talk. Not even having my brothers and me around her again made any difference to her. But once again, the prayers of a praying mother were heard. God heard my grandmother's prayers, and he answered them.

Slowly my mother recuperated, but she would always remain fragile, which probably explained why she struggled so when Dan rebelled. Depression came back with all the old threats, attempting to drag her in the depths of despair. With God's help, my mother fought back, getting the strength she needed to wait for her prodigal son.

What if I got like my mother did? Wasn't it in my genes? Wasn't I already fighting those dark thoughts of dread and worry? Wasn't I having problems sleeping?

The nightmares were so tormenting, leaving me in a cold sweat. When would they stop?

The sky darkened as I looked out of the window and saw the funnel cloud coming right at the house. I knew that the tornado was going to hit my home. I started yelling for my two sons to come with me to the basement, but as always, there was one who would not heed the warning. There was one who would not come when I screamed for him to come to safety. But I kept trying, yelling and risking my own life as the roof started to blow off and glass was scattering all around me. I frantically reached for Randy, grabbing his arm and running with him in a panic to get to the basement as the sound of the wind got stronger and stronger.

Then I would awake from my nightmare with my heart pounding. I was afraid to finish the dream, afraid of the ending. I awoke just before the end every time.

I was afraid. What if there was some hidden meaning in the nightmare? Of course, there was meaning. It was as clear as could be to me. I didn't need to tell a counselor about the nightmare; there was no need. The message was vivid and terrifying. I must lock up these thoughts in the jar, making sure that the seal was on more tightly. Maybe if I did this, the nightmares would stop.

Randy's friend Adam had been missing for a week, but Randy was not concerned. Adam disappeared for days sporadically all the time on a "heroin" binge. Adam had a serious drug problem, robbing him of good jobs and his relationship with his family. He had such potential, a hard worker, but his addiction was more powerful than anything in his life.

Randy met Adam in drug rehab a year ago. Even though the counselors strongly recommended that the patients not stay in contact with each other, these two still did. They went out to eat, and they talked on the phone.

I thought the relationship would come to no good since both of the men were weak. They were just substance abusers who were losing their way in the world. The stakes were high; there was a lot to lose, but neither of them cared.

But this time, Adam had been missing for a week now. Perhaps he was dead, in a gutter, or behind the cyclone fence. His family was going absolutely crazy. They thought that Randy knew where they could find their son. One night there was a sad message on the answering machine from Adam's dad. He was desperate to find his son. It saddened me to hear the pain in his voice, but I couldn't help him. But I knew of his pain and the fear of the worst possible nightmare, to lose a child.

Randy had gotten e-mails from Adam's wife, who was angrily blaming Adam's disappearance on Randy. It didn't seem to matter to her that Adam had used heroin for years and left town for days prior to even meeting my son. It reminded me of times past when I blamed everyone else for my son's bad choices. I had gotten angry with all the wrong people.

Drugs do not only affect the user, their usage of drugs slowly destroys the very souls of the ones that love them. The family members are ripped apart by feelings they cannot explain. We lashed out at all the wrong people, living with the thought that maybe others were to blame. The guilt was real, mighty, and as destructive as the drugs themselves. The wounds grew deep in need of healing, but there was no soothing salve to apply. So we just hurt!

We were living on a time bomb with no idea when an explosion might occur. But the explosion would come; just as surely as night turns into day, the explosion would come.

THE BLAME GAME

Somehow the lid on the jar had broken loose. The feelings inside were strange, dangerously out of control. Who loosened that lid this time? No one should mess with the jar or the lid. The feelings had taken on better disguises, making them more powerful. They waited for the still of the night, hanging on the walls of the bedroom ready to attack the powerless, when sleep would not come.

Finally after seven days, his friend, Adam, called, wanting to speak to Randy. He was alive, but he didn't seem too concerned over the torturous hours of worry that he had caused his wife or his parents. I knew because I heard their messages. I wondered what Adam would have thought if he could have heard his mother cry because she feared the worst fear—that her son might be dead. Anyone that reduces their mother to tears should have to go to hell and be forced to listen to a tape of her sobs, over and over again. His friend had joined the uncaring slugs whose drug usage was much more important than life itself.

Randy's reaction to his friend's disappearance was one of nonchalance, as if he had no fear that his friend may be dead. Didn't he know that drugs kill? Maybe Randy just didn't care.

Another argument was about to happen, and I was never prepared. We would engage in another duel with the same old useless words. Why wasn't he looking for a job? He always had excuses blaming all his misery on his shoulder pain. The need for pain pills was fast becoming his focus.

Randy was a good pitcher. He was a star on his high school's baseball team years ago. With an inexperienced coach, his arm was overused. One day, after he pitched a win for his team to earn its first banner in baseball, his shoulder started to hurt, but he was so elated that day, I don't even think he knew that he had damaged his arm. We were not aware of the harm that came to his pitching shoulder that day.

Randy was a senior in high school and was recruited by the baseball coach at a Division 3 college. I was so excited for him. He seemed on top of the world.

When the day came to take him to college, I felt all sorts of anxiety separation. I didn't think that I would cry, but after we unpacked his stuff and helped him get settled, I felt a heaviness in my chest that I couldn't explain.

What was with that? Hadn't I waited for this day? He needed to be out on his own, so he could grow to make something of his life.

He gave me a hug good-bye. I bolted down the hall as if I were being chased by a ghost. I could barely see the parking lot for the tears streaming like a river down my face. How foolish, nobody else's mom was crying, but I didn't care. I got in the car and waited for Jeff.

He came and didn't speak as we drove away. I sat stiffly in my seat, staring out the window, oblivious to the beauty around the college. We stopped to eat, but the food just wouldn't go down. I missed Randy already. Jeff put his arm around me asking me, "Are you okay?"

That was all it took to cause me to lose composure and shake with sobs. No, I was not okay; nothing would ever be the same now. My firstborn was out of the nest.

After two short weeks, Randy called from college, sounding quite depressed. He tried to throw the baseball, but his shoulder started to hurt again. He knew then that he had an injury. His dreams of pitching in college came to a heart-breaking stop. He wanted to come home.

The trip back to college to bring him home was as painful as the trip to take him there. His hopes and dreams were smashed. I tried to tell him that he could see an orthopedic shoulder specialist and get the injury corrected. He didn't seem to have a ray of hope left in him.

A few weeks later we saw the doctor who made plans for arthroscopy surgery to repair the tear in his labrum. The post-operative time was painful. The pain pills didn't seem to even touch his pain. Physical therapy was recommended early, but even after the first session, he started to complain again about the pain.

Physical therapy was quite the workout. They did "everything possible to rip your shoulder out of joint," as if to inflict more pain. Wasn't the therapy supposed to help? The exercises were painful, and the trips to therapy were getting farther apart. After weeks of pain, he went back to the surgeon to discuss the therapy and pain issues. The surgeon offered no solution. Randy and I called the doctor several times. The surgeon didn't even answer his phone calls. Then I wrote the doctor a letter, but he didn't answer. It was as if to say, "Oh, too bad." It was rather annoying, but eventually I gave up on communicating with the surgeon.

Sporadically, Randy would try to throw the baseball, still hanging on to his dreams, but each time it would hurt. I often felt that he didn't rehab properly, but he rejected that thought. His thought was that he needed pain pills. This was the beginning of more pain pill hell. The pills not only deadened the pain, they took his mind off the loss of the pitching arm. He got a feeling of comfort from the pills. He liked them.

The pills became a force that would rock his life, controlling his movement into a complex world, but pitch again? It wasn't going to happen. Somehow, he knew.

I thought that he should get his mind off the baseball dream and still get an education. We sent him to a local university and later to a community college. But depression sneaked in the back door. His world was collapsing around him. He didn't care if he lived or not. I knew those feelings well. They were dangerous and destructive.

Then the losses of both grandfathers within a short time were added pain. He loved his grandfathers so much. He had been the center of his Pop Pop's world from day one. My dad adored him. Pop Pop would play with him for hours on end whenever they had time together. I gave Randy part of his grandfather's name. They were quite a team.

Then sadly, my dad suffered many strokes. For ten years, he was not in the real world. It saddened everyone to see him waste away. Randy had been angry with God for allowing his Pop Pop to suffer.

Jeff's dad had been quite the athlete back in the forties. At age seventy-five, he could still throw a knuckleball. He seemed to be in the best of health. My boys adored him. He was inducted into the local hall of fame in the town he lived in. One day, while he appeared to us to be in his prime, a stroke ravaged his body, and within three weeks, he was gone.

The next sudden loss was Randy's relationship with the girl that he had dated for three years while in high school. Allison had been a good influence on Randy. They seemed to adore one another. Both of them were away at different colleges, but their relationship had taken a beating with all the campus distractions. One day, it was over!

Then the on-off relationship with Jessica, who had a crush on him for years, became another loss to Randy. It was over, all over. He could do nothing to change any of it.

So many losses with so much pain in such a short time came crashing down on Randy. It would have been tough on anyone, but he faced it all very badly, seeking refuge in all the wrong places.

For two years, the shoulder issue kept a dark shadow over his head. We made an appointment to see another orthopedic doctor to get a second opinion, who recommended another shoulder surgery; only this time, there was a long incision. Sure enough, he had extensive damage to the labrum. The surgery was done as an outpatient, but the pain was so severe that I had to take him back to the hospital to be admitted for IV pain medication.

The pain, the culprit, the ticket for pain meds resurfaced as if it had never been gone. The doctor gave him many prescriptions, which I found I had to dispense to him, since they were disappearing too soon. The pain issues were back with a vengeance and were there to stay.

The physical therapy was ordered again with the same ole tune; too much pain during the exercises, too much pain during therapy, a familiar scene. Once again, he quit on the therapy, but he had an agenda; he would take pain pills.

Randy heard about a pain management clinic in the area, taking the opportunity to make himself an appointment. I soon learned that he was given more pain medication than an end-of- life hospice patient. He had long-acting pain pills, short-acting pain pills for "breakthrough" pain, and pain patches. In the name of heaven, wasn't this a little extreme?

He was supposed to do physical therapy along with the pain pills, but soon enough the therapy sessions were farther apart, and the pain pill prescriptions kept coming. Didn't they see a sinking ship when it was going down? Randy wasn't dying; he had an addiction. Any fool could see that!

I was blaming the clinic for his problems. When would I see the light and be angry with the real reason? Randy was addicted. I tried to warn him that the pain pills would chew him up and spit him out, but he didn't listen. He found solace in the pills. They made him forget all about his shoulder and all the rest of the pain that he had bottled up in the jar. It was too much for him to handle as he became empowered by the curves that life had sent him. He had been beaten beyond what he could endure. He became lost in his own anguish.

The pain pills helped Randy forget that his brother Brad was recruited to pitch in college, that his brother had a well arm, and that his brother was succeeding in life. Randy never saw the sacrifices that Brad made to pitch. He never knew all the parties, sleepovers, and vacations that his brother had to say no to so he could play baseball all weekend. Randy couldn't imagine playing sixty-five games in a season in the heat. This was not fun and games; it was work.

He never knew about the criticism or the stress that Brad had to endure to pitch in a highly competitive, baseball team. It was not all the glory Randy thought it to be; it was tough. Baseball training was intense, with discipline and plenty of work. It was competitive with bucket loads of stress that was always there from game to game.

Anyone that ever made a success story had to work hard. That's what it was all about; training and more training, making yourself even better than before, breaking your own records, running faster, lifting more weights, and never giving in to the pressure. Brad would never stop trying. I knew that about him; it was strength that only a few possessed. It was endurance. It was the life my younger son had chosen. This life worked for him. He wanted the dream of playing professional baseball bad enough to never stop trying.

When Brad pitched, no one knew by the look on his face what he was thinking. If he got a bad call, he would just reposition his hat.

If a player missed a play, he never looked in their direction. It was a game of surviving. It was as if he had adapted a temperament, one that was needed in order for him to move forward, one step closer to his dream. He had chosen.

But Randy had high emotional responses to the point where I had never understood his infatuation with pitching, especially since he got very distraught on the mound. He would stare down his players if they missed a play or give the ump a look of disbelief over a call he didn't like. He would kick the dirt on the mound. His feelings were out jumping all over the baseball field. I could hear him muttering out loud; probably nothing good was coming out of his mouth. I wondered if he really enjoyed pitching or was it just a passing fancy. Did he think that we expected him to be a baseball player? Was this added pressure that he felt?

Even if it was, why did Randy quit on playing all together? So what if he couldn't pitch? There were other positions that he could play. He could hit a ball farther than anyone I had ever seen. One game in high school he cleared the fence of the baseball field and the trees with a homerun. The ball was never found. He could do something besides pitch, but he had quit. He had shut down on other potentials he had. He hadn't wanted to work hard and rehab; it was all too much for him to have to do. To quit was the easy way out and pain pills took the edge off the very thought of him never playing baseball ever again.

He blamed his misery on his "bum" shoulder. I blamed his misery on his pain pill-controlled universe. Whose fault was all this anyway? Who really was to blame? Addictions were taking over his life. He was losing control.

So there was much anger and blame still sitting in the jar. No one ever got a warning when one of them might seep out and explode, causing a flame of reactions that no one even understood. Soon anxiety and depression surprised everyone by swirling out of the jar when no one knew they were even in the jar. They became fixed on the whole house. They shook the walls, they cracked the foundation of the soul, and they were determined to destroy what sanity anyone had.

They robbed the sleeper, they killed the appetite, and they caused the heart to pound. Anxiety and depression ate away at the peace of mind until a tight band formed on the head that left a throbbing headache and a sense of dread for no apparent reason. They moved in, taking the house by surprise, and were not about to leave. They were a team, together, capable of irreversible destruction. They were to be feared!

THE WALLS

There were walls, individual walls around everyone in the house. No one was aware of the walls that had been unconsciously built by each member in the house. The walls were different sizes, but they had one thing in common—they were for the protection of the mind, to keep sanity intact. They could not be explained because the walls were invisible and were vulnerable to attacks. At the very best, the walls were weak, dependent on the seal of the jars that kept all the bad feelings hidden.

For three years, Randy's shoulder pain took over his life. By then Brad was in college. We soon became aware that Brad chose to stay at college more, where he was safe from the disturbances within his house. This was his wall that kept him free from the battle sounds within the house, free of wounds. He had chosen to stay away from the war.

There, Brad didn't have to hear about the pain within the house. There, he could pretend that everything in his world was just fine. He was pulling away, slowly, trying to find a place of better security for his own sanity.

He was coping in his own way, the only way he knew. He didn't talk about any issues within the house. Nothing was new about the war that had been raging for ten years, which was still at a level of intense heat.

His visits from college were brief, never spending the night in our house. He brought his girlfriend, Nicole, with him for almost all the visits. Maybe he thought he was safe from the war if he brought her since the battles in the house were hidden for a time. The dirty laundry was swept under the carpet, but just for a short time.

Brad knew that the foundation of the house was shaky with fingering cracks, ready to crumble and fall. He didn't want to watch. Maybe he feared what would be left if the walls fell down. Maybe he felt powerless to rid me of the pain he saw in my eyes. I tried to hide it from him, but he knew.

He didn't talk.

Jeff had his own wall, which I hated and envied the most. It was the best wall of all, a wall of detachment filled with illusions that everything would work out just fine. He didn't give in to anger like I did. He dealt with the war in his own way. He had wounds, but he never let them bleed. The wounds were hidden, bandaged tightly. He didn't lose sleep, he didn't lose his appetite, and he didn't fret over the war within the house. He didn't want to participate in the war, so avoiding the war made it all go away for him. He didn't see the need to talk about Randy. Anyway, hadn't we said all there was to say? What was left?

Jeff didn't want to discuss the road Randy was traveling. He coped much better with the deafening silence within his wall. After all, wouldn't talking about such things bring too much reality and pain? Wouldn't talking open the wounds?

I knew Jeff was hurting; we wanted our son to be successful, to make good choices, to start over, but each day, we didn't see any change. It was all so suffocating.

I knew that he feared Randy would die. God had spared his life so many times, but how long would this go on? What if the guardian angel grew impatient and ran off to help someone else's child? What then?

Maybe Jeff had more faith than I did. Maybe God gave him strength and peace, but I doubted that. I knew that his mighty wall was his protection. I hated his wall!

He didn't talk.

My son Randy, the one I worried so much about, what was his wall? Was it his room, where he could go and hide for hours? Was it his computer or the TV? Was it movies that totally took his mind off whatever was bothering him? They were all temporary fixes to issues that were sealed in the jar. They were his world of unreality.

Perhaps his wall only appeared if he drank alcohol. Maybe he relied on substances to help him build a wall that would protect him from the pain he had inside. He believed lies from the enemy, the enemy that sought to destroy his confidence and well-being, the powerful enemy that knew the weaknesses of everyone, the leader of the dark world, who wormed his way into the soul, robbing him of joy and peace. The enemy that never rested until the soul was destroyed with a lost spirit.

Randy's wall didn't seem to protect him from the enemy. Randy was in a spiritual war that left him powerless unless he looked to God for strength. His wall was too weak, filled with anger. He was dealing with feelings that even he didn't understand. He struggled to make good decisions. It was as if the choices were being made by a force that no one saw, by a force that was on a mission to ruin his very life. How could any wall be enough protection from such a force?

But the enemy was powerless, unless given the power. The enemy had snuck into the house in the still of the night when everyone was asleep. He had taken the house by surprise before the walls were even built. The house was unprepared for the attack.

Randy wasn't even aware who the force was. He didn't even believe in such things. How could he call on God to help him if he didn't recognize the enemy for who he was? He didn't have the armor on, the protection he needed to fight such a force. No one could fight the battle for him. It was his war. He was difficult to talk to, walking away if I tried. God was not the center of his universe, so he battled with what he had, a weak wall and a weak spirit. He was unable to choose the narrow path. He tried many times to do the right thing, but he became powerless over his own addictions.

He didn't talk.

Where was my wall? Where could I hide from the pain of my family falling apart? I loved to write. I hid in my work whenever I could. It was my solace and stress releaser. It was like having a session with a counselor, something I meant to do, but never did. I just wanted to write, write down all the feelings that were jumping around in the jar.

I wrote letters to Randy since he wouldn't talk to me. We were both so angry with each other most of the time. I had written him several letters, keeping the copies. I found a copy of a letter in which I had poured out my heart to him. I wondered what he did with the original letter. I never saw it after giving it to him. I thought maybe he had just thrown it away like junk mail.

Dear Randy,

How weird? A note from your mom, but as you know, I make myself feel better when I write things down, things that I can not bring myself to say to you without emotion. And so, I will write this and cry to myself, tears that you will not see.

When we were talking in the car today, as I was preaching about making things right, I became guilt-ridden over something I have needed to tell you for some time now. I knew at that moment that I needed to make this right with you, so before I even tell you what it is, I owe you an apology. Before you read on, I am going to tell you that I am sorry about the content of this letter.

About a month ago, I found my sapphire earrings, the ones that I accused you of stealing. I do not recall putting them where I found them, but I sat down looking at them for a long time, thinking to myself, *how could I face you and tell you that I was wrong?* I had treated you "like a criminal," accusing you of something that you did not do, even after you bitterly denied the accusation. I have kept this little secret of guilt in my heart and soul. Not a day has gone by that I didn't want to tell you, but I felt so guilty I couldn't look you in the face. I am even taking the coward's way out by writing a letter of apology to you. Please forgive me.

I have just asked you to do something that I never heard either of my parents ever ask. Believe me they could not have possibly been right all the time. When my brothers or I did anything that our mother did not like, she wouldn't speak to us for days. I think that I feared her wrath so much that I was as close to good as I could get. Then the day came when I ran off and got married. I recall coming home and telling her and Dad. I couldn't look them in the face because I felt guilty. I knew that the hurt was in their eyes. It was a very long time before we were able to talk about it. I know that my mother softened when I finally came home alone and close to a nervous breakdown. But this letter is not about me. I just wanted you to know how my parents handled things. They did the best they could.

When I have looked into your face these last few weeks and seen your clear eyes, I have been on cloud nine. When you told me that you hadn't drank in twenty-two days, my heart was singing. For don't you see that I have guilt to deal with as well? We are a lot alike. I feel that maybe if I had been a different kind of mom, maybe you wouldn't have had to face so many "rocks" in your young life. I feel that maybe if I had shown more love, everything would be different. I have listened to Satan whisper to me that I am not a good mother. Oh, how I have listened to him. He really doesn't have to try so hard to convince me. I am unsure of myself. My lack of faith in God opens up the door for lies to enter my head. Satan is not satisfied until he can destroy my very soul.

Satan wishes to destroy you as well; don't listen to his lies. I believe that God has allowed you to go through all these trials because he needs you for his work. What a powerful witness you would be! Satan wants you to get down on yourself. He wants you to believe that the people that love and pray for you every day don't really care about you. He wants you to feel bad about yourself. He is relentless, but he does not have the ultimate power. But we need armor to fight him, or he will win. We are all in the same battle, only in different ways. He knows our weak spot, and he goes for it.

When you were born, your dad would come home on his lunch break everyday just to see you. He never let anyone baby-sit you. He trusted no one with you. When we visited your grandparents, a place you dearly loved, he would worry about you being in the shed with Pop Pop playing with tools for fear that you may get hurt. Even now, when I have suggested certain jobs, he has expressed concern that you may get hurt.

Several years ago, a co-worker at your dad's job lost her sixteen-year-old son to a drug overdose. When your dad told me, we held each other and cried for a boy we didn't even know. Many times when you have slept for hours, it was your father that wanted to check on you. We confessed to each other that we were afraid that one day we might lose you forever. We cried.

Your dad may not say the right things or do the right things, but never doubt that he loves you or doubt that I do. Satan wants us to think that we have failed by succeeding in driving us apart. He will use anything to wreck a family, shaking the foundation of the home.

But I am determined to not let him win. I am not going to get the Mother of the Year award. I can live with that. I have done my best. Even though I know that's not enough, I will still keep trying to be the best mother I can be.

I have made a big start today by telling you about the earrings. The secret is no longer a burden to me, and I have God's forgiveness. I am asking your forgiveness now.

I know that this is getting a little long and you hate to read my "sob stories," but I cannot stop writing. I want you to know that I love you with all my heart. I have had difficulty separating my anger that goes to you instead of your bad choices. No matter what is in the past that is where it will always be. We can forget the past, move on, and start a new day as a new beginning, or we can let the past eat away at us and destroy our spirit, the spirit that drives us to do the right things.

It was great having you in church today; you looked so handsome. No one could have looked at you today with a hint of suggestion that you were anything but a regular church mouse, all clean-shaven with crystal clear eyes. I was so proud of you.

I wish I could take all your hurts away, but I cannot do that. I can only stand by and pray for you every day. My prayers are that God will use you in a mighty way. I pray that you will find peace and happiness in all your decisions. I believe that one day very soon, you will look at yourself in the mirror and be proud of the man you see and the choices you are making. Doing the right thing is a long walk on a narrow road. But with each good choice you make, you will find that you will feel better about yourself. Accomplish what you can so that you can find happiness and peace. Don't worry that Dad and me aren't noticing the steps you are taking. We are both aware because we see it in your face. You look healthy and drug-free. I will stay on cloud nine today as long as I can. For each day, like today, I will thank God.

I love you.

Love,
Mom

I had written that letter months ago, but he never said anything about it. He didn't talk. He didn't say that he forgave me. It was as if the letter had never been written.

I wondered what he thought or if he understood how guilty I felt when I had falsely accused him. Mothers are not perfect people. We make mistakes just like everyone else.

I never mentioned the letter either. I didn't talk. But the jar was getting full with feelings that were threatening to lash out and cause a mighty explosion.

The walls remained, day after day with each member retreating behind their wall of protection. No one was talking. There was no purpose in talking to a wall since the words would just bounce off as a worthless waste of energy. Words couldn't penetrate a wall and would crash to the ground. The wall surrounded the jar of feelings that only protected bad thoughts. The wall was dangerous, refusing to allow healing. The wall was a mighty deceiver, preventing peace by making the feelings in the jar harder to face.

It would have been a perfect day for a drive in the country. Just seeing the gigantic, gorgeous homes with horses grazing on the grass behind white fences seemed to make the ride even more enjoyable. Then the biggest thrill of being on this road was trying to get a glimpse of Cal Ripken's home. The trees made it very difficult to see the huge home nestled in the woods. Then the road did a sharp L-turn alongside the iron gates that blocked the entrance to the estate. I had to slow down to twenty miles an hour just to make the turn. Even though the trees were there, sheltering the home from onlookers, everyone knew the baseball legend lived up the hill. It would be impossible not to look and stare. There was always hope that maybe Cal would be coming down his driveway.

I had always wanted to see him. I went to Camden Yards once; I didn't see Cal play. It had been such a disappointment. I wondered if I was the only woman in this country that had never seen Cal in action.

Then the two-hour trip continued on as the scene looked more like a city with a mall, with huge buildings. I was looking for the street that would take us to one particular building. The fun ride was over, the scenery was gone, and reality was here.

This was not a pleasure trip, but a day of possible reckoning. There wasn't a cloud in the sky, yet I felt cold, as if it were going to rain. Once again Randy and I were in the car with an unhappy event about to take place.

At least we hadn't argued on the way. I let him listen to his music, as we seemed lost in our own thoughts.

I had been dreading this day of the MVA hearing to decide if my son should be driving or not. A judge, once again, would decide his fate. I hated going to places where lawbreakers or offenders congregated. I felt the unfriendliness as soon as we entered the building. The negative air seemed to be swirling around all the employees that worked there, or was it my imagination running wild? No, I was pretty sure that in order to be hired for a job in that building the employee had to be totally lacking feelings of any kind and had to score 95 percent or above on the lack of common courtesy. If not, they just wouldn't qualify.

The cool receptionist reminded me of the employees beyond the cyclone fence that I had met months ago. These employees were equally as unfriendly as the employees at the detention center. I thought back to the ordeal my brother Tom had endured when he tried to visit Randy in jail. It was almost comical now to think that he brought back to the check desk not only his framed certificate but copies of his sermons. There was no one like Tom.

The whole ordeal of Tom's rejection still angered me. If such treatment was experienced by law-abiding citizens, what kind of treatment did the lawbreakers get? The thought terrified me. I was so glad that the detention time was behind us, yet this place seemed to bring back all those memories that I wanted to forget. This building was a reminder.

The MVA building was actually a reprimand place, but a place of necessity. I felt the cool breeze as soon as we arrived.

At least we didn't have to walk through a metal detector or empty our pockets. I didn't have to send my purse along an escalator belt that took pictures of my lipstick or anything else that I had in my purse as it passed by the naked eye machine.

We walked up to the receptionist window where there was a huge sign reminding you to check in. There was a clipboard with a sheet of names and two pens. We wrongfully assumed that we had to sign in. As Randy picked up one of the pens, the unsmiling lady, who appeared to absolutely detest life itself, asked him, "Why are you here?" While holding the pen, he told her, "For a hearing." She replied, "You don't need to sign in. Put the pen down! The waiting room is around the corner." She dismissed us from her presence as if we were soiling her breathing space. It was a bad omen.

One could only assume she thought he was going to steal the twenty-five cent pen and sell it on the street for thirty cents to make a profit. He dropped the pen immediately, turning to give me a knowing look. We had both been the receivers of the same old attitude before. What else was new?

We walked into the waiting room as directed to sit down with the other lawbreakers. Most of them seemed to have a lawyer with shiny, leather brief cases. Randy and I didn't have anything, just a piece of paper with a few dates that my son refused to look at to help plan for this day. He never seemed to expect the world to come crashing down on him. This was his first mistake.

The people in the waiting room whispered to each other in low tones as if they were afraid someone might overhear their conversation or maybe someone would yell at them to shut up. Maybe there were surveillance cameras somewhere making sure that no one picked up a pen that didn't belong to them.

I hadn't been in the waiting room five minutes before I started feeling totally out of place. I hated waiting, being stared at, and the reason that we were there in the first place. I was getting on my own nerves as I watched the slow hands move on the huge clock on the wall.

I looked around the room, becoming aware that everyone had papers. Seeing the papers fast became a sad reminder that we were empty-handed. All too soon, I would learn that having no papers was not good.

We had arrived early for our 11:00 a.m. hearing, so there was plenty of time for the stress to escalate, which it did! By eleven fifteen, Randy's name was called. A lady with a clipboard walked to the door and stated his name. She then abruptly turned and walked away, leaving him no choice but to sprint to keep up with her. It was as if she had no time for being polite or for waiting for the worried lawbreakers to follow her.

The announcing lady was already going down the hall, totally missing the chaotic scene in the waiting room as I tried to join my son and caught my foot in the strap of my purse, almost causing me to fall face first on the floor. Luckily, I managed to free my foot and sprint down the hall in search of the two of them.

We walked into a small room with two chairs in front of a large desk; one chair was in the corner of the room. A lady judge walked in asking Randy, "Do you have a lawyer?" He said, "No." (She scared me a lot more than Judge Judy.) Did that fact somehow make everything all too easy? The judge motioned for him to sit down in front of the huge desk and asked me to sit in the corner where the mother of a lawbreaker should sit. It was as if I was in the doghouse and the corner was my punishment. This was a place where I could be seen and not heard, but I was given the privilege to watch the action.

The judge placed a tape recorder on the desk and spoke some numerical mumble jumble about the case to be heard. Then she began the proceedings by asking for his license. As Randy passed the card over the desk, it was painfully clear to me that the license would not be returning to his wallet. She asked for the license because she had every intention of taking it, adding it to her collection for the day. She had a job to do. The license was the only proof of who he was since we brought no papers for the hearing.

The judge asked all kinds of questions: did he work; did he go to school; did he go to AA meetings? There was a long list of questions. He had all the wrong answers. Randy had tried for months to get a job, but once the background check was done, he was rejected. He hadn't signed up for college because we didn't know if he would have transportation until the hearing was done. He needed the car to do all the things she asked.

How strange that working people and college kids are readily assumed by judges to be law-abiding citizens that don't drink and drive! I worked with people who stopped for drinks on the way home from the job. I knew that college kids drank, probably more than anyone really knew or wanted to know. One day soon, I was going to find out just how much drinking a college kid would do. As parents, it is a good thing we don't know what we may have to face.

The judge was quick with her decision, telling him that he would lose his license to drive for six months. She added that he needed some kind of medical examination. The MVA would get in touch with him afterward. Her job was to protect other people on the highways, just like the judges we saw in court. They didn't have an easy job. What did I expect from her anyway?

Randy seemed shocked by her verdict and her recommendation. He told the judge that he had been seeing a psychiatrist for months. She snapped at him, "You never told me that!" But would it have mattered at all? She didn't change her mind. He didn't have any evidence that he saw a doctor. We hadn't brought any documentation worth supporting his case. I, the invisible mother, had one of his prescriptions in my purse as I sat in the corner, but I wasn't allowed to speak. It was so hard for me to sit, listening to the drill, not being able to offer any evidence.

The judge never asked him about seeing a doctor. She had only asked about AA's. We have to assume that going to AA's meant that you knew better than to drink and drive.

The invisible mother had tried to interject the name of a drug rehab that Randy had completed, but the judge told me firmly that I was not allowed to speak. So I just sat in a corner keeping my mouth shut like a good invisible mother of the lawbreaker.

I started to feel some real pity for Randy. How much more would he have to face because of his bad choice to drink and drive? He had already lost the license for four months and spent forty days behind the cyclone fence. Jeff and I had agreed to put the club on the car for months as well. Now he was trying to get his life back in order, and he had nothing: no car, no license, no job, and no college.

I was starting to see how hard it must be for inmates trying to fit into society after serving their time, having no one to give them another chance. I knew Randy had done wrong; there was no excuse for drinking and driving. People died from the combination, victims at the mercy of drunk drivers. But he hadn't been drunk; he was barely over the legal limit, which five years ago wouldn't have mattered. He had been punished, more than once over the same ordeal, and now again today. Would it ever be over?

The judge was punishing me as well; after all, I wasn't a good mother. The judge knew that from the first moment she met me. Good mothers don't have to take their sons to such places. I was ignored through the whole process. I was in fact, the invisible mother. Did a person start to beg at this point?

What job did the judge think Randy would get? There were at least ten driver ads in the paper every day, but a clean driving record was a must. There were after school programs and day care, but a DUI meant that such a person should not be around children. Every job that he had applied for required a clean background record. Why would anyone hire him with a hazy background when there were others always around who had a good record? You know, the kids of good mothers. Did he even stand a chance?

Randy had already been to several interviews with hopes of being a prospect until the check was done. Then it was over as quickly as it had begun. No thanks. Rejected and turned away. He sent resumes via e-mail, but he wasn't what they were looking for in an employee. They always had excuses, which looked good on paper. But no matter what the reason, the end result was the same—no thanks, buddy.

I knew Randy well. I worried about the rejections. He would only be able to take so many before he shut down. He would throw up his hands and quit trying. He would be overwhelmed by giving his all-out effort yet being turned away again and again. Who could blame him? Didn't we all hate rejection, fearing it above all the other feelings we have? Wasn't rejection the most demeaning and painful to handle? People with good mental health felt the sting of rejection.

It didn't matter whether you brought it on yourself or not; the rejection got into your mind, making you feel just plain weird. It made you wonder if you were accepted or even loved for that matter. It left you feeling like a lost cause, waiting on the road for a ride to nowhere.

I felt all these things myself that day, but I knew that he felt even worse. He wasn't coping well with any of this and six months was an eternity for him. Six months was an eternity for me, too.

Once again, his choices had an impact on everyone.

The ride home was quiet with the music turned down so low; I couldn't hear what was even playing, nor did I care. I looked over at Randy, but he was looking out of the window. Was he thinking of his empty wallet with no money and no license? Was he thinking of being a passenger while his mother drove him around, again? How many times had we done this very thing? Today certainly didn't leave him with much dignity. I could only imagine how it felt to have someone take your license from you as punishment for a bad choice.

Would he learn anything from this? Would anything change in his life because of today?

We were almost home and as we were about to pass Arby's, he asked, "Mom, could I have something from Arby's?" He asked just like a little boy, who needed some comfort. I once again felt pangs of pity for him.

I looked at him saying, "I will stop and get you something because I feel sorry for you today. Not because of the verdict from the judge, but because you won't admit what is sending you to appear before the judge. Nothing in your life will change until you come to understand why your situation is what it is! But nothing I say to you seems to make any difference. If alcohol were doing to me what I see it is doing to you, I would run so far from it that it would never find me again. Its power is destructive! In the end, you will have nothing."

I looked over to him, but he might as well have been on another planet. The lecture fell on deaf ears, again. The words hit the wall and fell to the floor.

There was no reply.

"I'm going to blow my f——ing brains out," he screamed, running out of the house.

How many times had I heard him say those words? It made me wonder how many times that he said those words to himself. Could those words be ignored? What if he meant what he said? What if he carried out the very act of ending his own young life?

How I hated to hear him swear! He knew swearing agitated me, but he added those words for effect. He made his point, but was he bluffing or not? How could I be sure?

I wanted to try to save him, to protect him from the possible harm that he threatened upon himself, but how? He had tried before, did he really want to die or was he just thinking of ending the pain that he had inside of him—the pain that no one understood, the pain he hid deep inside, locked in a jar.

I was at work when the call came. I was unprepared for the call, a single call that could change one's life forever. I feared such a call.

A neighboring hospital emergency room doctor was on the line. As soon as I knew the source of the call, panic raced to my heart. I gripped the phone until my knuckles were white.

"Your son, Randy, is here. He took an overdose of pills. We have given him charcoal. He is fine now. You can come pick him up," were the detached words of the doctor.

I was not ready to end the conversation. I was distraught and had many questions, but there were no answers.

"How many pills did he take?" I asked, trying to understand what my son had tried to do.

"Plenty," answered the doctor.

"Well, shouldn't he stay there? Isn't he suicidal?" I pleaded for answers.

"No! He drove himself to the hospital, so he doesn't qualify for in-patient," was the unconcerned reply.

"How does a person qualify for in-patient? Arriving toe up to be placed in the chilly morgue? I want him to stay and get treatment," I pleaded.

The answers were all the same, total indifference. Then the doctor, who was tiring of the meaningless conversation, told me that the HIPAA law would not allow him to discuss anything else.

"HIPAA? This is garbage. How can I help my child if you won't tell me what I need to know? That HIPAA law is just an escape for you, but I am sure that you will send me a fat bill for this visit telling me why I should pay the hospital and why I should come get him," I replied in anger. What was wrong with this screwed up system? Since when is a twenty-year-old considered to be an adult person, especially when he lived with his parents who paid all his bills and health insurance?

I was getting more upset by the minute. I told the doctor that I would not come to get him since I was at work and that they should call his father.

"Your son has asked that you come alone," was the disinterested reply. So that was it. Randy was angry with his father, trying to punish him. He had played the trump card that caught the attention of his parents. It was a huge card!

I finally gave up since the conversation was going nowhere. The drive to the hospital was long. I thanked God for the guardian angel that had protected my child. Randy had second thoughts about ending his life by seeking help. Maybe the angel persuaded him to turn the car around and head to the hospital. I would never know what prompted him to turn the car around. This made him non-threatening, according to the doctor. How could anyone be so sure?

When I walked into the emergency room, I felt small and afraid as I walked along the curtained cubicles to find Randy. Then I saw him. His tall, pale frame, clad only in a hospital gown, was pacing up and down the small corridor looking for his clothes. Randy ignored me as I stood in front of him. He had nothing to say; he only cared about his clothes and getting "out of here."

His clothes were brought to the cubicle as I waited outside while he dressed. Then I went in sitting on the stool to wait for the discharge instructions. He didn't want me to be in there with him and told me to "go home!"

"And just how do you think that *you* will get home? Are you planning on driving?" I snapped at him as I felt the sting of the rejection that he had thrown at me. "And hand over those keys. You are in no shape to drive." I glared at him as I spoke. It was then that I noticed the charcoal on his lips. It was a reminder to me that he was not stable enough to think clearly. In silence, he passed the keys to me. I wanted to reach out to hold him in my arms, but I knew that he would resist. He was very distant from me at that moment, as I feared that I might lose him. I bit my lip to fight the tears, relieved when the nurse came in with the discharge papers.

The nurse only asked me one question, "Are you his mom?" Was that important somehow? It wasn't like being his mom gave me any privileges. I was surprised that the nurse gave me the papers, after all, wasn't this a violation of the HIPAA law? Randy was disinterested in the whole discharge process. I sensed that he was angry about something.

Was he upset that he was alive? Did he really try to end his life? These were just questions with no answers. It was all a guessing game. I wanted to talk to someone before taking him home, but he was protected by the HIPAA law. There was no support for me. I would have to deal with all of the events on my own.

I felt threatened. What if he had died? Kids killed themselves every day, but no one else seemed too concerned. We walked out into the night to get into the car.

I looked at Randy, who seemed so fragile. Would he talk to me? I wanted answers.

"Why? What were you trying to do?" I implored of him.

He was staring out into the darkness. Finally he answered.

"I only took a few pills, just to get a buzz. It was no big deal!" he answered, quite smugly.

How typical of him to minimize what he had done, but he was indestructible! He only took enough to get the attention he wanted. I learned later that he and his father had exchanged some unpleasant words early that day. I didn't even know what it was about, but they knew. Randy grew silent once again.

As soon as we arrived home, he went to his room, isolating himself. I stared at the closed door as I drilled his father, trying to find out what had happened, but there were no answers. The words that had sent our son to the emergency room were tucked away in the jar. The lid was tight.

It was a year later, before the trump card was played again. There was a mystery with the card since no one ever knew when it was going to be used. It caught everyone unaware. It was powerful.

Randy had two more weeks left of the college semester. I knew that he was unhappy. He hadn't made any friends. The depression he fought for years was overpowering him.

What poor timing that his first real girlfriend, Allison, of three years, ended their relationship at the height of his depression, or was that the cause of the depression? But when was a good time for a breakup? He looked so sad. I ached for him, even though he had betrayed her. He was going to pay. There would always be a consequence for a bad choice.

He came home one weekend. One look at him told me he was in trouble. His eyes were dull. He was suffering. I tried to talk to him, but he didn't want anyone to know how badly he felt. He was alone.

As I drove him back to college, I noticed bruises on his face. At first, I thought that he had been in a fight. I asked him about the bruises.

He looked away ignoring me.

I couldn't let it go. I knew that something had caused those bruises. I asked him, "What is wrong, Randy?"

He turned to me, speaking in a monotone voice, "I hit myself in my face with my fist!" I was shocked to hear what he said—shocked that he would hurt himself like this and shocked that he was in such pain.

I turned the car around to take him to the pediatrician that had cared for Randy since birth. Dr. Dandy was the primary doctor of children until they turned twenty-one years old. Dr. Dandy knew him well. The doctor saw him for only a few minutes before he came to speak to me. He told me that Randy was in a crisis. Well, that wasn't really news, but at least he was compassionate. Dr. Dandy and I looked at one another. We cried.

Randy hadn't even played the trump card, the suicide threat. There had been no warning. But it was there just the same, lurking in the shadows.

Once again, we had to go to the emergency room where two doctors had to verify that Randy needed an in-patient crisis intervention. We waited for hours. Everything was a procedure. We had to wait for the insurance company to say that they would cover the bill. What a system this all was, a system about money, not crisis.

This was a world of indifference. Upon admission to the ER, the nurse asked him questions like she had asked a million others in her career. She never looked up from her paperwork to glance at the poor mother, who was in a state of shock.

The cool nurse asked him, "Are you thinking of hurting yourself or others?"

He quietly answered, "Yes." The question she asked was really two questions. Which one was he saying yes to, hurting himself or others? Apparently, the end result was the same.

They put him in a room alone with a guard outside the door. Randy was considered a threat to himself and maybe to others, until a psychiatrist said otherwise. I could only look through the glass from the outside. He was curled up on the stretcher looking sad and helpless. It was ripping out my heart, but no one even gave me a second glance. No one offered him any food or even anything to drink. We just had to wait for the psychiatrist to come and evaluate the situation.

Four hours later, the doctor came. The psychiatrist dismissed the guard and made arrangements to send Randy to the nearest crisis center. The doctor walked right past me as if I were a ghost. I had to call out to him to find out what was going to happen. I knew at that moment if he mentioned the privacy trash to me I would surely knock him down!

He told me the bare minimum that soon my son would be transported to the center, which took two more hours.

The ambulance drivers came at last, strapping him on the stretcher. For some reason, this made me feel even worse inside. I felt a trembling like I was coming apart at the seams. This was a dream. When would I awaken?

The crisis center was the scariest place that I had ever seen. We entered via the basement entrance to a series of elevators with iron bars for doors. The basement was dark, secluded, and my heart was pounding as I followed the stretcher to the third floor after we passed a series of locked doors.

Randy was taken to another area to be searched for harmful items, while the nurse interviewed me. The nurse looked like she could moonlight as a carnival worker. She wore a short skirt with a low cut blouse that revealed a huge tattoo. She had on tons of makeup and long earrings. But underneath this outer appearance was a heart that was beating with compassion.

For the first time that day, someone looked into the tearing eyes of a mother who was drowning, saying to me, "I know this is hard for you. But he is safe here."

The tears that had been bottled up all day exploded in a rush while sobs began to shake my body. This was all too much for me to handle today, just too much, and two days away from his birthday.

The nurse reached for a box of Kleenex and touched my arm. "Remember," she said, "he is safe here! We will not let him harm himself."

He was safe.

The trump card became useful as time went on, serving a purpose for whoever played the game.

After his second DUI sentence, he was behind the cyclone fence for only one week when he called me, playing the trump card.

He called early one morning, saying. "I am going to kill myself. I know just how to do it. Can you find out where my soul will go after I kill myself?" His voice was distant. His words terrified me.

In a panic, I called the detention center. The trump card got their attention. They sent two guards to get him, locking him up for twenty-four hours in seclusion until a psychiatrist could see him to declare that he was safe.

Randy got so angry with me for calling, putting him through such "hell," that he made arrangements so I could never call there again. He had locked me out. He was angry. I had panicked, thinking he might hurt himself. I felt helpless to prevent his fall. I called so that he would be safe. Didn't he know that?

I had the fear grip my heart that I might lose him. That fear was always hanging in the air, even when he didn't play the trump card. The card was a real threat. How could I be sure that the guardian angel would protect him? Suicides happened every day, right in the home. Being in a home didn't make anyone safe.

Randy had thrown the card out again. I heard his words as he ran out of the house. There would be no peace as long as the trump card was usable. I heard his threat, but I didn't respond. There was nothing to say. I could not save him from himself.

The shadow was a dark cloud hanging in the house. It was real and could not be ignored. Was he safe in the house? I doubted that the house was a safe place. But where was the safe place? Was a detention center a safe place? I had to find it soon. I had to search a little harder, before it was too late.

Could we put blinders on our eyes, pulled shut to blot out what we didn't want to see? I saw what I didn't want to see, too much. I wanted to pull the blinds shut.

I asked God years ago to give me a special sense to know when danger was threatening my children, even when I didn't want to know, even when I didn't want to see. I had seen far more than I could handle. The sixth sense was the uncomfortable feeling I got in the pit of my stomach, appearing out of nowhere.

I could look into Randy's eyes and I knew. He was too calm, relaxed, too chatty, and lovable. He wasn't his usual bundle of explosions. Something was different. I knew.

The battle started with my aimless drilling of him with his serious denial. He played the part of being falsely accused. He used all his cards to throw me off the track. He lied!

Randy had become a con man of sorts, but he couldn't fool me. He offered to be drug tested to prove me wrong, but there was no need. I suspected painkillers. He was mellow, not complaining about his shoulder hurting. He had conned those blasted pills from someone, and he didn't even have any money.

There was a mobile mental health unit that traveled all over the county to help the less fortunate, the ones who didn't have health insurance or jobs. They passed out the medications without expecting any money. The pills were easy to get there.

I wondered who funded this unit and who the doctor was there. Didn't he know a drug abuser when he saw one? Maybe he didn't care. He just did his job and went home to his wonderful life or maybe the doctor felt fulfilled that he helped a few people along the way.

Addiction to pain killers was fast becoming a national epidemic. Heroin was taking second place for the first time in years. Cancer patients had been known to sell their own pain pills for groceries.

Pain management clinics were swamped with patients who complained of various chronic pains. These patients traveled from doctor to doctor, switching pharmacies to keep a stock of pain pills handy. They easily got prescriptions. These people were con artists.

Randy could convince any of his doctors to treat him with pain medication. I thought that he actually believed since the doctors wrote prescriptions this made the usage okay. He minimized that he was addicted to them.

I was starting to wonder if he even knew the truth. I saw how he walked. His voice was like a run-on sentence at times. His eyelids were half shut, as it appeared he was at peace with the world. I watched him as he sat on the deck during the snowfall, puffing on a cigarette, seemingly oblivious to the cold.

I knew that if it weren't for my constant harping on his behavior, he would stay in his make-believe world of peace. Yet, I was always ready to get in his face, ready to search his room, ready to throw out the trash if I found it. He was too clever for me as his hiding places kept changing. I suspected that he carried the pills around in his pocket at all times where they were safe, where I couldn't find them. None of my strategies worked. They had not worked in the past. They were never going to work!

.

I drove Randy to college one morning when the sixth sense came with a vengeance. I glanced over at him on the passenger side; he was half asleep. I asked him "Why are you so sleepy?" He blamed it on a restless night, but I knew that it was much more than that. He was lying!

There was still a glimmer of hope that maybe he was telling the truth, but I had been lied to so much that I wouldn't even recognize the truth. Maybe he was just tired, and it was all my imagination. That blasted sixth sense. I was starting to hate it, regretting that I had asked God for it. What good did it do anyway? What was the purpose in knowing the truth? The truth didn't make the drug abuse go away.

I thought back to the rehab last summer, (the second program) twenty-eight days to get drugs out of his system. The day of discharge he looked great! He had been so determined to stay away from "benzos" and pain pills, yet he was going to try doing it on his own, his way.

He had chosen to keep the same old friends. His lifestyle became the same again. When would it all end? Would he ever give up his temporary pacifiers to face life with all its issues?

When would he see the light?

Randy was a con artist of the finest. One day, he conned his dad so cleverly that it was days before the con was apparent. He ran out of the month's supply of the medication from the psychiatrist. It seemed that the psychiatrist had rules. If you break an appointment, you don't get the prescription. It didn't matter that he couldn't drive, depending on someone to take him to the doctor. The day before the appointment, he had to cancel the visit because neither parent could take him.

Randy had called the office several times, but no one would call in the mood stabilizer medication. It seemed that psychiatric medications could be stopped cold turkey anytime. He was in a panic, but he devised a clever plan…that had nothing to do with his mood stabilizer medication.

He called his dad saying, "The doctor called in my medicine. Could you drive me to the pharmacy?" Jeff took him, gave him the co pay and waited in the car. Randy walked out with the prescription bag, and they went home.

The prescription bag sat on the table for two days before my sixth sense came back to annoy me. I opened the bag to see a bottle of medications that was labeled a mood stabilizer. I looked closely at the bottle and opened it. I saw pills in there, but there was something very odd about those pills. The bottle was filled with a stool softener, not a mood stabilizer. I took the bottle and the receipt to the pharmacy to clear up what I thought to be a mistake by the pharmacy.

The pharmacy tech looked at the bottle and told me that the date was months old. She confirmed that the medications were stool softeners. He must have taken these out of our medicine cabinet. Then she added that Randy picked up a prescription for pain pills on that day. So my sixth sense was right, again. The only thing I didn't know was which doctor he'd convinced that he needed pain pills.

I walked back to the car and sat there trying to process what Randy had done. He apparently had the old bottle that was filled with the stool softeners in his pocket when he went with his dad to the pharmacy. He managed to have one of his doctors call in a prescription for pain pills. His mission to the pharmacy was to get that prescription filled. He had no interest in the mood stabilizers.

Once he got in the pharmacy, he paid the co pay and walked out as he cleverly switched the bottle of stool softeners that was in his pocket with the bottle of pain pills. He put the stool softeners in the pharmacy bag, and his dad had no idea that he had been conned. If it weren't for the sixth sense, I wouldn't have known either.

We confronted Randy, but as always, it was such a waste of time. He clammed up as usual, acting like he was the victim. He didn't even apologize for the trickery, feeling no remorse. He was a con man with no conscience. All that fine planning for a few pain pills that weren't even a narcotic. What lengths would he go to get something even stronger? The thought was rather disturbing. We were to find out later.

I had to wonder where Randy got his lack of morals and integrity. We had tried our best to instill values into our children, yet he didn't seem to care about any of these values. It seemed that he was all out for himself, whatever made him feel good, even at the expense of those that loved him the most. He seemed unaware that every bad choice he made bounced off all the family members. His acts of selfishness caused pain and heartache. I wondered if he was aware of his actions or their impact. I wondered if he knew the truth about anything.

Randy had become so good at telling lies that I could not tell if he spoke the truth, at least not by looking into his eyes. Yet, there was the weird feeling in the pit of my stomach, that nagging feeling that made me see, even when I didn't want to see. It always surfaced, even though I tried to push the feeling away; it always came back, even stronger than before.

Once again, he had lied. His dad had been the victim, caught totally unaware and unprepared for the medication scam. But it was so much more than just a scam; it was a lie, told to a trusting parent. The lie was painful! Where was the trust now? Would it ever be back? Didn't he know that we wanted to help him? We weren't the enemy. We loved him, but he always pushed us away. He kept us both at arm's length where he could not be reached. It was not a safe place for him to be.

The mother-son relationship had taken yet another beating in the bloodless war with more invisible wounds added to all the other wounds yet to heal. There was no "I'm sorry!" Why should there be; he wasn't sorry. He had the mind of a narcotic addict. He was desperate for pain pills. I would not understand for a long time, the guilt he felt over deeds he could not control.

I had been asked to read the poem "Standing in the Gap" to a prayer group of parents who were congregated at church to pray for their children. I didn't think that I could read the poem out loud since there was too much pain in my soul, but I had been asked to read it.

When I stood to speak, God gave me the words to say. I had my own little speech written down, but my eyes never looked at the paper. The words flowed from my heart, like God intended. As I looked over the small audience, I saw the parents huddled together with tears flowing down their faces. We were all hurting and fearful for our children.

We were in the same war. The pain was in their eyes. I knew that look, the same look I saw in the mirror everyday. We were parents who were losing the war with desperation for relief from the strain of the uncertainty. We worried for the safety of our children.

I spoke of my friend, whose seventeen-year-old son, mentioned on the dedication page, killed himself in his own bedroom and was discovered by his little brother. It had happened a month before I read the poem in church.

All the young people listed on the dedication page of this book were found dead in their own homes. A few of them died due to drugs, a few to suicide, and a few, the story will never be known. But what was clear is that they were gone. They were not safe with their parents in their own home. They had ended their pain.

The walls of the homes were not strong enough for the protection needed. In fact, the walls were weak and blinders were on. No one saw the end coming. If they did, maybe they could have prevented the fall. There was loads of guilt that had to be shoved in the jar with the lid. Those feelings were destructive, damaging to one's mental health, especially the parents. Even when parents hide the guilt, there were others always around who have perfect little kids. These parents did not understand the struggles of a parent whose kid was floundering. They were full of advice; after all, they did it right.

I was reminded of the book by Franklin Graham, the son of Billy Graham, who is one of the most famous evangelists of our time. But Franklin had been a rebel. He wrote about his feelings in a book entitled *Rebel without a Cause.* It made me realize that if a man of God like Billy Graham could struggle with a child, then so could anyone. I mentioned Franklin to someone once, who commented that they were not surprised since Reverend Graham was "never home." Once again, we see whose fault it was that a child resisted the teaching of his own father. If Reverend Graham had been a nine-to-five father, would Franklin have had anything to write?

Franklin wrote of his drinking, staying out late, and about his mom waking him for work with a firecracker under his door. Ruth Graham was tough. She probably stayed on her knees for hours at a time, just lifting up her son in prayer.

Franklin stated that he didn't want to follow in his father's footsteps. He mentioned the pressure of this, being the only son. God had given Franklin a free will, just as he had given to my son. Yet, Franklin had chosen not to obey his parents. Today, Franklin Graham is in fact doing the very thing he refused to do. He was taking his father's place. It was all in the plan that took years to cultivate, but it happened just the same.

It made me realize that there was hope. There had to be. Hope kept the mind sane by healing the wounds that no one saw. Hope floated over the top of the sealed jar. It didn't need to be in the jar since there is too much negative pressure that would stifle the hope— the drive that kept us going from day to day.

If Ruth Graham could survive the war, then so could I. I had to put on the armor and prepare to fight in a war that I already feared. I had to seek allies, wherever they were, to weaken the enemy, thus building my resistance. I couldn't fight the battle alone, or I would most surely lose. I must not be caught sleeping or I might be overtaken while unprotected from the force that threatened my very sanity.

There was hope. I must never let go of hope. One day, my son would see the light.

UNCONDITIONAL LOVE

I knew that I didn't have unconditional love. I wasn't even sure what it meant. Did it mean that no matter how many times Randy's decisions shocked me, that I should just act like nothing happened? But wasn't that what God was all about? Didn't he still love his children, even when we were disobedient? He didn't just love us when we were good, did he?

I heard about tough love. Now this was getting close to home, right on the front lines. But I wasn't tough, not even a little; neither was Jeff.

I saw a friend named Karen that I hadn't seen for twenty years. We only had a few minutes to chat. Karen "kicked" her daughter out at age eighteen. I was shocked, asking her why? She said that she and her husband were tired of the "aggravation" and disruption that her daughter created. Wow! Of course, I didn't ask Karen what the "aggravation" actually was, but it must have been quite serious.

I asked Karen about the other child, the younger one, a son. Once again, her answer was shocking. "Well, right now, he is home. But he is getting mouthy. We asked him if he wanted to go where his sister went." She was as solid a mother as there ever was. She had learned of tough love from somewhere. She and her husband just did what they had to do.

Karen was not sobbing with a broken heart or spending hours having a pity party, just the opposite. The facts were as they were. She and her husband moved on with their lives.

It was refreshing talking to Karen. But my home was quite different from hers since she and her husband were on the same page with the tough love. Maybe that is how they managed to get their child out of their house. They were a team with a mighty wall. Their child could not tear down the wall, which was forbidden territory.

No child should be allowed to disrupt the whole house, but Randy was more than capable of not only disruption, but of tearing down the walls. I knew why. Jeff and I did not agree on the game plan. Jeff thought that he could keep Randy safe in the house, but so did the parents of the young people on the dedication page, but it did not work! If I could interview those parents, would they have tried another approach? Asking such painful questions served no purpose now. They had lost their child. There was nothing but guilt, always the guilt. Their worst fears became a reality. Their homes had not been the safe place that they thought it to be. There was no safe place when a child was out to self-destruct. There was no shelter that would maintain a life when the life had no desire to be maintained.

I remembered the lectures that summer when Randy was in the second twenty-eight-day rehab. Every Sunday, we went to visit him. There were handouts and lectures. The lectures came from the same older woman, who was a recovering alcoholic with five children. All but one of them got caught up in substance abuse of some type. She had been in a war of the worst possible for any mother. Yet she had survived. She was telling us about surviving. Even the lady's husband had bailed out on her. He had taken the easy way out by leaving her, so he did not see the destruction of his own children.

She packed up her daughter at age eighteen, put her clothes in trash bags, and tossed them on the porch with a note saying, "Best of luck." She put out three other children as well. As she told her stories, she didn't cry or appear sad. She had done what she had to do, which ultimately saved their lives.

Sunday was our only visiting day. Brad always went with us to see Randy. There was a lecture time first that the whole family attended before visiting the member in rehab. The rules were very much like the first rehab Randy attended.

On one particular Sunday, she spoke on tough love. What a powerful message that day! She looked over the audience, stating so matter-of-fact, "Your child is at risk to die; he will surely die if you keep him in your home helping him drink and drug. Your only hope is to send him on his way, that maybe he will wake up before it is too late!" She glanced over the audience, possibly looking for our reactions.

She made it sound so easy, just pack a kid up and send him out, but where? To a gutter somewhere, not knowing from day-to-day if he was alive? What kind of love was that? Why did it have to come to that anyway? Why didn't he just wake up, seeing what a shamble his life was in, and start doing the right thing?

Deep in my heart, I knew Randy was not going to change while he lived under our roof. He was going to have to leave. I tried to talk to Jeff about it, but every time I spoke of kicking Randy out, Jeff delivered a sad story about a kid whose parents had tried that route. The kid got worse, or the kid killed himself, never a good ending. Jeff feared he was going to lose Randy as did I. It was all a useless conversation going nowhere, going around and around, causing angry feelings that had to be stifled in the jar before they broke loose and created an explosion capable of moving the house completely off the foundation. There would be yelling and lots of blame. No one would win in the bloodless war. The conversation of tough love was not going to take place. There was no tough love.

Tough love had been replaced by putting on blinders so one couldn't see the floundering of a child. There was no need to fix what was not seen. It was easier that way, at least for Jeff. He always had a ray of hope that Randy would tire of the dark world and come to the light. But I thought Randy liked his world of make-believe, of self-medicating to ease his pain. I did not have the vision that he would change anytime soon. I felt that he would have to be sent out of the house, out on his own. Only then would he wake up! It wasn't as if Randy was a baby; he was twenty-two years old. He needed to grow up.

Could we do what we had to do? We were weak, and secretly we both felt like bad parents. After all, Randy kept making bad choices. Who was to blame? My son was sinking in rough waters, paddling upstream against the current all alone. His relationships had fallen apart. What did he have now? He had pain that no one knew or understood. He couldn't find a normal comfort zone. He had problems making new friends. He created stress levels unimaginable by his procrastination of his college class deadlines.

His room was in total disarray. His class work and mail were tossed in a heap on the dining room table that he hadn't looked at for months. There were dates of doctor's visits with notes from the bank of being overdrawn. It was as if the whole lot was junk mail.

I referred to his lackadaisical attitude as the reason for creating his own hell. Was it any wonder that he was so anxious? He made me anxious. The stress bounced off the family. No one was left untouched by the huge mountains of anxiety. Anxiety had a way of attacking the spirit and leaving a hollow space that nothing could fill.

Anxiety had a way of loosening the seams of one's sanity by sneaking up on a weak spirit in the still of the night. It was empowering. It couldn't be hidden for long because the anxiety had a way of sifting out of the jar as it attacked the well-being of a fragile mind. It clouded the light, so only darkness hung around. It felt like a threatening doom with its end results so uncertain that one could not be prepared for the next attack. But there would always be another attack before the spirit had time to recover from the previous one.

Anxiety was supposed to be a symptom of depression, but I felt that the two were quite separate from one another. I got stressed and anxious at work along with my co-workers, but they were not depressed. What difference did it make? Even if anxiety and depression was the same thing, they were strong enough to cloud the thoughts and mess with your head until you fell down. They would batter the ship, tearing the sails, until the ship sunk to the bottom.

Anxiety was much too powerful to be held in the jar. It had the strength to rob the sleeper. Many nights, I heard my own heart pounding, rocking in my chest. I did deep breathing exercises to get the pounding to slow down.

I went to see my doctor, but he was disinterested in the anxiety I complained of, telling me that I was depressed. He even asked me if I was thinking of hurting myself. I stared at him in disbelief. What was he talking about for crying out loud? I was stressed, not depressed. He wrote a prescription for depression, telling me that I would feel better in a few weeks. It really didn't matter to him that I couldn't sleep or that in two more weeks of sleepless nights, I would be a basket case.

I asked him for something to help me sleep, which he refused to do. He said, "Those meds are addicting. You will sleep as the medicine kicks in." I felt like kicking him; now I was feeling depressed for sure. He should have asked me if I felt like hurting others. I would have said, "Oh, yes!"

I tried the medication only to have the anxiety worsen. Finally, I called the doctor's office asking for the nurse practitioner. I made an appointment with her to talk. Even though the nurse agreed with the doctor that depression was the problem, she changed the medication to one that would help me sleep and improved my appetite.

The deprivation of sleep was a dangerous loss when the troubled mind was deprived. How could I love or even exist without sleep?

Finally after three days of taking the new medicine, I slept. No more nightmares, just sleep. That was several years ago. I tried twice to wean myself off the medication. Talk about addicting, I was hooked on an antidepressant. What could be more addicting than that?

With each weaning down process, the nightmares returned, leaving me exhausted and wide awake. The nightmares were paralyzing to me. The dreams that were frightening seemed to be related somehow. Always I would be losing Randy. I could never save him. He was always out of my reach.

Maybe my dreams were just my inner thoughts created by the huge fear I had of losing him. It wasn't just a fear; it was reality. I felt him slipping away from me everyday and wished I could turn back the hands of time.

The meeting had been called by the middle school teachers in Randy's eighth grade classes. I went alone. I sat in the little circle with all my son's teachers, listening in shock as they filled my ears with every negative thought they had for him. One teacher suggested I send him to military school. The very thought made me cry, right in front of all of them. This couldn't be Randy they were discussing.

There was one teacher who didn't seem to share the negativity of the others. He thought that sending my son to a private school might give him the structure he needed to bring his focus back. He spoke with warmth in his voice. I cried again.

I tried to speak, but it was useless. What was there to say? They had said it all, but I loved my son. No matter what they said to me, I loved him. Someone had to have hope for him and believe in him. I would be the only one if need be. Was this the unconditional love? Maybe I had it after all.

Randy's last year in middle school had been a series of disasters. The principal of the middle school asked Jeff and myself to come to school for a meeting with him. Our son had been suspended for an "altercation." I didn't even know what the word meant. When I found out that Randy had been in a fight, I could hardly believe it. He never fought. He was passive. I always worried about him being bullied around. What a shock! He wasn't being taken advantage of; no, quite the contrary, he had become tough in the overcrowded middle school.

He had learned the art of survival and protection so that no one ever dared try to push him around. He had become tough. He hurt the other boy. He was proud of himself, and secretly, so was I. I hated to think of him being picked on because I had seen his passiveness over the years. Now I wondered where this tough guy came from. It was as if this other person in his body had erupted and there was no stopping him.

The principal wanted us to know that fighting was not acceptable behavior. I sat quietly listening to him while inwardly I smiled to myself. Randy was learning to take care of himself at last.

Later in the school year, Randy was kicked off the bus for a variety of bad behaviors. I saved the notes from the school, putting them in his scrapbook to show his children some day. The notes were descriptions and actions of a kid I didn't even know, my own son. Who was he becoming? What was it all about? What was he trying to say or do? It was becoming embarrassing, but I never stopped loving him.

Unconditional love comes from the heart of a mother planted there by a God, who loves his children the same way, even when they are unlovely. Love doesn't need to go into the jar; it just floats all around serving as a reminder that there is nothing greater or stronger in this world than love. Love is deep; it has to be.

CHILD IN A MAN'S BODY

I could hear the screaming and the kicking coming from the other side of our bedroom door. Our two-year-old was standing outside our locked bedroom door throwing an ugly fit in the middle of the night. How long would he persist? This was the fifth night in a row. We were exhausted and about to cave, but we had decided to take the advice of our pediatrician. Under no circumstances were we to allow Randy into our bed to sleep. He had his own bed. Randy had preferred to get out of his bed and to wander into our room for months now. It was frustrating. We were so tired.

The advice sounded easy when Dr. Dandy told me how to keep Randy out of our bedroom, but this was the fifth night with me sitting on the floor on one side of the door crying while I listened to my child beg and cry from the other side. I wanted to open the door to let him in. Wasn't that easier than this ruckus at night? It wasn't like it was really working! We were all awake anyway.

It was as if Randy knew that the big cave in was about to happen. After all, Jeff had to work and needed "uninterrupted sleep." Everyone was grouchy. Randy was creating a huge battle. Sadly, he was winning!

The same night, Jeff got up quite abruptly, opened our bedroom door, picked up our child, spanked his bottom, and firmly put him to bed. Randy responded as if he had been stabbed, screaming bloody murder. I was sure that all the neighbors in the complex heard his shrieks. That night, he stayed in his room but continued to cry for two more hours.

The next morning, I called Dr. Dandy. His little idea on how to keep Randy in his bed was just not working. I told him that Jeff had spanked him, which was the information that sent us both to his office for a conference. Obviously, we were showing the signs of child abusers of some sort. He wanted to talk to both of us.

We met with Dr. Dandy, but the advice was the same. He reminded us to stay firm, not to give in, and that our child was just trying to control us. He told us that our son wanted to get between his parents, sleeping cuddled next to me. Now what kind of nonsense was that? I had spoken to other parents of young children whose kids slept with them. What was the big deal?

The pediatrician kept returning to the control theme, reminding us, "This is a power struggle, and there would be many more. Some kids were just that way. This is a little battle compared to what may come down the road." I wondered what he meant by that remark, but all too soon I would be standing on that very road.

I wondered why raising kids was so hard? Why did everything have to be a battle? Why didn't Randy just stay in his room at night? He never wanted to go to bed at night. He was up, ready to start his day while it was still dark. I was exhausted and filled with feelings that I should never have had kids, that I should have stayed single and bought new clothes and new cars. That was the good life, and I was missing it. I had been good at being single; it was easy and not stressful. But being a mother was an exhausting job, one that never ended and one that I never felt good about with too many battles.

I shouldn't be battling with a two-year-old, nor should he be winning. He shouldn't be that clever. There was no justice in a child that could overtake his mother.

He fought me all the time. He didn't want to take a bath. Then he wouldn't get out of the tub. He thought of a zillion reasons not to go to bed: just one more story, one more drink, anything to stay up longer. He wanted to go to bed when he felt like going. He was tough. He could cave the warden of a maximum-security prison. He was already talking in complete sentences. Randy was the most strong-willed child that I had ever heard of; he was the king of manipulation already. I shuddered to think what was ahead for him and me. We were going to travel down the road that the doctor spoke of, the road of bumps and hidden mines. It was not going to be easy. I knew, even back then.

We somehow survived the baby days when I could just pick Randy up and put him in a chair for timeout. He would have to sit quietly for talking badly to me, or for some other infraction, to think about his deed. I wondered then, when he was allowed out of the chair, if he felt like repeating the deed, would he? I thought while he sat in the chair he was plotting his next adventure. He wasn't afraid of being in timeout; he wasn't afraid of anything, and he wasn't easily intimidated. He didn't seem to learn a lesson for having to suffer for his bad choice. Nothing changed the feeling of exhilaration in doing what he felt like doing at the time. It was a bad sign!

Randy was yelling at me at the top of his lungs, again, but he was not a little child; he was man. I could not pick him up to put him in timeout. Here we were, twenty years later, and the war was still raging. It was ugly. I wished I could turn back the hands of the clock. I would go to parenting classes to learn how to deal with a relentless child. I would say the right things and not get so angry with him. We seemed to push each other's buttons, plucking the last nerves in each other's tired bodies. It was a war.

I yelled angrily back at him. He was disrespectful to me, causing a rage to swell up in my mind. I felt like packing my bags and leaving

my home. I didn't have to tolerate his nasty tongue and bad language.
I wasn't Ruth Graham. I grabbed my coat and purse, running out to
my car to get away, so I could cool down. I felt like driving and driving, never to return!

Who would miss me? Brad had his college life, baseball, and his
girlfriend. Jeff was in his own little world of not noticing the turbulence in the house. And my yelling child, well he certainly wouldn't
miss me. I felt like he hated me most of the time, and whenever we
had a huge argument, he yelled, "You hate me, don't you? You might
as well say it!"

Whenever he said that, I would look into his eyes as the shock of
his words hit my heart like a dagger. Hate, never! Nothing he could
ever do would make me hate him, but there were times when he was
not easy to love. How could I explain that to him? What signals had
I sent him that made him think that I didn't love him? I hadn't meant
to, not ever, but I wondered if I had.

This was his interpretation of my feelings toward him. He couldn't
have been farther from the truth.

We were alike in so many ways. We even liked the same type of
people. Many times when I got a bad first impression of someone, he
felt the same way. I used to like the same teachers as he did. It was as
if we were of the same mind at times. It was eerie.

But I never liked one of his friends. In this, we were quite different. I always got a bad feeling whenever I met his friends. They
looked shady to me, whatever that meant. They didn't look me in the
eyes, like they were hiding something. They liked to party and keep
late hours. I got the sixth sense about them, even on the phone.

Wasn't I just blaming someone else again—the friends? It wasn't
their fault. They were just instruments of the enemy, used randomly
to sink my son. They were just the rocks that were not to be moved.
They were hidden bumps in the road. Only Randy could make them
go away.

We were angry with one another again, or were we angry with the situation at hand? Randy was grieving for his car with five more months to go, no transportation, and no job. He was angry with himself, but I was yelling just like him. One thing was for sure, there would be no caving with the car. The judge had his license safely tucked away. Maybe this was how his guardian angel was protecting him. He was safe.

"Why don't you just humble yourself and get some kind of job? You won't be driving in five months if you are not working. It takes money to drive a car around!" I had raised my voice as I engaged in the same frustrated conversation as if we had rehearsed the lines.

He hated to hear me tell him the same thing again, even if it was the truth. He started cursing, making me even madder. I slammed the door to blot out his words. I had jumped in the car to drive around, talking to myself. I was angry with myself for losing my temper. I knew how bad he felt about his losing the right to drive, yet I had to respond. Why had I reacted so badly when he asked me for a ride somewhere?

He wanted to spend a useless day with a so-called friend. I knew that he had tests to study for; after all, he was going to college. Jeff was giving him another chance to make his life positive. I was angry that Randy would even think of jeopardizing such a generous offer from his dad. It was time for him to grow up taking responsibility. Randy reminded me of a child in a man's body. He was acting like a brat who was too big to spank.

Well, the license was gone for sure. He had thirty days to appeal, but had never gotten around to taking the necessary steps. I decided not to help him. If he wanted his license, he would have to make it happen, but he hadn't. Now it was too late. He had five long months to sulk over the loss of the car, but it was out of my hands. The judge didn't think he should be on the road, so he wasn't. There was nothing left now but waiting. There would be no caving.

I hoped that in the remaining five months he would think about his deed, just like when he was a little boy sitting in timeout. He had time to think about changing, but would he get out of the chair and make the same mistake again? Hadn't his life become hell enough for him to give up alcohol forever?

I drove to the grocery store just to cool off, wasting some time before going back home. I brought in the groceries and started to put the food away when Randy walked up to me. He was talking, but he wasn't looking at me.

"Mom, I am sorry for how I reacted back there. I am just angry with myself for the mess I have gotten myself into. Just thinking about not driving is so depressing that I can hardly believe that I have to wait five more months!" He told me in such a sad voice that I almost cried.

I wanted to reach out to him to hold him in my arms, just like in his little boy days. I wanted to rock him gently in the rocker, read him a Bugs Bunny book, and listen to him laugh. I wanted to take him to the zoo to watch his face light up when he saw the monkeys acting all crazy or the elephants squirting water on the crowd. I wanted to hear that same laugh he had when he saw the elephant have a huge explosion of diarrhea that day on the field trip.

I wanted to turn the TV on to let him watch *Sesame Street* and *Mr. Rogers.* I wanted to take him to see his grandfather, so he could play in the shed where he worked with tools and made all sorts of boats.

I wanted to put little band-aids on his boo-boos. I wanted to kiss away his tears and make his life good again. Oh, to turn back the hands of the clock.

I wanted to sooth away all his hurts, but I couldn't. He had created mountains of chaos. Only he could get through all the mess. It was time for him to grow up and cope without me. He was no longer my little boy in need of my protection and direction. He had his own road to travel. He would have to travel without me. I had no part in his mess. He was alone.

The storm in the house had blown away as if it had never happened. It was days ago, and it was not mentioned.

I took Randy for another appointment with the psychiatrist. There was a lot of driving. We were in the car together for some time. He didn't say much, and neither did I. He listened to his music on the radio as we journeyed down the long road to the doctors' office. We must have passed a zillion liquor stores and bars, but this was a typical city.

I saw all the stores, but didn't think that he had even noticed. Then he surprised me with his observation and said, "You know, Mom, alcohol should be illegal. Look at all these bars where people just go in, drink, and then leave in their cars. Drinking and driving is just too easy. Just two drinks and your whole life can change."

I was too shocked to even answer him as I tried to take in what he was really saying to me. Drinking was so glamorized on TV with the funny beer commercials that even made me laugh. I still thought that alcohol should be banned from viewers, just like cigarettes. There was no glamour in a getting a DUI and no glamour in suffering from "black" lungs. They were both life changing and self-destructive. These were just bumps on the road; some people went around the bumps, and others hit the bumps headfirst. It was all about choices.

Randy was on the road alone, facing the bumps. He saw them and hit them, causing the force of the impact to send him plunging off the road. There would be other bumps just waiting for him, trying to catch him in a moment of weakness.

He was no longer in a little chair to think over his deeds. He was no longer a child. I could not come to the rescue. He was alone.

SECRETS IN THE HOUSE

There were secrets in the house. Everyone had them, thinking that no one else would ever know. They thought that their secrets were locked tight, to never leak outside the house, where they were safe. Secrets had a way of sneaking out by revealing themselves in odd ways.

Letting out the secrets would not be a good thing to do since everyone would know the sad truth. Others would know about the spiritual warfare. Isn't that why there were secrets, to hide the guilt and shame? Maybe the secret would never leak. The smile would stay painted on the otherwise sad faces to keep everyone else at arm's length. If they got too close, the secret may get loose. What good would that do?

I could tell when there were secrets in the houses of others. It was in their eyes. Sometimes, it was just the way the conversation flowed.

One day in church, I asked a mom, "How are the kids doing?" She responded, "They are alive, aren't they?" She wasn't smiling. What did she really mean? Did she mean that she was blessed that they hadn't been killed, or did she mean that they were blessed that she hadn't killed them? There was no answer since the mom just turned and walked away, harboring her secrets.

There was much left unsaid, but the words were not really necessary. I heard this woman's husband pray for their children in church that night in prayer meeting. I heard his voice crack as he cried out to

God as he struggled for words. There was no need to hide the secrets. There was pain in their hearts. It was so obvious.

This couple would not be sending out the newsy Christmas letter with the wonderful achievements of their family. Not this year, maybe never.

I wondered about those letters. Were they just smoke screens sent out to hide the secrets in the house, or were their kids that great for real? I decided to send out my own newsy letter that was full of jokes and lies. Was that my smoke screen, just a pretend letter to hide the real story?

In order to brag, a family had to be 100 percent functioning full-speed ahead in waves of perfection. We received three newsy Christmas letters each year; each one was two-typed pages long. I hated them. The letters were full of vacationing family time with tales of their totally focused children. I thought how nice it must be to have such a perfect life, to boast openly about it and send it to your friends. What was the real purpose? Let's not forget the picture enclosed taken at the vacation spot with everyone tan, smiling and hugging.

The letters were either a carefully devised plan to make someone covet their lives, or they were smoke screens to hide the little indiscretions that had popped up that year. I threw the letters away, but I always read them first. I didn't know why I even read them, but I did. They served no purpose.

I sat in church one Sunday as the pastor asked if anyone had a specific prayer request. One mother stood up, alone. She spoke with tears streaming down her face. Her words were unforgettable. She had lost one of the children mentioned on the dedication page. This was what she said that day.

"I have buried one son, and my other son is in jail," then her voice cracked. What pain she must have been suffering? How could anyone begin to understand what she was going through, certainly not the newsy Christmas letter people? She would probably never be the same again. Such losses crucified the heart.

She stood in front of a crowd letting all the secrets be known. She needed to let the secrets out as they must have been stifling her very existence. She felt no shame or lack of pride as she had lost those feelings long ago. She needed the love and support from others. She had humbled herself that day by laying her cares out for all to see. There were no secrets. One son was gone, forever.

Her husband sat still, offering nothing. Maybe he had nothing left to say. Maybe he was hurting, not knowing how to let it all go. They were his losses too. Surely, he felt them, but he didn't speak.

This same mom attended the prayer meeting in the church, alone. I remembered her. As I read the poem "Standing in the Gap," I saw this mom sitting quietly with the tears of grief and loss streaming down her face. The mom's face kept coming back to me as I spoke that night.

After the service, I went to stand beside the mom, putting my arms around her. There was no need to say anything. We cried together in each other's arms. There was so much pain, but there were no secrets left in the house. There was no need for secrets.

Some mom's had survival tactics living in serious denial. One such mother had lost one of the children mentioned on the dedication page. He had been found dead in his own bedroom in her own house.

I went to visit her in her time of grief. It was the first time that we had met, even though our sons were friends. I didn't know what to say to her, but I felt that I should go see her to take something for the family.

I sat listening to her talk about her son, but she had secrets that she was not about to share. She never mentioned he was a cocaine addict or a "cutter." Young teens cut themselves to ease their inner pain. How sad! The death of her son was a mystery to her and an autopsy would be needed. She knew that her son's asthma caused a respiratory problem. She never mentioned drug use as if it was not an issue, yet everyone knew about her son. The secret had been let out years ago.

Our meeting was eerie. She didn't cry. Her whole house was in shock; maybe she was too. Maybe this was her way of coping—believing that her son had died accidentally in his sleep. Maybe that thought kept her from going insane. Maybe that was the only thought she had left.

When Mary lost her sister, the shock was unimaginable. One Sunday morning, her mom knocked on her bedroom door. There was no answer. Death had snuck in the house, almost finishing its task while the ambulance was called. But the death angel won the war on the way to the hospital.

My friend and her mom had suffered a nightmare of the very worse kind. She had been in a bloodless war, and death had won.

Mary and her mom spent years fretting over Erin, trying to help, but nothing had worked. All their efforts had not saved her. It had all been in vain. They carried the load of pain on their shoulders for years. Now she was gone. They couldn't prevent the fall!

My friend blamed depression, causing her to seek relief through drugs. After all, there had to be a reason why someone trashed his or her own body. There had to be a reason why a drug user just would not stop their use for the sake of their family. Erin was a prisoner of drug abuse.

My friend spoke of trips to the psychiatrist and what a waste that usually was for her sister. It was as if they didn't really care. She couldn't find any support for Erin to help her stay clean. Did such a support exist? Did she want to stay clean?

The funeral had been sad to see such a young woman lay in a casket with a young husband and two young children standing close together. Oddly, not one of her so-called friends came to pay their last respects. It was as if they didn't really care either. Only her family stood by her in the end—the same ones that prayed for her everyday, the same ones that lost sleep over her, and the same ones who would mourn the loss forever.

Then there was Randy, who had cheated death more than once. He was just barely nineteen years old when he had his first car wreck.

The summer had been dry with a record drought, but on this particular night, the much-needed rain came in torrents. He was driving our car with a passenger, one of his going-nowhere friends named Jamie. It was just after midnight when Randy and his buddy decided to take a little drive just a few miles from Jamie's house. They had been drinking. Jamie wasn't even wearing a seat belt. The wet roads and the alcohol were a bad combination.

Randy went around a curve, lost control of the car, and spun out in a ditch and then on to the lawn of a young couple. Jamie was ejected from the car, wandering around the lawn confused with cuts and scrapes. Randy was at the wheel of the car, dazed with a bleeding nose. He had just gotten his first DWI!

The young couple called the ambulance. The two boys were taken to the nearby hospital. All these things, I learned of later that day, but that long night had been a nightmare for me.

This was the first night that he hadn't come home. I didn't even know that fact until the next morning when panic struck me as I wondered where he could be. Why hadn't he called? I went to work that morning in the same hospital where he was on a stretcher in the ER just one hundred feet away. No one told me he was there.

He had totaled our car that night. He was injured, he had been drinking, he hadn't come home, and no one thought that the worried parents needed a phone call. The police didn't call. The hospital didn't call. He was over eighteen, so parents were invisible people. It didn't even matter that the car was in our name. Wouldn't a courtesy call have been nice?

At 2:00 p.m. that day, I found out about the accident. Randy called me at work to tell me that he just got home from the hospital. Jamie's mom, who was so cool that she didn't even call me that almost fatal night, had picked them both up from the ER and gave Randy a ride home. This was the same mother mentioned in the earlier part of this chapter. Little did she know then that, she would lose one of her children to a drug overdose. It was years later that she almost lost Jamie to a drug overdose. To think how close she had come to losing another child. I wondered why all the secrets. It troubled me. I walked over to the ER to see if anyone would talk to me.

The ER doctor who saw Randy and Jamie was still on duty. I asked him if he had treated my son, but I doubted if he would give me any information. Maybe he felt sorry for me, standing in my scrubs, a peer of sorts. He asked me, "Does your son drink?" Then he told me that the police were doing an investigation.

Then I understood all the secrecy. Randy didn't want me to know why the accident happened. I was relieved to know that he and Jamie were not seriously hurt, but yet I was angry with Randy for making such a bad decision. I raced to my car to go home and see for myself that he was really okay.

When I walked into the kitchen, I saw him stretched out on the floor. His face and nose was swollen and bruised. He was complaining of pain, but once I saw that he was okay, I fought the desire I had to hold him.

Instead, I barked at him while he whined, "You are lucky that you didn't die and wake up in hell!" I regretted the words as soon as they came out of my mouth, but the words were out there, falling on the sad ears of a child who had made a huge mistake. He would remember my harsh words for years to come, and so would I.

It broke my heart every time I thought of what I had said to him. He interpreted my words to mean that I didn't care about him. He couldn't have been farther away from the truth. I cared, more than he would ever know. I responded as a mother in fear who almost lost her child. I was not even thinking clearly; I was in shock. I wished that I could have taken back those words, but the damage had been done. The words were swirling around in the air ready to destroy and confuse the fragile relationship between a mother and her son.

Didn't he realize how close he came to being killed? Suppose his friend had been killed that night with Randy at the wheel of the car? He would have had to live with that guilt for the rest of his life. All these thoughts were running through my head.

Why hadn't I just run to him and pulled him close to me just to feel his warmth? Why hadn't I just followed my instincts? What purpose did my angry words serve? They just made a bad situation even worse. He had wanted me to feel compassion for him, while I had shown him contempt. What kind of a mother says such things to a hurting child? Where was my compassion when he needed it the most? Where?

I went to the junkyard to see the remains of the car and to pick up whatever was left of the tags. I stared at the twisted seats, the broken glass, and the blood everywhere. I was amazed that the boys weren't killed. God had been merciful. The boys were not alone in the car that night; the angel of protection was sitting in the back seat.

Two months later, the police arrived at my door to give Randy six citations for that night. I couldn't resist asking the officer why he didn't call us that night. His answer was simple, "He is over eighteen. We have no obligation to notify the parents." I just stared at him, thinking that one day he may have a son stay out all night. He may wonder if he is alive or not. He will experience what true parent hell is all about, and then he will remember this day. I wished it on him.

The real story of the car accident remained a secret in the house for a long time. It wasn't something I felt like sharing with my loved ones. No one asked me what happened to the car; it was just gone as if it had vanished into thin air. I thought it was a secret that no one else knew, but they knew. Secrets had a way of finding their way out of the hiding place. Secrets lurked around in the house like dark shadows before a storm, just waiting for a chance to explode.

Secrets were dark pieces of information that everyone knew, but no one mentioned. The silence was a huge mask of the truth. It was easier for everyone that way. Secrets were not like the feelings kept in the jar with the tight lid; they could not be hidden. Secrets were far more dangerous and served no purpose.

REJECTION

Rejection, a word I came to despise, being defined in Webster's dictionary as: "to discard or throw out as worthless, useless, or substandard, cast off or out." Rejections left a sting that caught the victim by surprise so there was no way to prepare for or to ward off the pain that followed. Rejection lived in the jar tucked away in the bottom because it was too powerful to face, too complicated to understand. It just settled deep in the jar, refusing to move.

Sending both boys to a Baptist private school was a gigantic leap of faith as well as a hard decision. The school was a forty-minute drive. There would be sacrifices needed. Randy was entering the ninth grade and Brad the sixth. Randy needed the structure. I read their brochure before signing the rulebook. The school seemed to be more interested in rules than religion. I knew that it would be strict, but on the other hand, they would learn more about God in the school than I could ever teach them at home. They learned more than I ever could have imagined. Some of it came as a shock.

I remember how nervous I was when Jeff and I went to meet with the administrator to see if they would accept our children. Our main concern was Randy. His poor grades, poor relationships, and unruly behavior at the middle school made him a risk for acceptance. We were honest with the administrator, feeling that he must have sensed our urgency to change our son's environment. After the administrator talked about the school and its mission, he wanted to meet with

Randy before making his final decision to allow him entrance into the school program.

I fretted about that the whole way home, wondering how Randy would react, but it had to be done. He had to leave public school before he sunk down any farther. He would just have to go in for the meeting.

The next week, the three of us went, but the administrator only allowed Randy to come in his office while we waited nervously outside. The administrator did not want to meet with Brad. After about fifteen minutes, they walked out with the administrator smiling. He looked at us and said, "I'm cool, are you all cool?" Oh, yes, we were cool. It was a good thing!

On the way home, I recall Randy threatening us by saying, "I am going to be kicked out the first day and embarrass you both. You'll see." He was full of anger at both of us.

I told him, "You will only be embarrassing yourself. This is an opportunity to meet new friends and to get your focus back on your school work." I doubted if he was listening to me. I glanced at him as he sulked in the back seat with defiance on his face. This was going to be tough.

There were many differences in how the school was run compared to public school. We came face-to-face with many of them.

I was surprised that the school would not play sports against a public school. The administration felt that the exposure would not be a good thing for the children. I didn't think that there was any spiritual basis for such thinking. Didn't Jesus perform his greatest miracles with sinners around him? What about the adulterous woman at the well? Did her lifestyle entice Jesus, or was she transformed? He ate supper with the tax collector. He healed people on the Sabbath. Jesus wasn't contaminated by his association with the sinners, but their lives were never the same after they met him. Wouldn't the kids in the Christian-based school have a great opportunity to touch the lives of others by showing them their sportsmanship before games when they prayed together? What harm could come of that?

The school was totally affiliated with the church; in fact, the church ran the school. The handbook had no gray areas. It was a tight ship. Randy needed the tight ship and a tight line.

On the first day of school, I drove my solemn boys to their new school. Deciding to send both of them was my brother Wayne's idea. He felt that if we sent just one child, that child would see it as punishment. I didn't really agree with that thought, but decided to send both of them anyway. Brad was quiet as usual. In time we learned that he resented the change.

All day I waited for the school to call to tell me to pick up Randy, thinking maybe his threat was real. But there was no call. He stayed, he behaved, and it was good for him. I felt sorry for Brad having to miss out on public middle school and having to say good-bye to his friends, but I feared that he, too, might have gotten caught up in the wrong crowd. I just couldn't risk watching that happen again. Maybe someday he would understand. I had to protect him.

In the beginning, I was overjoyed with the school, but as time went on with Randy trying to cross the line, I began to realize that some of the attitudes of the teachers were just not the same as before. It was as if they had taken a dislike for any child who just didn't do the right thing or for any child who just didn't look the part of a good kid.

It seemed to me that a child in such jeopardy needed more love than the others, not rejection. Was that the way God treated those who committed a sin? Did he shun those who were lost, or did he die for those who were lost? Did they remember the parable of the hundred sheep? When one was missing, the shepherd left the ninety-nine looking for that one sheep. They had a Bible; didn't they read it?

There were two teachers that Randy came to love. These men treated him the same no matter what his behavior was; they just loved him. One was his coach, and the other was his English teacher. To this day, Randy still mentions these men because they showed him a Christ-like spirit that he understood. He felt God's love through these men. They had a true ministry, something that a child never forgets. All kids remember their teachers, even the ones that they didn't like.

It was the last day of school, the awards day. All the children of the school congregated in the church sanctuary to have their teachers stand up in the pulpit to give out the outstanding awards. Randy was not allowed to go because of a detention. He would not receive his award.

He had worked hard all year to earn that award. I was greatly troubled about their decision to not allow him to come to the event. I called the new administrator, who was by no means anything like the understanding administrator that we met four years ago. I called to plead with him to let Randy get his award. At first he was unbending. Then I cried, but to no avail. My son didn't deserve to come to the awards; it was painfully obvious to me. He was substandard, cast out.

While we talked on the phone, I asked the administrator if he believed that when he got to heaven that God would notice one of his own infractions, which I doubted he ever had, totally dismissing his achievements and sending him away. I waited for his answer, but he decided to think about it and call me back. I was convinced that he didn't pray about it, but discussed it with someone else, probably the pastor. Thirty minutes later, he called me. Randy was allowed to go in at the award time only. Then he had to leave! This was as close to bending as I had seen in four years, so I had to be satisfied. At least Randy got recognition for one of the good things he had done in those four years. He could stay a few moments but then rejection.

On graduation night, I beamed with pride as I watched him walk across the stage in the church to receive his diploma. Randy had managed to not only walk the line but got outstanding grades. He had done the right thing.

After graduation, he often received newsletters from the school. Each year the school had an alumni basketball game and letters of invitations were personally sent out to the alumni to remind them of the date. Randy loved basketball and played for the school four years. He learned from a fellow classmate about the game. All his classmates that played on the basketball team got invited via a letter, but he didn't get one. He thought that the letter would come any day, but it didn't.

What message was sent by the absence of the letter? He was substandard, cast out. The message was clear—rejection!

Two years later, Randy was floundering, trying to find his way in the chaos that he had created by drinking and driving. He had searched for a job, one that he felt he would be good at and enjoy doing at the same time. Even though I doubted if there was such a job, I had to admire his searching.

One day, he thought he had the ideal job. He went in for the interview. The staff "loved" him. He would be working with kids by tutoring them after school in a special program. The staff liked him so much that they allowed him to work two days before receiving the background check. He wasn't worried about it; he felt secure in this job since he had been honest with the employer.

Yet, I was worried about the DWI he had gotten two years earlier. It was a huge, dark cloud capable of sending down torrents of rain, which it did!

Randy was up early on the third day of work when the phone rang. I didn't hear the conversation, but I heard him slam his door shut and say, "Well, it's over."

I walked to his bedroom door, but he wouldn't talk to me. He stayed in his room for hours. I feared that they had told him not to come to work. Rejection, cast out.

Hours later, he told me about the phone conversation. I cried. It was so painful to see the hurt in his eyes, even though it was his own bad choice that made the situation what it had become. I wanted to call and ask them to reconsider, but Randy told me the same thing, "Mom, it's over!" They didn't even pay him for the two days he worked.

I just couldn't let it go. I called anyway. The lady was pleasant to me. She told me how much the other workers liked Randy. The decision was out of her hands, but she gave me the director's number.

He was not so pleasant. He was focused on the driving record. I tried to argue that Randy wasn't driving these kids anywhere; he was just tutoring them. I tried to tell him what a good mentor my son would be to these young people. He had been in public middle school. He knew about their battles. It seemed to me that he would be perfect for the job. The director stood his ground.

Then I threw in my own trump card by telling him about a nurse I knew that had a narcotics addiction at one time, was treated, and was now working back in the hospital. I asked him if he felt that the nurse should be allowed to work in a hospital. Before he could answer me, I said, "Well, she is back and could be any nurse that you or your family had at any time. You would never know. It would remain privileged information. What do you think of that?"

No. No. No.

Rejection! The answer was no. How could Randy deal with that rejection when I couldn't even handle it? It was as if I was rejected as well. I burst into tears every time I looked into his sad eyes. It was the kind of thing that ripped a mother's heart wide open. It was painful to see my child hurting. It hurt. It was rejection.

A few months later, Randy applied for a similar job. I warned him that the outcome would be the same, that he should just tell them up front that he didn't have a clean record. He preferred not to make that call, so I called. I talked to one of the interviewers, telling him about the DWI. He assured me that it would not be a problem. I was skeptical, telling him that the last job said the same thing. I didn't want to see my son go through this again. He encouraged me to have Randy come in for an interview, which he did. Two of the interviewers attended our church.

It was the same type of job, after school care, but with fewer hours. He was excited again, but the next day, the call came. No thanks, rejection, cast out!

So what kind of job could he get now? He was knocked down. I knew that he would have problems getting back up on his feet. He was starting to fear rejection, shutting down again. This was the easy way out for him; besides his friend alcohol would take his mind off the letdowns.

He would retreat to his world of unfeeling, the world of no pain, no rejection, no casting away. He would be numb. He wouldn't care.

His girlfriend, Jessica, had been infatuated with him since she was a preteen. There were no other boys in her life. She had eyes for only him. She saw no evil, no wrongs. She loved him unconditionally, lying to her parents to sneak out of her house to see Randy.

At first, everyone thought of it as a crush, but four years later, the crush had grown into a love that no one could get between. When Jessica turned eighteen, her parents began to accept Randy into their lives. Maybe they thought that they might as well since Jessica was determined to date him.

But as times before, Randy destroyed the faith that her parents had in him. He had become friends with Jessica's brother, Josh. They became party buddies. One day, Josh decided to come clean, confiding all sorts of stories to his parents. Sadly, much of it was true! There would be hell to pay.

After the information Josh gave their parents, they forbade Jessica to see Randy. They took Jessica's cell phone and the car keys. As a last resort, her parents sent her away to a Performing Arts College in California. It was all in the plan to rid their daughter of someone they believed was no good for her. He was cast out, rejected. He had brought it all on himself with no one else to blame.

I really didn't feel sorry for him this time. He had to learn at some point in his life that doing what he felt like doing may not be the right thing to do. He didn't think his party life was such a big deal. It cost him plenty.

He felt the hopelessness of never winning back Jessica's parents. They would never accept him back into their lives. There was no forgiveness, and anyway, he never asked them to forgive him. It was as if he didn't even care.

He had been rejected before. He knew the feeling well. To them, he was useless, substandard, and cast out, away.

I felt his pain, even if he didn't admit it to anyone. It was there. It was rejection.

THE EPIPHANY

An epiphany comes right out of nowhere and is capable of entering a fragile mind with a convincing apparition that causes confusion as to its very existence. It can easily become a scary reminder that maybe things are not as they appear. An epiphany chooses to come in the darkest hour of the night, leaving the mind and body on edge as to its meaning or impact on the life that is far from stable.

I had been praying for Randy to have an epiphany, a flash of insight, some kind of spiritual awakening. In a way, God had answered my prayer. I wasn't at all sure that there was anything spiritual, but it was supernatural, definitely catching his attention.

Randy was disturbed by his "bad night" as he told me about his experience. He knew that he wasn't dreaming, but yet the whole thing didn't seem to be real. He saw it, just the same.

I looked into his beautiful, brown eyes as he told me about his night. He admitted that he had been drinking more than "usual." I wondered what that really meant. It seemed that his drinking night had left him in some kind of stupor where he had some sort of vision that disturbed and scared him. He was so consumed by the vision, declaring that he would never drink again!

He didn't know if he had been asleep or what was going on, but he saw things in his room that were after him. He saw dark figures on the walls, looming closer and closer, trying to reach him to take him away. They were demonic, of that he was sure. They wanted him. He said, "I am never going to drink again."

Now why couldn't I just believe that my prayers had been answered? Wasn't that just a little too easy? Was he serious about quitting? Why couldn't I just be happy for that moment that he was sincere? I was afraid that something else would take the place of alcohol. I feared he would get depressed and seek refuge by another form of substance abuse. I worried about the temptation he was about to face.

I had prayed for an epiphany, one strong enough to open Randy's eyes, which it did. I still lacked the faith to believe that the very prayer I prayed had indeed been answered. Where was my faith when I needed it the most? Why did I allow Satan to get in my mind and create all sorts of doubts? Why couldn't I just live a day at a time? After all, Randy meant what he said, at least for that day. I had to be content and believe that his word was truth, music to my ears.

Then I started to worry about the epiphany. How long would the vision last? Wasn't it here today and gone tomorrow? Would the vision stay in his mind, or would it leave him alone while visiting someone else in the night? How long would the fear of the vision linger? Was it enough for him to stop drinking? I was just plain tormenting myself.

If God sent the vision, the epiphany, then it would last as long as necessary, as if it was on a mission of some kind. If it was just a dream, it would fly by like the hands of time and be gone. The details of dreams are soon forgotten, unless the same dream kept returning to mess with the mind. I knew about a recurring dream, the one that seemed to have the sole purpose of refreshing my own mind with anxiety.

I had the tornado dream so many times that I knew it was a dream while I was still in the midst of the dream. That dream served no purpose at all. It was just tormenting and evil!

Wasn't my tornado dream an epiphany of sorts? Wasn't it a flash of insight, an awakening? Didn't it make me sense a bad ending? Wasn't there reality behind the dream? Maybe this was my epiphany. It was scary. I hated that dream. It made me afraid. It was so real.

Two days later, Randy went out with his drinking buddy, and I worried. How could he be strong to fight the enticement of drinking with alcohol all around him? He would not be able to say no. I fretted the whole time he was out of the house. He did not come home that night.

When he returned the next day, I glanced up as he walked through the house. His eyes were shiny and clear. He didn't have to tell me that he hadn't been drinking. For three whole days, he had walked away from the potential destroyer of his young life. Maybe he knew all along that one day he would just give up the partying. Maybe he knew that he was not the kind of person that could drink one drink. He knew that alcohol was not his friend. I had wasted time preaching to him when he had always known the truth. The truth was all around him, reminders of what alcohol had taken from him. Had he seen the light at last?

It saddened me so much that I tried not to think about the past, trying to take a day at a time. I tried to look to tomorrow as a new beginning for Randy, but was it? There was always an ounce of doubt.

Randy left me a note, asking me to get him up early to go to church. It was the fourth day without alcohol. I was surprised and happy that he wanted to go. I got him up as he requested.

The ride to Wayne's church was almost an hour long. Randy was unusually chatty. He seemed to be in a great mood. For some reason, I had a feeling in the pit of my stomach that maybe his mood was not for real. I hated myself for thinking such thoughts, but he was typically moody and angry. The last place that he wanted to go was to church, yet he had asked to go.

Once in church, he was quite congenial even with people that he didn't know. I watched him as he walked up to an ex-girlfriend, chatting with her, while she sat with her fiancé. He would never do this on an ordinary day. I started to fear that maybe he was under the influence of something. His behavior was not like him at all.

He listened to the message about choices and consequences. What were the odds of that message being presented on that particular day? He was meant to be there.

On the ride home, he was still talkative, telling me that it was so great to be in church and not be hung-over from alcohol the night before. I listened, yet I doubted the personality he had that day. Typically, he would have been very anxious and sweating, but he was calm, cool, and charming. It reminded me of the times that he was on pain pills. Was that it? Or was it the new medication that the psychiatrist had him on now?

I liked the person he was that day more than the person who was volatile and withdrawn. But which one was the real Randy? Was his mood the kind that took over after withdrawing from alcohol? No, I knew better than that. Something was just not right.

Brad came home for a short visit that day. He and Jeff decided to hit golf balls. When they brought up their clubs from the spare room, Brad announced that four of his clubs were missing. Where could they have gone? They were the finest, most expensive clubs he had. The special club covers were still in their place, but the clubs were missing.

Everyone went about the house in search of the clubs, except Randy who went in his room for a nap. I felt the nagging in the pit of my stomach. No! I would not think evil again. There is no way that Randy took those clubs and sold them. I would not believe that at all.

I knocked on his bedroom door to ask if he had seen them. He told me that he borrowed one of them and that he couldn't remember when or where it was. The thought that he had taken them was start-ing to surface in everyone's mind. If he didn't, then where were they?

Randy never came out of his room, acting as if nothing was hap-pening as Brad and his Dad were still searching for the clubs. Either Randy really didn't know, or he did know and really didn't care. If he did sell those clubs, didn't he have an ounce of conscience?

The clubs were missing. I saw the hurt look on Brad's face when he realized the clubs were gone. I recognized the look; it was the same one I had when I "lost" my diamond necklace. It had just disap-peared. It was a violation. It was too painful to even think about with the kind of pain that one hid in the jar. It was a tiger that was too dangerous to be left unattended.

There was no proof. There was no confession, but the evidence was there. Four of the best clubs went mysteriously out of the house. Who would do such a thing? How desperate to take something of value that belongs to someone else and sell it dirt cheap for cash! Was that it? No, I just couldn't think of such trickery. Surely, the clubs would turn up!

I sat alone in the living room staring at the empty Taylor Made Bubble 2 suede covering that decorated the driver. The tears began to flow down my face. Brad took such pride in those clubs, always hav-ing them neatly arranged and keeping them clean. He had them in such order that he knew immediately what was missing. He looked at me with his soft, blue eyes. I saw the sadness there. It was enough to break anyone's heart. Why did it have to be this way? Where in the name of Sam Hill were those blasted clubs?

Maybe they didn't search enough. Maybe they are just misplaced. I wished that was the truth, but I knew better. The clubs were for-ever gone, probably sold for almost nothing, just enough to buy an illegal substance of some sort. Was that the truth? It was an act of desperation!

Brad and Jeff eventually left to hit golf balls at the range. When they returned, no one would have guessed that either of them was the least bit upset. I had three episodes of crying while they were gone as I stared at Randy's closed bedroom door. I was angry about something that I didn't even know to be factual. Then I was annoyed that there was no discussion about the clubs.

We sat down to eat dinner while Randy was still asleep. Brad looked at me and asked, "Why are you so upset, Mom?" There was no need to ask me that; he knew. As usual, Brad hid his feelings. He was not going to let the loss of the clubs change his life in anyway. He had always learned to cope, so his response should not have surprised me.

Brad even told me that maybe he had just misplaced them. We both knew better. He was much too careful with his possessions. He never broke his toys when he was little. He was always a pack rat.

One day, when he was five years old, I house cleaned his room. Afterwards, he walked in and looked in a special box, asking me, "Where is my little eraser?" It was just a piece of one, too little to see, let alone to use. But he knew it was gone. The eraser was just one of his little treasures, an inexpensive little keepsake.

I had to go hunting in the garbage to retrieve it, which took a long time to find. When I presented it to him, he suggested that I be "more careful when I cleaned." I promised, "I will be." It made me smile just to remember that day. I never threw out anything again.

He also saved his entire Christmas list, every year. They were his little collection. Collecting was his hobby. He had a zillion key chains and silver spoons from the different states where he played in baseball tournaments. He had cards from old friends and letters. His room was his shrine with all his trophies and awards. But he kept his golf clubs in the spare bedroom since they wouldn't fit in his little room. Now they had disappeared.

I knew that he would find a way to just let it go, but I knew that I would not have such ability. It was a violation, an intrusion, and an ugly scheme. Only a heartless, self-serving person, a desperate person could have done such a thing. Who in our house could have a need so great that hurting someone close to them didn't even matter? It was a process of elimination, but a waste of accusations since the guilty one would never admit to the crime. It was as if Randy had no recollection of what he ever did. But someone was guilty. I wanted those clubs back where they belonged.

I was too angry to talk.

The next morning, Brad went back to college. Whatever pain he felt was never expressed. He just took his reactions right out of the door.

When I got up, the anger was still in the air. Randy walked into the kitchen. I had only a few things to say to him, "You are a prime suspect, son. You have one day to cough up those clubs, or I will go to the police and file a missing items report!"

He walked away from me as if he could care less, yelling, "You are such a moron." Ouch, that hurt. So I was falsely accusing him. He was innocent. I had no proof, while he showed no desire to help locate the clubs. He had dismissed the whole ordeal from his mind. Deep down inside me, I knew that he had sold the clubs!

If I had to, I would have him arrested. I would do what I had to do.

HOUSING A CRIMINAL

We confronted Randy as he became explosive and defensive. He always hated it when we teamed up on him. He refused to talk to either of us or to tell us anything about the clubs. When we persisted, he got even angrier, which started the rebound anger thing that he was so good at by blaming the sad circumstances of his life on everyone else. He was working very hard on taking the focus off of the clubs. He spoke irrationally about his own brother, who he claimed was drinking, saying that we didn't even know anything about his lifestyle. Dear God, I couldn't deal with another alcohol issue. I dismissed that thought from my mind. Somehow he felt justified to do whatever he had done with the clubs.

He continued to complain about how pathetic his life was, about not being able to get a job, and about not having a car. I thought to myself, *Whose fault was that?* I asked him, "Why are you so angry?" His life was out of control by his own choosing. No one else was to blame. No one had messed up his life; he was in charge. Yet he was blaming everyone else for his problems. He was throwing out all sorts of smoke screens to steer us away from the issue at hand, the missing clubs.

He was in such a highly agitated state that we both knew it was futile to try to talk to him. I slowly walked away from the explosions that were popping in my head like firecrackers. In my heart, I knew that I just couldn't let it go.

I stopped by a pawnshop on my way to work to look for the clubs, but the ones I had hoped to find were not there. The man behind the desk had eyes that lied. I knew by looking into them. I described the clubs and gave him the names. He went in back to look for a short time. When he returned to the desk, he told me that they weren't there. He was lying!

I offered to pay for the clubs, whatever amount he paid for them, plus twenty dollars more. He was unmoving, refusing to acknowledge that the clubs were there. I sensed that they were right back in that room.

I started to get angry all over again. Why didn't Randy just tell us where the clubs were? He knew. I offered to give him cash for the clubs, no questions asked, if he would just tell me the truth. But did he even know the truth?

I was about to turn my car around, when my cell phone rang. It was Randy. "Don't go to the police! I will tell you where the clubs are." I was relieved at last. I would get the clubs back.

I waited a few days for him to come forth with the clubs, assuming that he had to go somewhere to get them. But the subject had been dropped. No one was talking. This made me even more furious. I was not willing to just let it drop. I would keep asking Randy until he got tired of hearing the same old questions. I would threaten him again with going to the police.

However, the next few days proved to be quite rough on the whole family. Our dog of sixteen years had to be put down. Everyone was sad! The clubs took a back seat of importance.

I waited until the morning of the dog's appointment to tell Randy. He never took such shocks well. We were getting ready to leave for the classes at the community college. I knew that I had to tell him.

He walked into the kitchen and I said, "Kiss the dog, good-bye!"

He looked shocked at first asking, "What are you talking about?"

I realized that this was going to be a most painful day. I told him that we had been talking about how pitiful the little dog had become and that the whole family heard her crying in pain during the night. It had to be done. Everyone knew it, but I was unprepared for his reaction.

He stood looking at me with tear-filled, sad eyes crying out loud, begging me, "Don't kill the dog, just a few more days, Mom. Please!" My heart was ripping apart. I knew that a few more days wouldn't matter. The dog was family. Everyone would miss her.

Randy picked up the dog and hugged her close to him with tears running down his face. I knew he would have a tough time with the loss, but I convinced him to go to his classes and try to focus on his work.

We drove to the college in silence. The only sound in the car was the occasional sniffing as we cried softly to ourselves. He asked me as he got out of the car, "What time is this going to happen?" But I refused to tell him. What good would that do? I doubted if I had the courage to take the dog at all. It was just so hard.

On the way to the vet, the little dog cried. So did I. The vet and the staff treated our Peproni girl better than a hospice patient could ever expect. The end was painless. I picked up my "sleeping" dog, put her in a soft blanket, and carried her home. I rocked her for forty minutes, still feeling her warmth, and sobbed out loud, all alone. I hadn't shed tears like that in years, not even when I watched the slow death of my own father. Not even when they zipped his dead body in a body bag and carried him out into the cold night.

My brothers and I had taken part in our father's funeral. I read an article I had written to a whole church full of people. I hadn't faltered. But when we buried the little dog, I tried to read the article about the sixteen-year-old little hellion with only the family in the backyard. I choked up so much; the words were barely understood.

How could the loss of our little dog stir such emotion? It was as if the tears had been locked away in a safe and someone had let the tiger out of the tank. It was as if I had been waiting for a time that I could just let all the pain go. Where had all these feelings been hiding? I felt a huge void in my heart. It was going to take all the strength in my body and soul to put the dog to rest in the metal toolbox I purchased for this day. I put the blankets around the little dog so that only her head was showing. She was just sleeping.

I touched the dog. I whispered to her, "Go find Pop Pop, girl!" I cried and then I closed the lid.

Randy called that same day to say he was skipping the last class. Someone was bringing him home. He couldn't get through the day. When he came into the house, I could tell he was under the influence of something. His speech and his gait were slow. His eyelids were half shut. He was feeling no pain. This was how he was dealing with the loss. Our little dog was just one more thing that was a big part of his life that was gone. I knew what he was going through. I felt the same pain. But life had to go on.

Once the dog was buried, I went right back to my crusade to get the clubs back.

I was on the way to work when I called Randy.

"Do not hang up this phone until I finish what I have to say. As hard as it was to put down the dog this week, it will be much harder for me to go to the police, but I will do what I have to do. Where are the clubs?"

He hung up the phone. I called him back.

"I asked you not to hang up! You have until 1:00 p.m. tomorrow to tell me where the clubs are. If you don't, you will be escorted out of this house."

I hung up the phone, sitting in the parking lot crying. I cried for my dog. I cried for Brad's lost clubs. I cried for my crumbling family. I cried for Randy, who just would not do the right thing.

That night when I got home, he left me a note. He sold the clubs three months ago to the very pawnshop I had visited. For some reason, he didn't want anybody else in the family to know what he had done, like it was a secret that should never be told. Did he expect me to put the secret in the jar with the tight lid? Didn't he realize that everyone knew already? This was a secret that would be told to all the injured parties. Did he know that the violation of the clubs hurt us all? I doubted it.

I feared the worst; I would never get the clubs back. It saddened me deeply, but I decided that something had to change.

I looked for a locksmith in the yellow pages, making arrangements for him to put dead bolts on Brad's and our bedroom doors. I was determined that never again would Brad or myself be violated in such a way in our own home.

I felt like moving away and taking Brad with all his little treasures, but I knew that he would not come with me. The locks were all I could do. It was only a temporary fix like a small Band-Aid on a gaping wound.

Jeff decided to take an active part in Randy's deed by having Randy pay for the missing clubs. There had to be a consequence. This was better than going to the police for now.

Once again Randy had been spared being arrested. Jeff had saved him, but I wondered if he was really saving him at all. Our son had no remorse. I thought that he got off quite easily. He had lost his right to live in the house. He was overcome by his addiction. He had lost control.

The locksmith came on a Saturday while Randy was asleep, putting the dead bolts on the doors that I had requested him to do. Jeff put the remaining golf clubs behind the locked door.

For some strange reason, Randy pretended to be asleep during the whole loud ordeal. Finally, he got up and went down to his computer. After the locksmith left, he must have examined the doors and walked into the kitchen, looking puzzled.

"Why are the locks just on your doors? What about mine? I can't even close mine all the way!" he stared at us in disbelief.

We both responded at the same time by telling him that the locks were put on to keep him out of other people's rooms, so he couldn't steal things to sell. I added, "We are thinking about taking your door off the hinges."

He exploded with a long string of cursing, bolted into his room, very angry, slamming the door for effect. Somehow, he had become a victim. We were making his life "hell!"

It was all about him, his feelings, and his life. He never tried to make his wrongs right. He could have told his brother that he was sorry. He could have told us where the clubs were in the very beginning, but a con man has no conscience, no remorse. He didn't seem the least bit upset. He had managed to hurt the closest people to him in the whole world. He didn't seem to give a damn! It would be a long time for me to realize that Randy was dealing with guilt and shame. The power of his addiction was strong!

I wondered if Randy even noticed that the whole family lived with keys in our hands. I wondered if he noticed that all the cars had clubs on them. I wondered if he really understood the need for dead bolts. He wasn't the victim. His family members were prisoners in our own home. Nothing was safe in the house. The medicines were locked in a large safe, along with watches, baseball cards, and any other collectibles that would fit. Wallets were never left unattended. Charge cards were locked away, along with the checkbook.

It was bad enough that he had sold his nice digital camera, camcorder, and multiple CDs and DVDs. They were his to sell, but they had been gifts from us to him at Christmas. It still felt like a violation in knowing that he wanted cash that badly. Would the power of his addiction destroy him?

Jeff and I added all the new keys from the dead bolts to our key rings. The reality of such locks being needed seemed to hit us both at the same time. We sat at the kitchen table staring at the two piles of key rings. It was a sad way to live!

All the keys were just cover-ups to keep the crimes from happening and to prevent further violations of one's privacy. But weren't these just efforts on our part to keep Randy from going to jail? We were housing a criminal, our own son, who did desperate things to get cash. Who was he becoming?

The sting of Randy's loud cursing still rang in my ears. It was painful to hear him talk such trash to the two people on earth who loved him the most.

The next morning was Sunday. Randy left another note for me. He wanted to go to church with me telling me that he loved me. This was his way of apologizing, but was there any remorse? He just assumed that I would just forget his harsh words to me as if it never happened. He should have known better. I was hurting. The pain was not going to leave anytime soon.

I wondered how long I would have to tolerate his behavior! He was out of control just like his life was and living in the house was nearing the level of torture. The clubs had just added more pain to the jar that was getting so full that I knew it might explode anytime. When would this nightmare be over? How much longer?

I got dressed for church, stopped for a second looking at his closed door, and walked past. I left without him.

IN THE SHADOWS

There was one in the house unnoticed most of the time. There was a quiet one, not joining in the war, not participating in the yelling, seeing no purpose to any of it. For years Brad felt the tension with insane levels of stress within the walls of the house. He heard the arguing. He felt the anger and the pain, but no one noticed him. He tried so hard to stay on the good side of the battle, trying not to cause any more stress. It was a huge burden for him to carry. I knew.

Oh, the times that I wished I had just taken him away from the whole mess, some place where he would be protected from the angry words that hovered around in the house. I wished that for myself, too, but I had always known that he would stay with his father. I couldn't afford to lose him, too. Leaving would mean saying good-bye to everyone. If I left, I would be empty-handed. It was much too high a price to pay, but I feared the loss would be unavoidable.

He stayed in the shadows, the invisible son.

Brad had found a way to cope, his way, through the years. Whatever made me think that he didn't sense what was really going on in his own home or that he was not affected by it all? His quiet outer shell was just a disguise, a mask. He pushed his own feelings aside, choosing not to join the forces in the war. He would not fight. It was futile to him. He was going to suffer down the road. Feelings that are bottled up inside of us are never safe.

Brad was sensitive to my feelings. There were times when the tension in the house was at peak levels. He would say to me, "Mom, let's go for a ride." Together we would leave the nightmare behind us to just ride away. He would ask me what music I would like to hear; it was all about me. Perhaps he sensed that I might leave. He wanted to prevent the escalation of events in the house by temporarily getting me away for a short while, allowing me to calm down and think clearly.

I often looked into his beautiful, blue eyes and wondered where he had developed his ability to soften the hurting of the soul. Brad didn't inherit Jeff's ability to have a brain spasm over a flat tire. He didn't inherit my ability to become highly agitated over a leaking pool. His personality was all his own. As much as we would have liked to take some credit for the young man he had become, we couldn't.

There had been times when Jeff and I joked that he was not our real baby. We laughed, feeling sorry for whoever got our real child. There was one thing for certain; we would not trade. We would keep this guy. We needed him, so we could have a day or two to feel like good parents. The days were so few. Brad had become our sun on a cloudy day. It was a lot of pressure to put on a child. Perhaps it was too much pressure.

I remembered bringing Brad home from the hospital. I knew instantly that he was totally different from my firstborn. After two weeks, I hadn't even heard him cry. He never got colicky or went off in screaming fits like Randy.

I even called the pediatrician one day, "Dr. Dandy, there is something definitely wrong with my baby!"

He replied, "Such as?"

I starting muttering some nonsense like this, "He never cries. Not even when he is hungry!" I was petrified that Brad had some neurological problem.

Dr. Dandy laughed at me saying, "Wasn't it just a few years ago that you called because your other child cried all the time?" He made me laugh; yes, that was me all right. He assured me that Brad would cry, which he eventually did, but not much.

The pregnancy had been anything but normal. I went into labor at twenty-six weeks. Every move I made caused contractions. It was a stressful time for me since I worried about my unborn child most of the time. He was born early even though I had been on bed rest for months. I awakened one morning in a pool of blood and was rushed to the hospital for a caesarean section. He swallowed amniotic fluid during the surgery, which sent him to the NICU for as long as I was in the hospital. My nerves were plucked when I finally got him home. I think maybe I was suffering from post-traumatic stress!

I expected him to be a total disruption to the household like my firstborn had been, but he wasn't. His temperament was mild. He was easy to please, sleeping through the night as soon as I got him home.

I tried to think back to his early years, trying to remember if he had ever been punished. The times were rare. He didn't like to cross his parents, seeming to enjoy pleasing us. He cared what we thought about him.

As he grew older, I noticed that Brad never engaged in the conversations when we were upset with Randy's actions. He stayed out of the picture. He was in the shadows.

Sometimes, he would just retreat to his video games for hours. The games were his temporary escape. He became invisible.

One day, I heard some yelling from downstairs where Brad played his games. The yelling was sporadic and agitated. I was shocked to hear his angry words. Could he be so annoyed with the game he was playing or was it just a release for him? Was it a time to lash out when he thought no one heard? But I did. I heard.

I noticed that he became another personality while playing his non-violent games. They were just sports games. I didn't like to hear his frustration, but was his behavior a reminder of the bad feelings that he had bottled up inside him? I would call downstairs to him suggesting that he take a break.

For a short time, he would quiet down, becoming invisible once more.

Brad became somewhat lost in those shadows as Jeff and I became burdened with the struggles with his brother. I didn't think he noticed the invisible war, but he had wounds just the same, covered with temporary bandages that were becoming loose.

One night, I went to his high school to watch his basketball game. I loved to watch Brad play. It was a great escape from the sadness at home, which was always threatening.

I walked into the gym and sat down in my favorite spot to watch the game. The basketball players were on the floor warming up, but Brad was not there. *How odd,* I thought. Then I saw him walking toward me in his school clothes. He sat down beside me. I was puzzled as to why he wasn't in his basketball uniform and was about to question him. Before I could, he spoke first. I was blown away by what he said.

He sat looking straight ahead, as if he was reading a note card, with his arm around my shoulders. All of his friends were sitting a few feet away. I couldn't help but notice they were watching us. Then he spoke to me in a tone that I had never heard from him. It was as if someone else was talking from within his body. The voice was a monotone, while his face was expressionless.

"Mom, I've flunked off the team," he said solemnly, refusing to look at me.

I knew he was joking, but there was nothing funny about what he said. I hit him on the leg in fun while I threatened, "I am going to call your dad to tell him what you just said, so you had better tell the truth and get dressed for the game!" I held up my cell phone as if to make the call. He never looked me in the eye.

Then it was true. Why hadn't I been able to see it coming? There was no note from the teacher of that class, no warning, nothing!

This had to be a dream. It had to be just another nightmare!

When the reality hit me, I stood up, walked out of the gym, and sat in my car. I cried. I called Jeff and gave him the bad news. We were both in a state of shock. I decided to go back inside to watch the game since going home after learning that Brad wasn't playing was just poor school spirit. It was a struggle for me.

At least six times during the game, the tears swelled in my eyes as I saw him sitting on the bench in school clothes. He was one of the high scorers on the team. He was needed. The sadness was overwhelming, but I knew that something was just not right with Brad. He had been invisible as long as he could. He was over the limit.

What made me think that he could cope with all the stress in the house? He wasn't coping. It was painfully obvious.

That night Jeff and I waited for him to come home to sit down with him to talk about the whole mess. Now we had to worry about him. Brad was no longer in the shadows. It didn't seem real!

The walls of the house were cracking. This was the last straw. Our quiet son was hurting too. But was this really a surprise for me? I had seen the pain in his eyes. The whole family was hurting. Our lives were spinning out of control.

Brad sat at the kitchen table between us. We asked him to tell us what was going on in his life and to be honest with us.

At first he didn't talk much, but when he did, his words were shockingly painful.

He began with his head down, saying, "Sometimes, I don't even want to come home to all this stuff! I hate what is going on here all the time!" His voice choked when he talked. I thought that I would die. His crystal blue eyes were shining with tears.

He felt all of the pain. He had held his quiet suffering inside of him. He was in some kind of emotional overload. He had stopped caring about schoolwork, even though he needed good grades for college. I couldn't understand why he would sabotage his own future. He had taken all he could. Now his suffering was clear to us and depression was obvious.

I went to the school counselor and talked to the administrator. It was difficult to discuss such painful stories. I listened to myself as I was describing my dysfunctional family. There was substance abuse in the house. It had created a war big enough to penetrate even the quiet one, the one in the shadows, the one with the huge smile.

Brad had become a terrific actor. He had been living in the pretense that his family was intact. He sheltered himself as long as he could. Now he was showing signs of emotional stress. He couldn't hide it any longer from us. His wall of protection was coming down.

Brad's baseball scholarship was for a college close to home, but the distance was too far for him to commute. In the fall, he would be living on campus. In time, he had managed to bring up his grades, getting back on the basketball team at his high school. He seemed to move on with his life. He was anxious to move into his dorm room. He had found another escape. For that I was so thankful.

I envied him. He had a place to seek refuge far enough away from the pain in the house. He kept himself busy with workouts, school, and baseball practice. He chose not to come home. He had a place to hide, a place of quiet, a huge shadow.

The next year, he met a girl who was as genuine as any person could be. When he brought her home to introduce her to us, I fell in love with her as soon as we met. It wasn't like I planned to like her so much; it just happened. There was something unique about her.

We developed a special bond. We often talked about what would become of our relationship if one day there was a break up with Brad. What a sad thought that would be! We agreed that we would always stay in touch. I know now how unrealistic that was.

Brad's visits home became fewer and fewer. When he did visit for a few hours, he brought Nicole. She was his insurance that the house wouldn't explode. She was a ray of sunshine that God had sent to the house.

The following summer, Brad came home from college to live, but Nicole stayed on campus since she was taking summer courses. She came to visit us several times a week, driving back to her dorm at school. Sometimes, she left late. For her to be traveling the roads at night alone was not a good thing. It was too dangerous. I worried about her safety. I asked Nicole to feel free to stay in the spare bedroom and leave in the morning. She could have stayed the rest of the summer, and it would have been fine with us. She was such a joy to have around.

As the summer went along, Nicole came to stay on the weekends. It was as if she had been sent to ease the pain in the house. She was contagious. She had such warmth. She was the calming medication for the house. When she was around, it was like having doubles of Brad. Her laughter rang through the house, bouncing off the walls.

Everyone was on his or her best behavior when she visited; after all, no one wanted her to think that her boyfriend's family was dysfunctional. But she knew all the secrets. She was always ready to listen. Never offering any advice, she just listened like a good friend would do.

Having her around brought the realization of what life would have been like with a daughter. I would have liked to have her as a daughter. My first mistake was assuming that someday she would be.

She became a part of the family so quickly that it seemed that I had always known her. Becoming attached to her had been so easy that I was afraid that maybe I had scared her away by latching on to her so tightly. If she minded, she never let it be known. She returned the love as strongly as it was given to her.

Jeff and I referred to the spare bedroom as Nicole's room. Her visits became the highlight of the summer. The summer flew by and soon Brad and Nicole were back at college.

Then the clouds returned to block the sunlight.

Brad was back in his own private shadow. He got a nice apartment on the campus, and he had Nicole. He was content to be away from home or what was a shell of a home. Then he got busy with baseball season. The first week his shoulder started to hurt.

The thought of another child with a pitching injury was almost too much for me to bear. I called Brad to see how he was coping and offered to take him for some of the tests down in the busy city.

We had directions, but the city was always a maze. We were together in the car for a long time. He was great company. We waited forty-five minutes for the test, while we sat together talking about the mess in the house.

Neither of us saw any sign of change in the house. It was as explosive as it had been for the past few years. Now Brad was injured and might need surgery. I felt as if my house was under an attack of some kind. When would all the stress lighten up?

The possibility of surgery was a real threat. I talked to him about pitching and red-shirting that year. He seemed to be coping well or maybe he was hiding it from me, not wanting me to worry about him. How typical of him, to think of me when he had to be upset about the whole shoulder thing. He saw Randy's career change overnight and how Randy's life was so greatly affected. Now what was in store for Brad? No one knew, only God.

I knew one thing for sure though: Brad was a strong young man. He would find a way to get through all this. Somehow he would. He always did! But did he?

SOMNUS, THE GOD OF SLEEP

The ride home from college was unusually quiet with the soft music playing on the radio. I couldn't even hear the lyrics, but I could hear the deep, throaty respirations with each breath Randy took as he drifted into sleep. His mouth was open and his head was tossed around as the car made a few turns. He was in a totally relaxed state. I never saw him fall asleep so soundly in a car. I glanced over at him. The sleep was unnatural. Was it was drug induced? He was somnolent, causing me to fear that he may be dangerously sleepy. What if he died in his deep sleep? What if his respirations got fewer and fewer as his diaphragm got so lazy with drugs that he just went into the last sleep of his life?

How could the medications that the psychiatrist prescribed make him so sleepy? He was fine when he walked to the car. How weird! Maybe he was just tired.

I awakened with a start early the next morning glancing at the clock. It was four thirty, but I was wide awake. It was as if someone told me to wake up and listen, but there was no voice and no sound in the room. I lay there for a moment and then decided to turn over to go back to sleep, but sleep wouldn't come.

Then a disturbing thought came to my mind—the DVDs were gone. How ridiculous! Why was I thinking of something so crazy in the wee hours of the morning? I knew it was of the devil trying to rob me of sleep. I tossed and turned as I tried to get the thoughts out of my head. Eventually, I fell back into a restless sleep.

All too soon my alarm rang. It was time to get up and start the day. I felt uneasy for some strange reason with my first thought on the DVDs. Over the past few years, we had accumulated at least thirty. Most of them were gifts to Randy that he had selected for Christmas gifts. I had only one, *Pretty Woman,* which was a gift from Randy at Christmas two years ago. It was such a thoughtful gift. He put a lot of thought into my gift, surprising me that he knew what my favorite movie had been. I was touched by the gift, and I treasured it. Why was I even thinking about that DVD now?

I went into the kitchen to get my morning coffee, but the DVDs kept coming into my thoughts. I went downstairs to make sure they were there if for no other reason but to get that nagging feeling in the pit of my stomach to go away. Certainly they would be on the shelf.

As soon as I entered the family room, the bare shelf caught my attention. I walked over seeing three DVDs on the floor; all the others were missing. He must have let his friends borrow them or maybe someone moved them upstairs to the entertainment center. Maybe Jeff put them in the huge safe. I would call and ask him.

I hated calling him at work since he always seemed annoyed at being disturbed, but I was so sick inside that I just had to know the truth. Jeff told me that most of the DVDs were upstairs. While we were on the phone, I checked. There were two in the entertainment center, which meant that only five were in the house. The rest were gone.

It was bad enough that he had sold his own DVDs, but he had sold mine as well. Jeff had one DVD that was a gift from Randy, and it was there. How odd that he hadn't sold that one, but he had sold mine, another sad violation. Was there anything untouchable in the house? I felt like vomiting; it was as if I had stomach flu.

I had to go to work that day, and Jeff told me that he would talk to Randy. I had to be satisfied with that, but I wanted to confront him myself. I was angry again.

The next day, I asked Jeff how the questioning went with Randy. He told me that Randy didn't say much. Of course he didn't, what was there to say? He was selling anything that he could get his hands on. It was another act of desperation. What had he done with the cash? I couldn't wait to confront him myself; he would not get off so easily with his sorry excuses.

I got up early the next morning to take him to the new psychiatrist. Randy was always changing doctors. He didn't like the doctor that he been seeing, and I knew why; this doctor was not so easily snowed. He had probably seen kids like Randy before, not buying into their lies. He probably knew a con man as soon as one walked through the door. I guessed that he had seen a few in his career. I wondered how the doctor could sift through the drug-seekers or how he treated them once he discovered their little secret.

I decided not to talk about the DVDs until we were on the ride home. It was hard not to get into an argument that I knew would ensue if I even mentioned them, but I had to ask anyway.

Randy came out of the office, got into the car, and was talkative. He was very happy with his new doctor. He handed me the next appointment card with the new prescriptions. The doctor had increased the antidepressant medication.

The silence was back! When we were halfway home, I opened the conversation with this, "It was nice of you to sell my DVD." I glanced over at him waiting for a response.

"Well, you never watched it anyway," he replied.

His reply struck a nerve, almost causing me to pull over the car to punch him. I knew that I was in dangerous territory. I knew better than to speak when I was so angry.

"So you feel justified, then. Is that it? The DVD was mine, not yours. You had no right to sell it," I told him as calmly as I could. Then I asked him, "What did you do with the cash you got for the DVDs?"

"I go out with my friends. I don't need to tell you anything," he answered as he stopped talking and looked out the window.

His silence just seemed to anger me even more. Why did he always have to play the part of the victim like I was harassing him for no reason? Wasn't he sorry even a little for his selfish deed? Did he even remember taking the DVDs?

I wondered if he could even look at himself in the mirror. I understood why he never bothered to get a job; why go to all that trouble when he could just sell his earthly possessions and everyone else's in the house for almost nothing? But what did he do with the cash?

"I want my DVD back," I told him.

"I'll buy it back when I have the money," he said.

Yeah right, I thought to myself. *When will that be?* I felt emptiness inside me as I glanced over to him. It dawned on me how sad the scene before me was at this time. Who was the passenger in my car? The young man sitting beside me looked like my son, but the man inside him was someone else. That man was desperate, and he was a thief with no conscience and few morals. That man was stooping to an all time low. But what had he done with the cash? I was just learning about the conscience of an alcoholic, a narcotic addict, and a benzo abuser. He was an addict! There was no conscience!

I went to the pharmacy to fill his new prescription when suddenly it dawned on me that somehow, he had gotten other prescriptions. I could not understand why I had such thoughts. The sixth sense was still around. Where did those crazy ideas come from, and what was the purpose of it all? Yet, I couldn't let it rest.

I went into the pharmacy seeking out the pharmacist, trying in a clever way to get information. If I were calculating and careful, the HIPAA protection for the guilty wouldn't come into the picture. I spoke with the pharmacist asking him, "Did Randy pick up the other prescriptions already?" He replied that he had. Then I went out on a limb asking him, "Did he pick up the pain medicine also?" The pharmacist told me that he picked that one up and the Xanax as well. I asked him, "Oh, did Dr. Laydbak prescribe them?" Sure enough, I was right. He had gone to another doctor, had a free visit, like a homeless patient, and had gotten all the medication he wanted and then some. It had been so easy.

So that explained his somnolence on the ride home from college. He was heavily medicated with dangerous medications within his grasp at his own disposal. He had no control over these substances, and he knew it, yet he had been taking large doses for weeks. Later that day, I found an empty bottle in his room. The prescription had been written for 100 tablets. No wonder he never felt like doing any homework or even taking a shower. He just ate and slept. He was pitiful to look upon, and I felt like moving away. Jeff and I had to come to terms as to what we were going to do with Randy.

I dreaded talking to Jeff about Randy because we never agreed on a course of action. If the truth be known, our disagreeing was a huge reason why our son never hit rock bottom. But I didn't intend to help Randy get drugs by supporting him under my roof. He had to go.

Surprisingly, Jeff and I talked calmly about him for the first time in years. It was decided that as soon as he finished the semester that he would have to go. We would tell him together.

The conversation with Randy was brief. As soon as it was mentioned that he would have to go, he jumped up, stating that he was leaving soon anyway. Yeah right and where was he going with no job and no car? For sure, the car would not be going with him. If he chose to be a slug, he wasn't safe behind the wheel of a car. The club was on to stay.

As he pranced out of the room, I had an insane thought. I asked Jeff to sell Randy's car, and this is how I suggested it be done: One day, the car would be sold and gone. Randy would come to realize that it was gone and ask where it was. I would say that I didn't know. He would persistently ask. I would say that I remembered using it a time or two and that I didn't remember what happened to it after that. He would get a look of pain on his face when it dawned on him that his car had been taken and sold right under his nose without his permission. Nothing he could ever do would get it back. He would have been violated and justice would have been served. The very thought of it gave me a feeling of power. How sad that such a thought made me feel good! What was wrong with that picture? Was that a Christian spirit? What kind of mother was I?

I just wanted revenge. I wanted him to feel what I felt. I wanted him to be hurt, as I was hurt. I wanted him to be wronged and feel the violation. He was long overdue.

Convincing Jeff to sell the car was not going to be easy, but I would work on that as long as necessary, which was another waste of my time. It was not going to happen, and I knew it.

While Randy was at college, I walked into his room. I glanced around at all the mess and the musky odor like someone homeless lived in there. It was a gorgeous day and a perfect time to wash the sheets on his bed. Once I got started, I went into a frenzy of cleaning the bed. I stripped the bed of everything, including the mattress pad. I turned the mattress over. I sprayed all the pillows and the mattress with Lysol. I washed the linens and the mattress pad, hanging them on the line to dry. The spread was too large for the washer; it was dingy and smelly. I decided to take it to the laundry mat.

My cleaning binge was like an unconscious effort of mine to cleanse Randy. I would rid the room of all the dirt. His room would be fresh and smell good again without a hint that it ever looked otherwise. It was a reminder to me how easy it was to get something clean.

I brought the wet spread home and put it on the clothesline. The wind blew strongly, and the odors of his bed linens just floated away, right up in the clouds.

After everything was dry, I wrestled the mattress to get the linens back on, but I never relented. I sprayed the spread with his cologne and put it in the dryer for a last minute effect. It worked like a charm. I put it on his clean bed and stood back in the doorway to smell the nice aroma. His bed was clean. I wondered how many times I would attack his room in episodes of useless energy.

Then I realized what a waste that all was since he hadn't showered for days. I wanted to put him in the bathroom, lock the door, and not let him out until he smelled like the linens. Didn't he care what he looked and smelled like for crying out loud?

Why did it bother me what he looked like or smelled like for that matter? They were reminders to me that something was just not right with him. I kept getting the signals from a power unseen to warn me about him. It was all in a plan to help him somehow. Only, I didn't know how. Nothing I had done so far had helped him. As a matter of fact, I only made things worse. He interpreted my efforts as invasions. It had all been such a waste, just like the other times when the room cleansing was only a temporary relief.

I didn't recognize that the above symptoms were depression. Did depression lure him into drugs, or did drugs send him into depression? Jeff and I didn't agree on that either. He excused Randy's actions, blaming it on depression. I blamed his depression on drugs.

Now he had enough medication in his possession to take his own life, causing me to worry that he might do just that very thing. There was no way to control his use of benzodiazepines. He managed to get prescriptions from doctors. He was a sly fox. He used our prescription plan and stole from us to pay the co-pays. He was full of lies and deceit that defined him as the con artist he had become. How low would he go?

I knew that the benzos and the narcotics would control him. He wanted me to think that he took only what he needed for his "shoulder pain" and that he only took Xanax when he "really got anxious." I thought that maybe he actually believed that he had it under control. He was listening to lies from the enemy—the one who sought to destroy him. Randy was losing the battle with substance abuse, taking away his very soul.

Randy's door was shut. He had been in bed all day. He woke up long enough to eat some junk food and drink a glass of milk before he went back to bed. His hair was greasy; he hadn't shaved. He was such a mess to look at, enough to break anyone's heart. I was losing the battle too.

Jeff and I had several discussions that weekend about how much Randy slept, or was he really asleep in his room? We both feared that closed door—the door of mystery, the door of possible doom. It wasn't the door itself, but the fear of possible harm that could come to our son behind that door. There was always the fear looming about, causing the heart to pound and the head to throb. What if we entered an empty room?

Why didn't this stress just go away? Why didn't Randy just see the mess he was making of his young life and come to his senses? Why didn't he know that everyone that loved him was hurting?

His choices were casting dark shadows on the house. Now Somnus, the god of sleep, was trying to take control. Somnus was drug-induced with a grip of steel that was stronger than death itself. He would not let go of Randy.

He was the god of the dark, lurking in the shadows, totally out of sight. No one saw him, but he was there just the same. He had taken up residence in Randy's room. I felt his evil presence when I went in there. I knew he was there.

The battle raged on and I was losing.

Stains are ugly reminders that something is not right. They refuse to go away. They become a focus; even after vigorous cleaning, there remain empty spots where the stains were created. Stains are stubborn. They are simply blotches that special attention would not erase. Stains leave a mark in your mind before they start to fade. To lift the stain is tiresome, but it can be done. The marks, however, remain forever, leaving their worrisome memory behind. The memory lingers over the empty spots as if to cause some kind of pain for its replacement. In a way, the memory serves to torment.

I walked down to the basement just to smell the sweet aroma of the new carpet. I waited almost twenty years to replace the ugly, blue tweed carpet. The old carpet had taken an extreme beating with the many years of use. There had been at least four floods down there, not to mention the spills, occasional vomit, and unexpected sprays of urine. My boys and their friends had spent many nights on sleeping bags, nestled on the floor.

The ping-pong table had been rolled over the floor many times. The ceiling tiles had been ripped by the ping-pong paddles of tall kids playing a vigorous game in a room barely large enough for the table. The carpet was disgustingly filthy. I had been elated to see it tossed out on the lawn. I neglected this room for years because it was too massive a clean-up job. There never seemed to be enough time to get the job done.

New things are like treasures that you are afraid to touch for fear of causing some kind of permanent damage. The new smell sends out an electrical message to tread softly.

I walked all over the family room, rearranging furniture and wiping off the dust. I stood back glancing at the newness of the room with the new paint job and the beautiful carpet. I had a zillion pictures to put on the walls, but instead, I just wanted to see how clean everything seemed. I didn't want to clutter the room.

Jeff complained about the color of the walls telling me that they were "pink." I knew for sure that I hated pink and had not chosen pink, yet I secretly agreed that the walls did have a glow of morning sunrise. I figured that once I put up all the pictures, I could hide the pink glow somehow.

I hadn't wanted to fix up the family room because I felt that Randy, who treated the basement as if it was his very own apartment, would trash it. But Jeff was sick of looking at the messy walls and the stained carpet. Today had been the day to renew the room. I loved the look. The room was beautiful. I was elated.

That night Jeff and Randy got the computer working and the TV, which was the main focus of the family room. Randy also thought of the downstairs as a personal bachelor pad, where he could sneak in women of the world at all hours having private little parties. He was responsible for most of the destruction down there. He even managed to destroy the recliner. The elevating foot would not go back to the sitting position remaining halfway out, making the chair look like a piece of junk. He never admitted to breaking the chair, but as always, he was the one that got the blame. He was an easy target since he occupied the room 99 percent of the time. He was the one who seemed to have short-term memory loss. Even if he did the damage, he never remembered.

I walked out of the room and back upstairs at last to go to bed.

The next morning, as soon as I was fully awake, I opened the basement door to go downstairs to once again admire the newness. Then I saw it, a dark, ugly stain beside the computer chair. At first I thought it must be a shadow, but as I got closer to the spot, I became aware that something had been spilled.

I stood over the spot looking at it as if staring would make it go away. I knelt down touching it; it was still damp. Someone had tried to wipe it clean by rubbing something over it, which caused it to get even larger. Stains on that type of carpet were supposed to be lightly sponged and treated.

I stood up. Instantly I was angry with Randy. He had spilled something on the new carpet the very first night. I went running upstairs to ask him about the stain, but he was silent as if he had no clue.

I walked into the kitchen where peanut butter was smeared on the cupboards, the knobs, and the framework. Then it dawned on me what had happened last night; he had been drinking. Even worse, he was mixing alcohol with all the other medicine he took. What in the world was the matter with him? Didn't he see the danger in such a mix? No wonder he lost his coordination and his balance.

I was so angry with him that at first I couldn't speak. He didn't apologize, as if he had the right to do whatever he wanted downstairs.

I threw my hands up in frustration and glanced at the clock. Time was slipping away, and I had to take him to college. I was about to explode on him. I knew that the anger was seeping out of the jar.

I was an absolute nut. I told him that he was a baby, that he was irresponsible, and that he didn't care about anyone but himself. To make matters even worse, he thought my tirade to be amusing having the audacity to laugh out loud. This infuriated me even more. I was wasting my breath!

As we arrived at the college, he jumped out of the car in a hurry to get away from the brutal tongue-lashing. But he didn't escape the last remark I had for him, "And by the way, the deadbolt will be locked at night when your father goes to bed. Your bachelor pad is closed forever!" I doubted if he really cared what I said. I watched him in the rear-view mirror as he walked away.

I cried the whole way home. The stain was a violation.

When I arrived home, the carpet guy was there to put hardwood floors in the living room upstairs. As soon as I saw him, I asked about the stain on the stain-free carpet. He was certain the stain would be easy to clean.

I purchased the chemicals he suggested, working on the ugly stain for two hours that day, but all my efforts were in vain. The stain refused to go away. It was the ugly reminder to me that I had been violated somehow, leaving an ugly mark.

I whined so much that day, muttering to myself, that the carpet man took notice. I guess he felt sorry for me because he finally told me that he would cut the stain out and replace the small area. I felt like an utter fool but was very happy with his suggestion.

The next day, the stain was gone, but I looked at it carefully. Oh yes, I could tell that the patch was there. I could see the yellow seam, which was a mark that no one else could see. The spot was still a thorn in my flesh. I just couldn't let it go.

The deadbolt was a done deal. We locked our son out of his little domain. I had a feeling of sadness—another lock, another key, and another violation. When would it all end?

The stain was just a small area just a "little coke," but it had created a huge mess. The little spill had a big consequence. I wondered if he understood why the entire house was starting to look like a Federal Bank with locks and safes. Did he know that he was the one being locked out, or did he even care for that matter?

I picked Randy up from the Christian school, where he was doing his mandatory community service. He had eighty hours to do for filing the false police report and with three days left before the deadline, he had completed barely eight hours. Didn't he care if he went to jail? He didn't seem to mind that thought at all.

I glanced over at him as he thanked me for picking him up. Then he started to talk about his day. There was a play at the school, and he seemed moved by the message. His voice cracked when he spoke as he stared out the window.

"I believe in God and everything, but I have done so many bad things that I think that God has turned his back on me," he said sadly.

It pierced my heart to hear those words. He was listening to lies from the enemy. I told him that Satan wanted him to think that God had turned his back on him. That's what Satan was all about, destroying our faith in God and causing us to fall.

I doubted that he was listening to me. He just sat looking out the window. I could see his beautiful dark eyes that were shining with tears. It was enough to break the heart of anyone. I even forgot about the stain on the carpet.

I became aware that he was still filled with guilty feelings about his past. He would never believe that God would forgive him if he couldn't forgive himself. I was filled with guilt as I looked at him that day. Had I forgiven him for the past? If I had, then why did it all keep resurfacing?

Could he feel God's love if he couldn't even feel my love for him? What kind of mother was I anyway? Why did I get so upset over a stupid stain? But it wasn't just the stain; it was the state of mind that he was in when the stain left its mark.

Stains were like sins that only God could wash away. The sins would be tossed into the river to never be remembered again. Oh, the sweetness of forgiveness!

The day had gotten off to a horrible start. I set the alarm to get up early to take Randy to do more community hours. He walked into the kitchen and asked me to pick up his pain pill prescription before we left for the school. I refused. We argued for days about the pills and my concerns that he was addicted to them since he wanted the whole day's worth of the pills, so he could chew them like M&Ms.

He sulked in the car. He was agitated about the pills; he was edgy, and so was I. I was so tired about the arguments over the pain pills. He was so proud of himself for giving us the actual prescription. He admitted that he couldn't control his use of them, but I knew that he liked the pills because of how they made him feel. It wasn't about the pain in his shoulder; it was the feeling of euphoria, the trick of the pills on the brain.

I looked over at him. Tomorrow would be his birthday. Was he ever going to grow up and get his life back in order?

He kept playing with the radio, and for some reason, he brought up his license. He seemed excited that in a few more months, he would "be driving."

I turned to look at him, saying, "You have to pick one, either drugs or driving, but not both. You shouldn't be behind the wheel of a car!"

Another argument started to arise. He reached to change the radio station again, and I pushed away his hand; then, the explosion! He yelled a string of cursing, and the lid of my jar flew off. My hand struck him right across his mouth as I told him to "shut up." If only he had. He had both of his arms over his face to protect himself from my swings. It was as if Satan was hissing at me, daring me to swing harder.

A new string of words flew out of his mouth. I was violently out of control. I pulled the car off to the side of the road. Every time he cursed, I hit him, over and over, warning him to "shut up." But he didn't stop cursing, and I couldn't stop hitting him. It was as if years of repressed anger had come thrashing out of me. I was horrified by my own rage.

Only by the mercy of God did I finally gain some self-control. I sat back in my seat in a state of shock at the horrific scene that had just taken place. He was in shock too. He kept looking in the mirror at the marks on his face. He had marks; I saw them, reminders of my insanity.

Then he cried. He would soon be twenty-four years old, and I had made him cry.

I had hurt him deeply, and I knew it. He looked at me as he wiped his tears, telling me, "I have always thought that you hated me; now I know that you do!"

It wasn't hate that had jumped out of the jar; it was fear, anger and rage. I was desperate to try to save him from drugs. I was insane with worry, and I had struck him, as if by hitting him I could shock some sense into him. I was losing my sanity for sure!

We arrived at the school. He got out and slowly walked inside. I just sat in the car, watching him walk away. I started the slow drive home, but I was shaking so much I could barely drive. I cried out loud to God, "What have I done?"

I realized that my mental health was in serious jeopardy. I couldn't get a grip on myself. I kept reliving the scene in the car as if a video was being played in my mind. What had I done? Would he ever forgive me?

I couldn't even bear to tell Jeff the whole story since as soon as I told him that I struck our son, he went bananas on me. He would never have done that if he had known the fragility of my mental health. No sane person would have attacked his or her own child.

I sat down and wrote Randy a note, but I couldn't even ask him to forgive me since I could never forgive myself. The letter was lame—a feeble attempt to excuse my behavior.

Somehow I managed to get to work, but as soon as I walked in, I started to tremble again. My insides were jumping as I fought for control. One of my peers noticed that I was crumbling. We went off to a room to talk. I relayed the story of the scene in the car. It sounded like a movie. Who was that woman back there? Who had she become?

I got through the shift, which was the longest day of my life. I slowly walked to the parking lot in the dark to sit in the car, not wanting to go home. I wasn't safe anymore. I was losing my mind. I looked at the clock in my car. It was one o'clock in the morning, and today was his birthday.

I pulled into our driveway at 2:40 a.m. The lights were on in the house. Then I saw Randy sitting on the sidewalk smoking a cigarette. He didn't seem to notice me, and I was wondering what I should say to him. The guilt was tremendous. I was so sorry for what I had done.

I walked up to him, touching his face and straining in the moonlight to see if I had left marks on him, but I couldn't see. I told him, "Happy Birthday! I love you!"

Then I cried as I spoke to him.

"What I did to you in the car must never happen again. I will never do that to you as long as I live. And the only way to make sure of that is to leave you, which I know that I must do." I turned to go inside when I heard him speak.

"I deserved it, Mom. Don't leave," his voice sounded slurred. I wondered if he was under the influence of something.

I wondered if he knew how sorry I was for the insanity. I scared my own self as I realized my poor mental health and the fear of never being able to control my own actions.

I walked into the house, alone, and sat down at the kitchen table, trying to control my shaking.

A few minutes later, he came inside. I looked at him. The first thing I did was scan his face for marks from my uncontrollable slapping earlier the day before. There were no visible marks, but I was sure that marks were still there, wounds that went deep into his heart. I had inflicted those wounds. I would live with that scene for the rest of my life.

What a sad beginning for his birthday!

THE RISK

On Randy's birthday it saddened me to see how impaired he looked the whole day. His eyelids were half shut; his speech was slurred. He wanted to go to the mall to pick out some "cool" clothes. I thought that was a great idea, so he could toss the new things on the floor of his room with the already large heap of dirty laundry. I had decided to leave his room as it was—in total disarray.

On the way to the mall, he snored at times. I tried to focus on driving, but I could hear his rhythmic breathing. He was feeling no pain.

He had his whole day planned while he appeared to be in a pain pill-induced peaceful mood. I hated the way he looked, but I still felt so bad about my attack on him a few days ago that I was quiet, not wanting to start another catastrophic event. I feared the rage I knew was still inside me.

Later that day, our family went out to eat to celebrate his birthday. We invited Nicole, the insurance that everyone would be on his or her best behavior. No one wanted to have an ugly confrontation in front of company. She knew there was pain, but she played the game and was quiet. Everyone knew that Randy was impaired, but everyone chose to ignore it. We were all just trying to get through the birthday without an argument.

It was a struggle, a real drain for me to be in a good mood the whole day. I kept thinking about how I had attacked my own child.

What kind of a mother did something like that? The scene kept playing in my mind so much that I couldn't even look my own son in the eye.

I was fighting for my sanity, and the struggle was wearing me down. If only I could just go away and pretend that none of the sorrow was real.

What was left? The guilt was heavy. My soul was crushed, with an empty jar remaining. There was no need for a lid now. What good would a lid do? The feelings had jumped out as if they had been waiting for the worst possible time to erupt. There had been a mighty explosion. The lid was nowhere insight. The house was in some kind of aftershock. The attack had been the most powerful with no signs of recovery.

I walked around the house like a zombie. I felt dead inside. I was being destroyed by my own fit of rage. Now I had to live with the insanity that took place in the car. I didn't know who that angry woman was, but she was out of control. That woman must never appear again, not ever. I had to take that woman out of the house, where the rage would not be a threat. The next time she might be more vicious. She could not be trusted.

How could I tell Brad that I was leaving the family? Would he understand that I was dangling on the verge of no return? Would he forgive me? Would he know that my leaving was not an option?

For eleven years, I fought the forces that threatened to tear down my house. I had lost the battle. It was over. I would have left years ago, but I couldn't bear leaving my Brad behind. But he was no longer a baby; he was a handsome, young man. I stayed, enduring beyond what I was actually capable of, because I couldn't bear to leave him. Today, I had surrendered. I had to leave. I was convinced that Randy could have cared less.

I had to have some time to think, to clear my head, and to decide what to do with the woman that was capable of such madness. That woman, who was filled with anger, was still lurking about, possibly waiting to explode again. She might lash out for no apparent reason. She had the potential to snap, being brittle and untamed. Where had she been hiding all those years? I couldn't bear to talk about this woman. That woman was me!

I decided to write Brad a letter. Maybe he would understand after I told him what I must. The letter was long overdue.

My dear Brad,

You are so very dear to me. Don't ever forget that I love you and I always will. From the day you were born, you have been a blessing to me. God knew how much I needed you, and I am so glad that I allowed your father to persuade me to have another baby.

I can hardly believe that you will be twenty-one soon. You will be a man technically, but you have actually been a man for a long time. You are a confident, motivated young man who has always been capable of empathy for others. This is a gift that only God could give you. Empathy and sympathy is not the same thing and only a few people even know the difference.

I can't tell you how sad I am to have to write this to you. Leaving our home is a hard thing to do, and I have fought until there is nothing left of me to avoid this day.

I am not going to blame your brother for my lack of self-control. The woman in the car was a maniac, full of anger. I don't like her at all and neither would you. I pray that you never see her as she was that day.

But she is inside me, where she has been for a long time. She has been hurt, and she has watched you get hurt. She is full of pain.

I regret that I did not leave a long time ago. Maybe, I could have spared you the violations that you had endured. Maybe, if I had left three years ago, things would have worked out differently.

I never imagined that you would be hurt, too. We have all suffered. Your dad and I are deeply saddened by your brother's choices that will affect our lives for years to come.

I know that what happened last week between your brother and me was meant to be. It made me realize that I needed to get away for a while. I need some space. He and I cannot exist under the same roof anymore.

I will not be far away. I want to see you as often as you would like. We will have breakfast, lunch, and dinner anytime you like. (And you do know who to call when you need cash!)

I am still your mom, even though I will not be in our house. I love you the same as always and no one can ever take that love from you.

I love your father, but I have allowed our relationship to suffer, as I have been tortured deep in my soul about a wayward child. Our marriage should have come first, and I pray that you will always remember that when you are married. Children should not come between you and your wife.

I cannot imagine you having a child capable of causing such pain in your house. I pray that you never know what it is like to watch a child sink while you stand by, powerless.

I know that for now this is what I have to do.

Please forgive me. Maybe something good will happen if I leave—a risk I have to take!

My love forever,
MOM

After I wrote the letter, I read it over and decided that I should go see Brad at college to talk over the mess in the house. He deserved much more than a letter. I called him and arranged to meet for dinner.

As soon as we sat down in the booth, he asked me why I wanted to talk to him. Somehow, I knew that what I was going to say would not be a surprise to him, but how would he react? It was such a risk.

I tried not to cry as I tried to explain my insaneness in the car. I talked about the woman inside me that was full of anger. I looked into his soft, blue eyes for a sign of how he was feeling.

He sat listening quietly as I told him that I needed to get out of the house so that I would not feel such uncontrolled rage again. I felt the tears swell up in my eyes.

"I support you 100 percent, Mom, if you are leaving because of my brother. But if you are leaving Dad, I will not support that," he told me in his usual calm fashion. He didn't appear to be alarmed by what I had told him. He had known!

A huge sense of relief took over my troubled soul as I looked at my baby. He was indeed a fine young man.

We both said everything we had to say.

When I took him back to college, he hesitated a moment turning to look at me. He hugged me, kissed me, and said, "I love you, Mom."

I cried the whole way back home, tears of relief and tears of sadness.

Writing the letter was the easy part, but walking out of the house was going to require power from an unseen force. I loved the way the house was starting to look. The recent upgrades made everything more cheerful. I was getting a new piece of Queen Anne furniture that would hide the TV and the DVD player. The hardwood floors were shiny. The new carpet smell was still in the family room downstairs. I didn't want to leave. It was going to be the hardest thing that I had ever done in my life.

Was this just a bad dream? Surely, I would awaken in the morning and feel the relief in knowing that I just had the worst nightmare of my life.

But the dream had gone on and on, refusing to end. It was real.

I thought that I should write a letter to Randy, the one who was lost, the one on the high seas, the one I had trouble communicating with most of the time. He was in the battle alone now. I had surrendered. I had given up the fight.

My dear Randy,

By the time you read this, I will already be gone. The episode last week in the car convinced me that I needed to get away. I have done what needed to be done.

The woman in the car was on the brink of insanity. She was out of control, full of rage and anger. She must never come back! She must not live in the house. She is not safe.

She was a mother bear trying to save the life of her cub. She was fearless and strong with the power to injure. Her cub was in danger. She wanted to save him, but she could not see for the anger inside her, the anger that had been tucked away for a very long time.

The war that you and I have been in has gone on for too long a time. I have tried to save you, and you don't want to be saved. I have lost the battle. I gave it my all, and it wasn't enough.

Now, I must leave the house to try to stabilize my mental health. Last week made me aware of my own fragility. I haven't been able to help you, but I must try to help myself. I can no longer live with locks on the doors and clubs on the cars. I have lost my freedom in my own house. This is no way to live.

In my failure, I have asked God to take over, by sending the angel of protection to watch over you, keeping you safe. God is waiting for you to rely on him, just like he waits for me to turn you over to him.

I have tried to fight the forces that got into your life, messing with your mind, but the forces were too massive for me. I was fighting a losing battle. I know now that only you can save yourself.

You won't be the first young person who got caught in the trap of substance abuse, and you won't be the last. When you are ready to ask for help, it will be there.

When you are tired of the quick fixes, you will look for a lasting cure that only God can give. If you try to do anything on your own, you will fail, as I have. You must ask for help, so you can put on the armor that you will need to fight.

The force is too great for you alone. The force is driven by Satan, as he desires to watch you fall down. Don't give him the power; he doesn't deserve it.

Do not doubt that I love you. The love I have for you hasn't changed since the day you were born. I fear for you, that you will be lost forever and that you won't be found.

The fear has overpowered me in a way that I cannot explain. The fear came out with a vengeance last week. I have taken the fear with me, where it is safe.

Take care, my son. I will love you always!

My love forever,
MOM

I packed my bags. Deep down inside me, I was praying that Randy would miss me and become so upset that he would change the down hill course of his life completely. But I knew that there was only a small chance of that happening since I was always the thorn in his flesh, trying to wedge myself between him and the substance abuse. It had been a pointless tug of war.

He had chosen what mattered to him. Jeff had chosen as well by allowing Randy to live in our house no matter what he did or didn't do. Now I had chosen. I had chosen to leave.

Then I wrote the last letter to Jeff.

My dear Jeff,

What pain we have secretly suffered as we have watched our lost child flounder. Neither of us knew how to comfort the other and so we went into our separate worlds to lick our wounds.

We tried to handle it in our own way, each of us with different ideas. We were never a team. We were divided, and we fell.

I regret that I put Randy's needs before yours. I should not have made him a priority, and our marriage took a beating that caused us both pain and suffering. I cannot take back the years of neglect, but please know that I never meant to cause you more pain than you were already having. I got caught up in Randy's problems, and I couldn't let go. But through it all, I have never stopped loving you.

There is no need to blame each other. Our child has a free will just as we have. He has chosen, and there is nothing we can do to prevent his fall. The path that he is on is self-destructive. He knows that, but only he can choose a different path. If only he would.

The woman in the car last week was the scariest person that I ever knew. She is always hanging around, hiding, and waiting. She has no agenda since she is sneaky, thinking no one was aware of her. But she showed her face last week! She must never return.

Please forgive me. The fear for my own mental health is real, and I need time to get myself together. Hopefully the distance between Randy and me will be good for all of us.

Each day, I will ask God to show me the way so that I may do the right thing.

I will miss you and our pretty little house, but I will not miss the fighting over how to save a child who doesn't want to be saved. He is not a baby anymore. He is a man responsible for his own actions. We are not to blame for his choices. He has created his own hell, and there will be hell that he has to pay.

Please forgive me for leaving, but I have endured all that I can. I have become a shell of a woman, and I do not know the woman inside me. She is not nice. I know that when I leave, she will go with me. I have to face her and deal with all those feelings that created her. I am prepared for the battle ahead of me.

When Randy changes his ways or is no longer in our house, I will return, if you will have me.

Take care of yourself.

My love forever,
Love, Me

I cleaned the entire house one last time. All the laundry was done. I stood in the living room admiring how nice everything looked.

I stood alone in my house as tears slid down my face. I was leaving the whole family with the hope of saving one. What if I lost all of them? It was a huge risk.

I picked up my bags and put them in my car.

I locked the door and left.

THE NOMAD

Stress was like bonding glue adhering to the body and not letting go. Sometimes, the stress hid, convincing everyone that life was good. Stress was sneaky since it liked to surprise attack by demanding attention and refusing to be left alone. It had to be reckoned with and gotten under control before it devastated its host.

What made me think that sweet release would come to me if I left my stressful house? The stress came right along with me as if I have packed it in a suitcase for travel. At first, I was deceived. It felt so good being away from the stress. I wasn't forced to think about my crumbling family or about Randy. I didn't have to see his self-destruction. I didn't have to sit in a car with him, worrying about my bitter anger. I didn't have to see his depressed state of mind.

After one week of quiet time while I was totally unprepared, the stress hit me with full force. I became fully aware that leaving the house of stress meant absolutely nothing. I brought all the baggage of my sad family right with me. Even though I was not in the house, the bad feelings were still inside me.

I felt new anger for being forcing to leave my home of twenty-five years. As usual, my anger was directed toward Randy. He was old enough to be out on his own. He should be the one to leave. Why didn't he go instead? I had allowed him to run me right out of my own home.

I missed my home. The house was almost cheerful as the new things hid the stress and unhappiness. The light paint and light flooring made a soft glow of brightness that was merely a disguise for the darkness.

The outer appearance covered the inner turmoil, but only for a limited time. Only a stranger would be tricked by the shell of a house. A stranger would not see the cracks in the foundation that threatened to make the walls of the house come crashing down.

All my reasons for leaving seemed to make no sense to me. Randy was still in the house and nothing had changed. He started calling me on the phone. I knew as soon as I heard his voice that I had never really left the stress behind. The stress was with me, but much worse this time as if it had gained double strength in just a few days.

I got reports from home by phone that made me feel like a quitter, an outsider. Brad and Nicole were stopping by my house after his baseball games. I was left out of the picture. I was nowhere. I had no home!

I felt as if someone had died. There was a void that I could not explain. I wanted my life back, such as it was. At least I had a home. The anxiety became overwhelming; depression was taking a strong hold. I was sinking fast. I couldn't come to the surface. The sadness was suffocating! I wondered if Jeff felt the same way. I needed comfort, and I needed it from him, but we were emotionally distraught so much of the time that neither of us was ever in any form of mental stability to help the other.

We had decided before I left to keep the lines of communication open, but there was a strain. We both felt it when I was invited to my own home for a cookout by Brad, who was as much a stranger in the house as I was. It had only been a week, but yet it felt like an eternity. I was nervous having to walk back into the house that was no longer mine. I wasn't sure that Jeff wanted me to come. It was all so weird.

We sat around the table, but I felt out of place. It was so unnerving that my insides were jumping and my skin was tense. Jeff and I avoided eye contact. We were both hurting, and neither of us knew what to do as if we were paralyzed by shock.

The conversations were awkward and generic. I hated the bad feelings. Could these feelings possibly be worse than what I felt before I left? What was I going to do? I asked myself that a million times. I wondered how Jeff felt. I was afraid of the answer.

The next time that Jeff and I spoke on the phone, I thought that his voice was different. He sounded like me—lost. I told him, "I missed you!" He replied, "I feel as if someone has died." I knew that feeling so well. I decided to go back home, to all the chaos, to all the explosions, and to all the emotions that I thought were left in the house.

I had to try again. Maybe Randy would turn his life around. Maybe he sensed that he was partly responsible for my leaving. But would he?

How was I going to prevent an unpleasant encounter with Randy? What if he and I got into another horrible fight and I totally lost control? What was I doing? This was a far worse risk than before. I already knew that I was out of control. That woman inside me was just waiting to go nuts. I knew it. It was a worry and a reminder of my fragile mental health, but I decided to go home anyway.

Jeff greeted me at the door. We held each other for a long time as if to comfort the other. Regardless of how badly the state of our marriage was in, we still loved each other. We both had doubted that for some time now. We were struggling to hang on as we had always pulled apart in a crisis. We went off to our own comfort zones to seek refuge.

In order to deal with Randy's many issues, we had to stand together. We were mightier as one. We needed that armor to fight the enemy who was entrapping our son is a web of destruction. What could we do to help our child? We couldn't help him see the light.

The two weeks that I was gone, I stayed in the empty in-law quarters at Tom's house. I promised to watch their children on a Friday night so they could go out for the evening. This evening happened to be the same evening of the day I went back home, but I had promised them a week earlier. I had to keep my word, so I went back to baby-sit for a few hours.

They returned at 8:45 p.m. I was in my car ready to go back home when my sister-in-law came running out to me with her phone in her hands looking worried. The call was for me.

Randy was on the phone. He was talking fast, telling me that he got stung by a wasp and that his lips were swelling. He wanted me to go the pharmacy to get his medicine the doctor had called in for him. I couldn't possibly get to the pharmacy before it closed; I told him so, thinking that he was being dramatic as he had been before. Besides, he wasn't allergic to bees. I didn't even panic.

Randy got his friend Derek to get his medicine as I was driv-ing home. I was not prepared for the sight of Randy when I finally arrived. He was on his bed with the door open in the dark, laying flat on his back. I turned the light on, seeing the worst reaction to a bee sting that I had ever seen.

His entire body was deep red with huge hives. He was talking hoarsely. He didn't open his eyes. I ran to the medicine cabinet to get him some Benadryl, which he swallowed fine. He had already taken the Prednisone from the pharmacy. He scared me. My heart was pounding. I was afraid that he would go into anaphylactic shock. What if he died? Panic seized my heart. What if God took him from me? I was going absolutely nuts. What a scary welcome home!

Somehow, people know if they are close to dying. He asked me, "Mom? Am I going to die?" I reassured him over and over, but I didn't want to leave him alone. I stayed by his bed for several hours to make sure that he didn't get worse.

I looked at him, touching his forehead. He said, "Don't leave me, Mom!" I told him that I would stay with him until he started to improve. I sat there thinking to myself, "What if I hadn't come home?" He may have died, but the angel was there watching over him. The angel protected him until I got there. It was a close call.

After an hour, he didn't get any worse and drank some water. He wanted to go to sleep. I sat there watching him in the dark, listening to his breathing. He still needed me; I had to stay and help him.

The next morning he was much better, but the fear was still in my heart. What if I had lost him? One bee could have changed my life, just one bee. What was God trying to tell me?

As part of my returning home, Jeff and I agreed to seek outside direction to help our family cope with Randy.

We asked our pastor to set up an appointment with the pastor of recovery from our church named Drew. Drew had been through years of addictions with a powerful testimony. He was my light. If God could change him, then there was hope for my child!

Our first meeting with him was in private. He knew that Randy was creating a life of hell for all the family. His recommendation was what we already knew. Randy had to leave our home. There was no other way. We discussed how we would present this to Randy and set up a time for Drew to come meet with the three of us.

When Drew arrived at our home, Randy reacted with indifference and agitation. He sat across from us at the table with his arms crossed, totally unscathed by our concerns for him. We laid out a plan that he had to get a job, get drug counseling within a time frame, or he would have to leave. He begrudgingly agreed, but I thought that he would agree to anything to get us out of his hair. I doubted if he would do what we asked. Why should he? He had done whatever he wanted without consequences for so long that he knew a weak wall when he saw one. He would find a loophole, looking for that one thing.

Within a few weeks, he surprised us by getting a part-time job and committing to an outpatient drug program. He seemed to be making an effort. He was just one month away from getting his license back. Surely, he saw a light at the end of a dark road. Things were starting to come together. So why did I feel so uneasy? The feeling in the pit of my stomach was back, preparing me for a storm that was about to blow.

It had been eleven years since our family had a vacation. We had all kinds of excuses. The truth was we didn't want the worry of taking Randy and one of his friends. As a teenager, he wanted a friend along, but who in the name of heaven wanted the responsibility of someone else's kid who was as big a worry as our own? We ended that battle by not going, which in the long run just punished ourselves.

I missed the ocean so much. When the opportunity to stay in a nice condo on the Bayside came along, Jeff and I decided to go. At first, we were going alone. Then Brad and Nicole wanted to come for the weekend, which was fine with us, but what about Randy? What should we do with him? We didn't want to take him along since his idea of fun would be to go out on the town every night, worrying us to death.

Randy surprised us by saying that he didn't want to go with us. He had to work, seeming very comfortable with being left home alone.

It was an opportunity for him to show us that he was accepting responsibilities. He could prove himself to us by taking care of our house while we were gone. Jeff was very uneasy about leaving him home, but I was persuasive by telling him that we shouldn't allow our son to ruin our vacation. I told Jeff that it was a good time for us to get away to spend some much needed time together.

As the time grew closer for us to go away, I noticed that Jeff was shaving the time that we would be gone. We had the condo from Saturday to Saturday. He lined up some kind of golf tournament on the Friday during that very week, which meant that we had to come back on Thursday. At first, I was annoyed, but some vacation was better than none. I had to be content with the time we had.

We left Randy a note the morning we left for the ocean.

Dear Randy,

Please feed the Beta fish and take down the trash Sunday night. Take good care of our house!

Love, Mom

I didn't feel good about leaving either. He was just too glad to see us go. He was interested in how long we would be gone asking several times. I believed that he had an agenda. I was starting to fret.

I pushed the bad feelings from my mind as we drove to the ocean. Brad and Nicole were meeting us there for just two days. I was convinced that we would have some rest and much needed relaxation.

On the second day of the vacation, we hadn't heard a word from home. We both wondered if this was good or bad news. Jeff and I called separately, thinking the other didn't call. We both got the same type of feeling from the calls; our son was just too chipper at 10:00 a.m. in the morning. The worry was mounting. There was a heavy cloud of concern hovering over the vacation. Had we been fools to leave him home alone?

Did this prove to be another bad idea on my part? I was the one who was going to take the heat for this!

MY BROTHER'S KEEPER

We took the stress and anxiety in the trunk of our car to the ocean. Every worry that we thought we would have by taking Randy was not near as bad as the worry of leaving him home alone! Something wasn't right at home. We were so certain that we started making plans to cut our vacation shorter.

On the third day of the vacation, Jeff was at the height of his anxiety by asking Brad to go by the house to "check on things." Brad and Nicole were only able to visit us on vacation for a few days due to their college schedules. They were driving back that day.

I was in total disagreement with Jeff. I worried more about Brad having a confrontation with Randy than I did with what Brad would find at the house. Material things could be replaced, but relationships—sometimes they couldn't be repaired. The damage could be irreversible.

Their relationship had already taken a beating. Things between the two of them had not been right since the golf club incident. Who was going to make it right? We had all been violated in some way, yet the one doing the violating sought justification in everything he did. Randy seemed to have some kind of distorted entitlement. He always felt that he was wronged first, minimizing his own actions. It seemed to be a huge cover-up for past deeds left hanging around with no remorse.

I had no idea how the mind of an alcoholic worked. I didn't know that they processed thoughts and deeds in a way that non-alcoholics such as me would not understand. I also had a long way to go to understand the mind that was addicted to opiates!

On the fourth day of our so-called vacation, Brad called. He spoke with Jeff. I could tell by the look on Jeff's face that things at home were as bad as we had expected.

Brad had done as his father asked. He stopped by the house and found the front door wide open with the air conditioner blasting and no one home. He took a tour of the house and saw a tremendous clean-up job. Not wanting us to come back from vacation early, he decided to wait for his brother to help him clean the house.

After a short time, Brad saw Randy come through the door carrying several packs of beer. It became clear that a party was about to begin. There was no need to clean the house since the party time was far from over.

What a mess! We put Brad right between his brother and us. He was torn about calling us, but he did what he had to do!

The house evidently revealed a continuous party as Brad told his father what he saw. I knew the vacation was over. We hastily cleaned the condo, packed, and headed home.

The four-hour ride back home was tortuous. There was anger in the car, bouncing off Jeff and me. We said all sorts of horrible things to each other. I was angry that we had to leave. Jeff was angry with me because the vacation was my idea and so was leaving Randy home alone. We were in fact "idiots," or better yet, we were prisoners again. We couldn't even leave our own home in peace.

As bad luck would have it, we ran into a roadblock from an accident that caused an hour delay. Then we hit a rough storm with torrents of rain and lightening. I was scared to death, afraid that maybe God was so angry with us that he was going to end our very lives that night for saying curse words to each other.

We sat sulking in our own little worlds. Our conversations had ended as soon as I said, "Randy has to go since he refuses to obey us or respect us." The silence in the car was unbearable.

Finally, I broke the ice saying, "You aren't going to ask him to leave are you?"

The answer was solemn, "It'll be hard." *Really,* I thought to myself, *I will have to do it myself.* I would have to pack him up and take him somewhere, but where?

At last, we pulled into our driveway. The lights were on with the front door open. Jeff walked in first, and I followed close behind. The kitchen had me in some kind of trance. Dishes with days of food stuck on them were piled up in a clogged sink that was about to overflow. My shoes were sticking to the floor.

As we walked into the living room, there were three strangers relaxing in front of our new high definition TV. Randy was nowhere in sight.

We asked them who they were, and they politely introduced themselves. They must have thought they needed to give us an explanation as to where our son was because one of the young men volunteered to tell us that Randy had "gone out for more beer."

As I stood on the sticky hardwood floors, I was livid was agitation. I ordered them out of my house, and they left. We continued with our tour of our home.

The toilet in the bathroom had overflowed, and someone put piles of paper towels on the floor to soak up the water. The guest towels had also been used to clean the mess. Three of the lounge chairs had been broken to pieces. The grill was out in the rain with no top. The curtains had been knocked down. What a sight! I was overcome with despair at the massive cleaning job ahead of me. As we waited for Randy to come home, Jeff busied himself with the mail, leaving the cleaning to me. Why did I have to do the cleaning? Randy should be the one to clean; after all, he made the mess.

Our car was in the driveway. I knew as soon as Randy saw the car, he would choose not to come inside. I busied myself with a three-hour cleaning job that did not even begin to rid my house of the mess. I was bone tired and so stressed. What in the world had he been doing while we were gone? Did he drink all day long? It appeared to be that way.

By 11:30 p.m., we knew that Randy would not be home that night. The lectures and questions would have to wait until he decided to face us.

After a restless night, I got up, pausing by Randy's open bedroom door. He had not come home. Well, he couldn't stay away forever. We would wait.

We sat at the kitchen table drinking our coffee in silence when we heard him turn the key in the side door. He walked past us as if we were ghosts, heading to the bathroom to shower.

I wondered if the much-needed conversation was even going to happen. I could picture Randy going on to bed to sleep the day away with nothing being said about the spoiled vacation. I could feel my agitation level rising by the moment. He would not escape my wrath, even if I had to go into his bedroom. No sir, he would not get off this time!

As soon as he walked out of the bathroom, Jeff called to him, asking him to come into the kitchen. He slivered in like a naughty little puppy, not a twenty-three-old man, to sit down at the table.

No matter what we asked him, he seemed oblivious to any problems that he may have caused. We asked about the three people in our house who told us that he went out for more beer, yet he denied that a party was about to begin. He didn't even notice that the house was clean. He told us, "I planned to clean up!"

The conversations with him were going nowhere. I finally said the words to him that no one wanted to hear, "You have to go, son. Call one of your friends and make plans now to move out on your own. You have lost the right to live here. It's over."

I could tell by looking at him that he was upset. He didn't want to leave. This was a nice place for him to stay. He had a bed, food, and transportation when he needed it. He wasn't about to go without a fight. We thought, *Well, at least he has a job so that he can make a little money to buy food.*

He spent the day making a few calls with no prospects of staying anywhere. It seemed that his friends like to party with him, but they didn't want to live with him.

Jeff asked him, "Do you need a ride to work?" Then it dawned on us that maybe he didn't have a job anymore. If he drank everyday while we were gone, he probably got fired. We confronted him; sure enough, he "forgot" to go to work and "forgot" to go to the outpatient drug center.

Now he was penniless, jobless, and homeless. What a mess! Was this rock bottom or was he going to try to float to the top? Somehow, I knew that Randy would find a way out of the mess. I wanted to see what that would be.

That same day we found out from Brad that Randy called him, saying all kinds of horrible things to him. Randy was angry that his brother had "ratted" on him. It must have been ugly. Then hours later there was another phone call from Randy apologizing to his brother, but the damage had been done.

Why had we allowed Brad to get in the middle of all this mess? He wasn't his brother's keeper. Nothing good was going to come of this situation. The distance between the two of them was growing farther apart. There was pain on both sides, pain that the other didn't understand or even know existed. It was sad for me to watch. I was angry with Jeff for involving Brad, but wasn't I always angry?

My house was falling apart as I stood helplessly by watching the turmoil. How in the name of heaven did it come to this?

As expected, a day later, Randy had a plan. He needed drug rehab and wanted to go to Christian rehab that specialized in addictions. He heard about Keswick, the Colony of Mercy located in New Jersey, through my brother Wayne, who knew the man who ran the facility.

There were several problems with this rehab. First, there was a long waiting list and second, it was out-of-state. Something kept nagging at me that the provisions of his DUI probation stated he couldn't leave the state, but I couldn't find it on the paperwork.

I drove Randy to the probation officer while I sat in the car and waited. I could tell as soon as I saw him coming out of the building that he was told he could not leave the state. He would have to get his rehab in the state that he resided.

He sat sullen, staring out of the window. How many times had we done this very thing? He was depressed and rejected, and I did not know what to say. I couldn't make it better. This was his mess, the bed he had made for himself. Now he would have to sleep in that bed. But had he learned anything?

As soon as we got home, Randy called his lawyer who advised him to write the judge who had passed the sentence for the DUI. Randy wrote a two-page, typed letter with several admissions that he had violated probation by drinking alcohol and that he needed drug rehab. We had no choice but to wait for the reply from the judge. How long would it take for the response? What would the response be?

One week later we were still waiting for that response. Brad stopped by one evening to get some groceries for his apartment. He sat upstairs with me talking about everything except his brother, who was downstairs watching TV. Two hours later, Brad was about to leave with no communication between him and his brother. It saddened me.

How many times had we heard Randy tell us that we loved his brother more than him? It just wasn't true, but as events happened in their lives, it always appeared that Brad was favored. He got "all the breaks." Every good thing that happened to Brad seemed to make Randy do something more destructive to himself as he attempted to hide his pain.

It was easy to see the jealousy. One child never gave us a moment of concern, seeming to want to please us and make us proud. While the other child wanted our attention more, so much that he was satisfied with negative attention. To Randy this was better than none.

I looked at Brad and said, "Have you spoken to your brother since the day you came to the house to check on things?"

"No. There is nothing to say," he replied solemnly. He was hurt as we all were with the fences of communication breaking down. The mending would be a time-consuming effort. I couldn't patch their relationship. I couldn't even repair my relationship with Randy. We were beyond talking.

I tried to communicate with Brad about substance abuse. How it created a lot of pain and heartache. I told him the way someone acts while drinking or drugging is not the real person. It is a if something evil was inside them, something out of control, something angry and full of rage, something confused and distorted. He listened to me, but he didn't say anything. I wondered what he was really thinking. It worried me.

The new wounds were deep. There had been bad feelings for years now, anger and jealously. These feelings were destructive and a menace to anyone's mind. No matter what I said, I couldn't fix their relationship.

This was one more reason for Brad to choose not to come home. What a high price we were paying by keeping our rebellious child in our home—too high a price to pay!

We were in a war with divisions that would take a mediator to decide the rights and wrongs. How had it come to this? My family was dysfunctional, the kind of family that I had read about in books or had seen in movies. This didn't seem real. Where was all this going? Where was the light? Where was the relief from this agony?

THE BUREAUCRACY

There was a nagging feeling of potential frustration about to shower my hopes of getting Randy in the New Jersey rehab. The waiting list was enough of a worry, but there was so much more. I could sense the whole scenario would go bad. Maybe it was just the feeling of doom that lived in my mind all the time, or maybe it was the reality of bad dreams coming true.

I knew that the longer it took for the rehab to happen, the less likely Randy would be to get the help he needed. Wayne called the rehab daily, pleading Randy's case. He spoke with the man who ran the facility, a man that he had known for years. Everyone was working to get my son in sooner, but the rehab was out-of-state. This was a problem bigger than a mountain that couldn't be moved. It was red tape; it was bureaucracy, a killer of time.

We waited for the judge to reply to the certified letter that Randy sent. We got the signed card from the mailman that the letter had been received; now the painful wait. I had a copy of that letter, but I had not read its contents. I walked over to my computer and started to read the letter.

July 27, 2006

Honorable Judge,

My name is Randy. I appeared before you in court on September 6 of last year for my second DUI within five years at the age of twenty-three. You sentenced me to two months in jail or drug rehab, which at that time seemed unfair. Now I thank God daily for your ruling.

Since I was released, I wish I could say I have been cured from drinking due to all the terrible things that I saw in jail, but I am not. I enrolled back in college and with nights of drinking and being high at times in class, proved to be my folly. I was far from "letting go." As things progressed, alcohol became my passion.

Everything came to a head about two weeks ago when I had a four-day straight drinking binge. Then follow that with the shakes and full-blown alcohol withdrawal. It was then that I finally decided that I was tired. I realized that I would not graduate college if I didn't give everything up. During the past few weeks, I have been in contact with my uncles here in Maryland. I had remembered one of them mentioning a Christian rehab program in New Jersey in which my uncle was friends with the man who operates the facility. The place is called the Colony of Mercy at America's Keswick.

Before I go any further, let me explain a little of my family background. I have a devoted Christian family and extended family. I currently have two head pastors as uncles and another is a youth pastor. The youth pastor mentioned was also an alcoholic like I am. Since I graduated from a Christian high school, injuring my pitching shoulder, everything has changed. I became lost and had a void. I drew away from God and could feel it inside. To fill the void, I used everything possible besides putting my faith in God. I have been lost.

Through many counseling sessions with my uncles, we discussed Bible College (when I was clean for a month or so) and many other options for me. Also during that time, I had a second shoulder surgery and became addicted to painkillers. I had to go to rehab if for nothing else than to detox off those terrible things. It was secular and twelve-step based. We read through the Big Book and the Narc Anon books daily. I felt I was replacing the Bible, but I got through the program only to give up the pills but to continue drinking. The drinking got worse.

I went to my AA meetings, and I didn't see God there. I needed God back in life. As my parents and extended family eventually stopped asking me to go to church, I didn't care. I had my alcohol.

During one of the meetings with my uncle, I had quit drinking for a couple of weeks. (This was right after being arrested for the DUI for which I appeared in your court.) My uncle told me that since I took alcohol out of my life, it would come right back if I didn't fill it up with something good, like church, the Lord, and his Word. I didn't listen. And sure enough, the alcohol came back in full force. And it was only up until two weeks ago that I finally cried out to God, my uncles, and my family for help. I want nothing to do with alcohol or anything anymore. During these past two weeks, I have been in constant contact with my uncles, in prayer and the Word. Something has happened to me.

As stated before, my uncle suggested a while back this Christian recovery center. In this letter, I will have enclosed all of the information about the site. It is a beautiful place that I already have admittance in enrolling. Everyone has prayed about this, and Keswick called today and were pleased to welcome me with open arms. There was only a few weeks waiting list. My prayers were answered.

But today, I went to see my probation officer, Mr. Sliver. He said I couldn't leave the state for this rehab. I did not understand. I was devastated. I called my lawyer, who told me that most probation guidelines would not allow anything out-of-state, but that I should write you right away. He said you would be understanding and that you also write people back very fast.

Even with a good recommendation from my out patient drug/alcohol program counselor and complete compliance with your probation, he would not let me go for whatever reason. I am in no way a risk of violence or flight. If I were permitted to go, I would check in with him as often as possible. I would adhere to every aspect of the program and come right back, finishing probation with my three AA meetings a week and continuing the outpatient rehab. I just feel so strongly about this place and where my soul will be when I return.

Your Honor, I have served my time, abided by every aspect of your probation and will continue to do so. I am asking you and begging you to allow me to go to New Jersey and start my life again where it was throughout high school with the joy of Christ in my heart and a clear mind. I am asking you to allow me to start my journey in life. Like I said before, I am tired, and I feel stronger than anything I've ever felt that God has led me to this wonderful place.

As I said before, everything about this program will be enclosed. It's no cakewalk at this program either. They have strict rules of conduct. I feel so strongly that I need to get away from this environment and just concentrate on what is most important to my life, which is Christ.

Again Your Honor, all I can ask is that you see that I am genuine, have a strong and caring Christian family who all want me to go to this place in New Jersey for at least three months. Please search your heart and allow me to start my journey and allow me to go. One choice on your part will change my life. Thank you very much in advance. Your decision will be in all our prayers.

Sincerely,
Randy

NOTE: The entire point of this letter is to request that you allow me to go to New Jersey for three to four months for this recovery program. Upon completion, I will return home and continue with the terms of your probation. My reasons for this request are already mentioned.

I read the letter over and over. It was powerful. After a few days, Randy called the office of the judge. His secretary told my son that no letter came. Randy told her that we have the certified letter card signed, but when he went to look for it, the card has disappeared from our house. While he was on the phone with the secretary, I searched and searched. It was gone. How in the name of heaven did that happen? The secretary told Randy to send another letter. Time ticked by.

We were determined not to give up. I told Randy to print out his letter, and I would hand deliver it to the judge's chambers that very day. As he was printing out his letter, I decided to write one as well. One more letter couldn't hurt anything. My letter was brief and to the point:

Dear Sir,

My son has written a letter to you, and as I read the letter, I felt the need to add a few things. I know that you are a busy man, but the matter has become urgent.

Last September, my son and I, along with our lawyer, sat in your courtroom. I was deeply moved by your concern for Randy's well-being. I knew that you were aware of his need for drug rehab. As a matter of fact, you ruled for him to go to a sixty-day drug rehab called the "Garden," asking the court representative if a bed was available that day.

To make a long story short, one week in the Detention Center, while he waited for the clearance to be accepted at the "Garden," withdrawing from alcohol, pain pills, and psychiatric medications, Randy made a hasty decision. He decided to stay in jail and work, shortening his sentence by a few days. I seriously doubt if he was even mentally competent at that time.

The DUI has cost him his freedom. We allowed his temporary license to expire, which was suspended for ninety days. He went before the judge for a MVA hearing. She suspended his license for six more months. The six months is over today. He could go to the MVA, getting the license back, but he has chosen not to by expressing his need for drug rehab.

I wish that I could say that going to AA's and seeing a probation officer has made a change in Randy, but it hasn't. He needs intensive rehab. He has finally seen his own need.

Presently, he has no health insurance and drug rehabs are very expensive, but the Colony in New Jersey is operated strictly on gifts. The waiting list is eight to ten weeks. Randy is on the list, and we are praying for an opening much sooner.

We were made aware by Mr. Sliver, his probation officer that Randy could not go there. I am asking that you consider this rehab as part of the healing process in my son's life. The drug counselor has highly recommended in-patient rehab for our son. We all want what is best for him.

The Colony is a four-hour ride with a 120 day minimum stay and longer if needed. If he shows a lack of development, he will be dismissed from the program, making room for someone else who truly desires the help.

I understand that there are policies of the probation and that he can't leave the state, but we are asking that you consider this program as a much needed part of Randy's recovery.

Jeff and I believe that the extended rehab is needed, and more importantly, our son has realized this as well. We assure you that he will stay in the rehab as long as they feel necessary. If he gets dismissed, we will notify you and the probation officer immediately.

The Colony's waiting list is long. If they call to say Randy can come and we decline because we do not have permission, then he will be put on the bottom of the list, and the process begins again. As you know, everything is a process.

The Colony is not a vacation. I believe that the time Randy will spend there will enrich his life. He has struggled with addictions for many years. If he gets the help he needs, then he can come back into society and function to his potential. I shudder to think what will become of him if he doesn't get treatment soon.

We await your ruling in this matter and thank you for taking the time to read this letter.

Sincerely,
Randy's parents

I folded both letters rushing to the courthouse to hand deliver the letters to the judge's secretary that day on my way to work.

I called home later that evening to find out that the secretary had called to tell Randy the letters were not signed. How in the name of heaven did we forget to sign them? Jeff and Randy had to drive back to the courthouse and sign Randy's letter; of course, my letter served no purpose since I couldn't sign it. But wouldn't you think that somewhere the original signed letter that we mailed was lying around somewhere in that courthouse? This was a bad dream, full of frustration and unbelievable red tape.

The next day, Randy spoke with the secretary again. She told him that the judge did not understand what we wanted. Didn't he even read the letters? We had spelled out our request, hadn't we? A hearing date was set to discuss the matter. That very morning, the Colony called to say that a bed was available. They had accepted Randy into the program. We had to decline while we waited for a hearing. Randy's name was removed from the list and the process of admission had to be started again. For the love of heaven, where was the support?

Somebody please wake me up from this bad dream.

Two weeks later, Randy, Jeff, the probation officer, and our lawyer went to court for the hearing. When they arrived in the courtroom, they were told that the judge was sick, thus postponing the hearing. Now this was really getting nuts. I suspected that the judge had never missed a day of work in his career, and today of all days, he was sick.

As they walked out of the courthouse, the probation officer was full of information that he had kept to himself all these weeks. He apparently knew more about the law than even the lawyer. He said that the judge would not rule in the matter unless he suspended the four months remaining in the probation sentence, but since the crime Randy committed was so "serious," the state of New Jersey would not allow him to come there anyway. He added that if our son had been arrested for possession of marijuana, he would have a better chance to leave the state.

It seemed that a DUI made Randy the type of criminal that other states tried to keep away. You would have thought that Randy wanted to go to Atlantic City, New Jersey and play serious poker on a mini vacation.

I didn't believe a word anyone said anymore. Who could I trust? We waited out another two weeks for the rescheduled hearing. With each passing day, the hopes of Randy getting to go the Colony became a dream that was drifting like the clouds, going farther and farther away. I could see that he was losing hope, and even worse, so was I.

The hearing finally happened, and the end of the dream. The judge clearly stated that he had no say in the matter of our son leaving the state. There were interstate compact laws that he had no jurisdiction over; slap, bang, and rejection!

Why in the name of heaven were we even there? There was to be no rehab, no recovery, nothing. The probation was becoming like an outside prison, where Randy could walk around, but couldn't go through the door. The Colony was just another dream, another chance for help that slipped through our fingers, totally unattainable.

Randy was caught in the bureaucracy web, and the probation officer, the head bureaucrat, could do nothing to help him get drug rehab.

What was wrong with these people? Where was the help?

THE HEDGE OF THORNS

The dark clouds of doom were following me everywhere I went, sneaking into my bedroom in the darkest hour of the night into my dreams. Something bad was going to happen to Randy. I couldn't shake the dread and fear that welled up in my soul.

I sat in church beside my mother, crying!

"Mother, he is going to die. I just know it," I sobbed to her while she held me in her arms.

She replied to me, "No, honey, God will watch over him. We will pray for the hedge of thorns to protect him." But I was inconsolable.

On the way home from church, there was the same eerie stillness. Jeff and I seemed to be lost in our own little worlds. But before we got home, he admitted to me what he had prayed to God, the same prayer that I had prayed. We told God that we were willing to die if our death would cause our son to change. It was a sad prayer from two desperate people. My eyes filled with tears at the thought of such sad praying by two heartbroken parents.

Randy seemingly got over the rejection news from the probation officer about the rehab. He got another part-time job and convinced us that he was ready and responsible enough to drive. I had many misgivings about him driving, but Jeff argued that the "law" said he could. It had been six months; surely he had learned a valuable lesson.

Maybe that's what bothered me the most. Had he learned a lesson? He never seemed to learn from the losses he had already received from his abuse of alcohol. I thought he was still at risk.

Randy and I had several conversations about his driving. He was very convincing.

"Mom, I could face eighteen months in jail if I drink and drive. Do you honestly think that I would take a chance in being sent back to that horrible jail again? No way. I know better!" he had earnestly exclaimed.

Deep in my soul, I didn't believe him. I knew enough about people that drank and drove. They didn't have the sense to know that they were even impaired. The alcohol robbed them of logic. They knew no fear. That's why they got into a car. The drinker was unaware of his own danger or the danger to others. The conscience part of the brain was dulled from reality. Who in their right mind would get into a car impaired with the risk of murdering themselves or others? That's why they get more than one DUI; they just don't get it.

So Randy was driving again. He had his license, had kept his job, and managed to save the money for one month's car payment and the insurance. It all looked good, but I was far from feeling any peace.

One afternoon he invited his friend Josh over for the afternoon before they went to work at their job. They were waiting on tables in a small restaurant, but it was work.

It seemed that his friend wasn't driving either, but neither were several of his friends. They were a circle of binge drinkers, and they were dangerous drivers.

The two of them were downstairs on the computer. They sounded like schoolgirls, giggling and being silly. For some reason, their voices annoyed me. Soon, they came up, left in Randy's car for about fifteen minutes, and returned, going back downstairs. They appeared to be secretive, like naughty little boys who were stealing cookies before supper.

One half hour later, they came up to go to work. They seemed to be quite happy. I thought that I heard tires squeal in the front of the house, but I was sure that it wasn't Randy's car. He would not drive fast down our rural development with little kids always riding bikes and playing; he had more sense than that. I dismissed it from my mind. But someone burned rubber from fast acceleration in a car because I heard the noise. It was unsettling.

The next morning Jeff told me that there was an away message on Randy's computer from his friend Josh, the young man that had gone to work with Randy. He wrote, "I have never been to work drunk before!" I was right about my anxiety; they were drinking downstairs in the daytime, but surely Randy wouldn't drive if he had joined his friend in drinking. I couldn't convince myself that only Josh drank while my son watched since Randy had driven them to work.

This was our first warning. He had his license one week; already his safety and the safety of others was a huge worry.

One week later, our family decided to have a special dinner and eat out. We would be celebrating my birthday and our twenty-fifth anniversary. Where did the time go?

Randy was doing more of his community service at a different church this time. I called him and invited him to meet us for dinner. He drove over to the restaurant. As soon as he sat down, I saw it. He was impaired. His eyelids were half shut; he was jovial, talkative. He was not himself.

Not wanting to ruin our dinner, I walked up to Jeff at the salad bar and whispered to him to get Randy's keys, so he couldn't drive his car home. He looked at me in bewilderment. So that was it; I was the only one that saw the way Randy looked. I walked back to the table as I continued to stare at Randy in disbelief.

As time slipped by after we finished eating, it was apparent to the rest of the family that he was indeed impaired. When we stood up to leave, I followed close behind Randy. I spoke in a low tone to him,

"You can ride home with your dad, or I will drive you home in your car!" He looked so shocked and questioned, "Why?"

This agitated me. I barked at him, "Just get in the car!" The ride home was brutal as he kept asking why he couldn't drive. He kept saying that he had paid the month for the car and the law said that he could drive. He denied being impaired. I stopped trying to reason with him. What was the purpose?

As soon as we arrived in the driveway, I got out, opening his trunk where he had tossed the club. I slammed it on the steering wheel with unnecessary force. As far as I was concerned, he would never drive again.

A couple of days passed with his increasing agitation over the club. He called me on my cell phone while I was on the way to work to give me an ear full. He was so angry! He hung up, yelling, "F——you," loud and clear in my ears. It was as if Satan was sitting in the car waiting for me to explode and get angry with God for the mess in my life. But I recognized that the words coming from my son's mouth were prompted by Satan, who was having a glorious day observing the chaos.

Next was the meaningless conversation I had with Jeff. He felt that Randy should drive to work at least and after all, "The law says that he can drive. So what can we do?"

"But we know better. We know he shouldn't be driving. If the club comes off, it will be on your hands. I refuse to be the one to take that responsibility," I replied with a new calmness. "I will no longer argue with you about his driving. It's over. I do suggest that you sell his car since you are part owner and have him get insurance in his own name. He is high risk, and you are liable." There was no reply.

The next day, the club was off. He drove to the courthouse for a hearing to explain why he hadn't done his community hours on time. The judge had given him a year to do eighty hours for a minor charge. He had done thirty-five hours, so he was in violation.

Apparently, he expertly explained to the judge about not having his license for so many months, as convincing as any high paid lawyer. The judge was sympathetic and gave him two more months to get it done. I could hardly believe it. I knew that he would wait until the new deadline was close before he would even think of doing the hours. It was as if he didn't care if he went to jail or not. What did he care about?

Later that day, he got a call from work. He had lost his job. He had several reasons why. I had heard them all before: the boss never saw anything good he did (welcome to my world), the people he waited on one night yelled at him and made a scene (welcome to my world). The work place could be a tough place. I warned him that he had to always be alert and at his best to do a good job, but he never heard a word I said. My advice was just wasted words on a floundering soul.

That same day, I got a phone call from the outpatient drug rehab. The lady on the phone asked for Randy. I told her that he was not available, asking who was calling, even though the name of the rehab was clearly on the caller ID. She told me that she could not give me that information. I went nuts on her.

"Listen, lady, I know this is the drug rehab calling. If you have something you should share with the parent who is letting him drive a car, you should do so now!" I spoke sharply to her.

She politely told me that the HIPAA law would not allow her to discuss Randy with me. Oh, I was getting nuttier by then.

"Do you realize that he is driving a car? He obviously tested positive on his urine drug test. That's why you are calling. Who are you protecting, the guilty? You certainly aren't protecting the innocent people on the road, the same road that he may be driving impaired on. If he has an accident and kills someone, it will be on your conscience!" I informed her.

She was unmoved by my tirade and told me it was out of her hands. The law would not allow her to "discuss the case."

I was not about to give up the fight. I told her, "I will have that law modified before the day I die, so people like you could stop protecting the wrong people." I slammed down the phone and paced the floor in the agitation of my own creation. Who was I really angry with?

She was just trying to do her job, and the HIPAA law put restrictions on her like the rest of the world.

The doom was more threatening than ever before. I felt my skin crawling. I was jumpy inside and outside of my own body again!

I drove down the road to our home at 2:30 a.m., my usual time to return from work. I couldn't help but notice how dark the night was, especially without streetlights. I saw several deer lurking, so I was cautious when I neared home, which was the time I was the most tired.

When I got into the house, I noticed Randy's bedroom door was open. The light was on downstairs, but I couldn't even hear the TV. I doubted if he was down there; then I thought to myself that he might be drunk or passed out. I was too tired to face that possibility. I grabbed a snack, and at 2:45, I went to bed.

The next morning, I woke up early around 8:00 a.m. As soon as I walked out of my room, I noticed that Randy's door was the same way as it was when I went to bed. Hadn't he gone to bed? The lights were off downstairs. As I walked into the kitchen, I noticed his car keys were gone and so was his car. I thought that maybe he had gone on an early job interview, but the doom was weighing me down.

I called Jeff at work to ask him where Randy was, but he didn't know. Something was not right. In an effort to block out the bad thoughts, I decided to go for my hour walk in our neighborhood.

This was my quiet time—a time that I prayed a lot, a time that I prayed that Randy would not kill someone while he was driving. There was such a sense of doom. Where was that coming from?

It was such a beautiful day, so fall-like with a few leaves falling. I felt more relaxed the farther I got down the drive. Then I passed the house of a neighbor who lived about five hundred feet away. His lawn had tire tracks. There was glass everywhere and flares. At first I thought, *He must have had some party last night,* even several mailboxes were askew. Then I saw the tire marks on the road, one single set of black marks and the other tire marks were on the lawn. Someone must have lost control of his or her car. Somehow, I knew who it was, but I kept walking and praying.

At the end of my work out, I passed the same house again. The owner of the house came out, looking right at me. I could tell that something was on his mind. He walked in front of me.

"Are you Randy's mom?" he cautiously asked.

"Yes. Why?" I asked with my heart pounding so loud that I could hardly hear myself speak.

"At 3:30 this morning, your son lost control of his car, hit the mailboxes, and then he hit my car. The air bags blew up in his car, and he isn't hurt," he quickly added.

"Then where is he?" I stupidly asked. I knew. Why did I ask?

"The police did an alcohol breath test. They took him to jail. I'm so sorry," he looked at me with pity in his eyes. He couldn't possibly know what this accident was going to cost Randy. This was his third DUI charge.

My mind was going nuts as I wondered if Randy was alone in the car, but the neighbor assured me that he was alone. My prayers had been answered; no one was killed.

I talked to my neighbor awhile, trying to process what had happened. He told me that Randy told the police that a pinecone hit his windshield, causing him to lose control of the car. The neighbor said that the police thought that he was speeding since the tire marks indicated that he may have been driving seventy miles an hour. In the name of heaven, what was he thinking? But of course, he wasn't thinking; he was drinking. It was believed that both cars were totaled. They had been towed away.

I sadly walked home to call Jeff to give him the news. I was especially angry with him since the club was not on the car. This whole scene could have been avoided. The real blame belonged on Randy, yet I was still ready to scream out at everyone else.

The doom was here with a vengeance. All my fears were real. I thanked God that Randy's life was spared. The hedge of thorns and the angel of protection had surrounded him, protecting him from physical harm once again.

Life had suddenly become painfully simple. God took the car from Randy because we as his parents refused to do what we knew was right. God took Randy away from our home because we had failed to keep him safe. We were unfit parents. The truth hurt.

I walked down the hall to his dark room. I heard the soft rumble of the ceiling fan. I turned it off listening to the silence. I glanced at his room that was still in disarray. Dirty clothes, books, and papers were all over the floor. The room exemplified his lifestyle, a life going nowhere.

I reached down to pick up his portable cardboard organizer that I bought for him to help him organize his paperwork. When I lifted the handle, it was heavy and the organizer fell open. I heard the crash of a bottle as it slammed on the floor. The bottle landed with the label facing me. It was an empty bottle of Vodka.

I sat down on his bed with the empty bottle in my hand, and I cried.

The Potter had given the gift as a loan. Was he going to return to take the gift away?

THE ERUPTION

Once again Randy could have been killed with his parents the last to know. To think that the accident happened a few houses away and we were unaware. An even worse thought was that I had driven past the very location of the accident just minutes prior to the collision. What if he had collided with my car? The very thought nauseated me.

Randy was once again behind the cyclone fence. I feared that his stay would be a long time and wondered if he suspected the trouble that he was in.

That morning the phone rang. The caller ID said "pay phone." I reluctantly answered, saying, "Hello?" It was the exact recorded message that I had listened to so many times last year:

"Medix has a collect call from the detention center from;" then I heard Randy say his name. "If you refuse to accept this call, hang up now. If you accept this call, do not accept call waiting or you will be disconnected. If you accept this call, enter one now." I pushed one. "Thank you."

"Mom?" he asked quietly.

"Randy, are you alright?"

"Yeah, I'm fine, but you need to come bail me out today. I have a job interview at 2:00 p.m.," he told me, acting as normal as any day of the week, not like someone who had just wrecked two cars, and not like he was in jail with charges of a DWI. What in the name of heaven was wrong with him?

"We are not going to bail you out. You will have to stay until the hearing," I told him as calmly as I could. But the conversation went around and around as he came up with all sorts of ideas on how to get the bail money.

"It's not about the money. We told you that if you ever went back to jail, you would have to stay there and finish your time. You are on your own." We had no control over him; we couldn't help him. We surely would not bail him out.

I listened to his outrage and cursing that felt like a violation to the point where I hung up the phone. At least he was making it easier for me; since he was so disrespectful to me, saying no wasn't as difficult. If he had been remorseful in any sense of the word, I would have had a hard time not going to get him. If he told me that he was sorry for all the pain he caused us, if he told me that he deserved the punishment and was sorry for all the years of pain. No, he was a caged animal wanting to get out that day, the same day of the accident.

He called me several times, asking the same thing; when were we coming to get him? I tried to avoid saying no again by asking him about the accident. He told me that Josh was downstairs with him, and they were drinking. Randy decided to give him a ride home. He was on the way back when a pinecone hit the windshield of his car, causing him to lose control.

"Why didn't you just ask me to take him home? I was up anyway. Why did you drive?" I implored of him, but he had no answer.

I was clueless in understanding the mind under the influence of alcohol.

I wandered around the house for two hours like a zombie. I was on a rampage. This whole scene could have been avoided. I was angry with everyone that I knew. I was out for revenge, totally out of control. I had almost lost my child. Someone was going to hear what I had to say.

The first person to get a taste of my wrath was Jeff; after all, he had taken off the club. I drilled him as to why the club wasn't on at night, blaming the accident on him. I was crying and irrational. Why wasn't the club on the car? We were just unfit parents, both of us. Now Randy was taken from our home. I had lost my child. In my fit to keep him safe, no one was on my side. Now he was gone. The pain was unbearable.

I wasn't satisfied just blaming Jeff, so I went to see Randy's probation officer, the head of the bureaucrats. I hated walking in that place where people sat all around to report in as part of their probation resulting from breaking the law. They lived on the wrong side of the law. There were consequences.

The stone-faced man behind the glass didn't see the necessity of my wanting to see the probation officer, but I insisted by telling him that I would wait all day if I needed to. He saw the crazed look in my eyes and probably viewed me as a nut. He told me to sit down and wait.

Before long, I got to go into the probationer's office. He was sitting down at his desk. As soon as he looked up at me, I slammed his door shut and went off like a rocket.

"Do you know why Randy isn't here to see you today? He is in jail being charged with a DWI. He wrecked his car and a parked car at three thirty this morning. The air bags saved his life. You are a lucky man today that he did not get killed or that he didn't kill someone else," I paused for a breath, but when he tried to speak, I went off again.

"If he had gone to the drug rehab in New Jersey, this whole catastrophe would not have happened. But no, he couldn't go to the rehab; he was a criminal. So he had to stay close by, driving a car and risking killing himself and others. How insane is that? So much for your bureaucratic nonsense. I was about to say some very nasty words. I had almost cussed, and I hated cursing.

He sensed my insanity and requested that I sit down.

I replied, "No, I will not, sir. I have just begun. You just sit down and listen to what I have to say. You had it within your power to actually help Randy. You knew that he needed it, but no, it looked good on your little paperwork for him to bring in AA meeting stamps. It looked good on your paper for you to come visit our home for your three-minute visit. It looked good for you to occasionally drug test him. I know that the one you did was positive, but what did you do about it? (Actually, I didn't know that for sure; I was just going nuts.) You knew that he violated probation, and what did you do about it? Nothing, you did nothing.

"You let him drive, that's what you did. I don't know if you are a praying man or not, but you should get on your knees and thank God tonight that your conscience isn't eaten alive by the guilt you would be having if there had been a death in that accident, some innocent person on that road at that time. Did you know that I just missed the accident by a few minutes? It could have been my life."

Every time I paused to take a breath, he tried to speak. As soon as his lips started to move, I went nuts all over again.

"I could have lost my son this morning. Do you possibly feel any regret that you said no to the rehab in New Jersey?" I glared at him in my anger, knowing he had no control over that interstate compact. I was irrational!

He looked kind of pale. He told me the same story that he told my son. Once he let a young man go to a rehab in Colorado, and this man killed someone. As soon as he said that, I went nuts again.

"In the name of heaven, that story has nothing to do with Randy. Let me tell you one. Some old lady in a hospital somewhere hung herself on her vest restraint, resulting in her death. As a result of that, nursing homes cannot use restraints and hospitals have to have a severe heavily documented reason to use one. Do you know what we all do now? We just let them fall, splitting open their heads, and fracturing their hips. What do you think of that? Do you see any sense in that?" I barked at him.

"You have a waiting room full of young people for you to see. You have it within your power to help them. Don't close you eyes when they violate. Look closely at those AA stamps. Those stamps are full of deception. There is nothing you can do for Randy now. But maybe you will remember this day when a parent came to you and asked where in the name of heaven the support was? Why didn't you call us if a drug test was positive? Who were you protecting? I'll tell you who; you protected the guilty, and the innocent were at risk. This is a sad excuse for a jurisdiction system that is supposed to keep the public safe."

I threw up my hands in despair. There wasn't much left to say. With tears flowing down my face, I left his office. Mr. Sliver had no say on whether Randy could leave the state. It was a law, and he had just tried to do his job. I wasn't ready at that time to see that reasoning. I didn't find out until later that day that Mr. Sliver went to visit Randy in jail. But what could be done now?

I was far from lowering the level of my agitated state of mind. The outpatient drug rehab was next door. I bounced in there demanding to see Randy's drug counselor.

She was a beautiful young woman. As soon as I heard her voice, I knew that she was the one that had called my home a few days ago. I began my loud talking as before and asked her if she knew what our son had done that morning at 3:30 a.m. Of course she didn't, so I elaborated in the same way as I had done in the probation officer's room a few minutes ago.

She tried several times to find a quiet place for us to go because people were all over the run-down little building, listening. After all, it was entertaining to watch a person go insane on someone else.

Her reaction was different from the probation officer as she didn't seem to be the least bit intimidated by my nutty accusations that she knew that Randy had a positive drug test or that she refused to tell me. Thereby, he was still driving a car, putting him and others at risk.

She asked, "How do you know if the drug test was positive?"

"Because I live with him," I snapped at her, "And you knew. What did you do about it?"

She got defensive, asking me, "Are you blaming me for your son's accident?"

"Blame, I'm not talking about blame. I'm talking about accountability. You knew! I told you when you called that he was a danger to himself and maybe others. But you had to throw in that HIPAA trash, which only makes your job easier and mine harder. Thanks for nothing," I turned to leave as the tears started to flow again.

I guess as that point she felt some pity for me and asked, "Are you okay to drive home?"

For some reason, that made me angry all over again, and I retorted, "I'm not impaired, my dear. I'm angry. There is a difference." I walked out, slamming the door.

So far, I had gone nuts on three people, but who was I really angry with? Whose fault was all this? Randy was responsible, yet I was attacking everyone else in my path.

I thought I would feel better after the tirade, but I didn't. I wanted to know where the car was so I could get the tags or so I thought. Deep down inside me, I just wanted to see the car. Somehow it was closure for me, not that I was attached to the car at all. I had to see the car.

The police barracks was a few miles away, so I went up to the glass window to inquire about the car. I was calmer by then; certainly, I didn't want to go nuts and be locked up for my insane accusatory attitude. I am sure that must be against the law.

The officer took a second to glance at me, causing me to fear that maybe the probation officer or the drug rehab counselor had called to report me for my lack of self-control. I was wearing a T-shirt with the writing, "The Good, The Bad, and The Blond." Didn't that just about say it all?

He asked me, "Was the owner at the scene of the accident?" and I said, "Yes." He then told me that the owner knew where it was towed, so he didn't see the need to give out that information to me. Dear God, the insaneness was back.

"Sir, the owner is in jail. I have no way to speak to him, and I need to find out about the car," I tried to sound like a desperate mom, not the "blond" crazy woman that had insulted at least three people in the past hour.

He and I had several conversations that went nowhere. As I realized the hopelessness of finding out where the car was, I asked him what Randy was charged with. He replied, "I can't give out that information due to the HIPAA law. He is of age."

Snap! "Oh, that's right, but you can give it out to the newspaper, and I can just read it at home. Thanks for nothing. By the way, his father is co-owner of that car. Do I need him to call you to find out the status of our car?" I inquired with my heart pounding so loud I thought that I might die.

He went to his computer and wrote down the name of the towing company. He handed it to me through the little hole in the window without even a glance in my direction. That glass annoyed me, but I had to assume that insane people like me came in there often causing such disturbances that the officers carried a gun for their protection.

A fifteen-minute hassle over the overrated HIPAA law! Someone needed to do something about that law; it was out of control.

I pulled in front of the fenced-in area with broken cars all over the place. Then I saw the little, crumpled car. The windshield on the passenger side had indeed been hit by something, but I doubted if it was a pinecone. It must have been something hard like a stone.

The front end of the driver's side was totally twisted with the tire pushed into the engine area. The air bags were deflated looking like dead balloons. For some reason, the door was locked. I unlocked the door, got in, and sat at the wheel of the car. Immediately, I thanked God for his protection over Randy. Once again, the angel had been in the car. He was safe.

For the next week, Randy called everyday with a new angle to get out of jail. There was a payment plan with installments, or we could take out a lien on the house. Then we could co-sign the bail bond. He would pay us back. He would get a good job and hire a real good lawyer. He was making all kinds of plans all that revolved around his bail. But it wasn't about the money; it was about our home not being a safe place for our son. We didn't help him by bringing him back home; he was only getting worse.

By the end of the week, he called me before I went to work to say that he was going to get "hurt." That some of the guys had been in a real prison. They tried to steal his food and "stuff." It broke my heart to hear these things because I was afraid for his safety. Good God, wasn't he safe anywhere?

I told him again that we would not be bailing him out; he cursed in the phone, again, before he hung up.

My prayers to God were those of anguish. I wanted God to protect him and do whatever it took, yet this had happened. God took the controls and somehow, I felt even more pain. When would this bad dream be over? I was exhausted.

THE GLASS WALLS

Glass walls were much better than most walls since you could at least see through them. You could see what was on the other side, but you couldn't touch it. You could see someone, but there wouldn't be any hugs or kisses, just a telephone and a booth of glass. I hated this place. This must be hell.

The first two days of Randy's incarceration were unbearable. He called from a pay phone, telling me that he was in isolation without a TV or even a book to read. He didn't know why he was placed there. Just like the first jail trip, he hadn't had any of his medications. Once again I knew that he would be withdrawing from benzos, alcohol, and painkillers. The threat of a seizure came back to haunt me. I started to fret with each passing day, regretting not bailing him out of there.

Then he called to say how sore his throat was, that his lips were cracked and he was sick. When I asked him about seeing a doctor, he told me that he had to wait a few days for the doctor to come in for regular hours.

I worried that he may be dehydrated. What if he developed strep throat and became septic? They would probably just let him die without calling us. My mind was driving me crazy. I fretted constantly. Finally, Jeff called the detention center for me and spoke to the nurse. The conversation was brief, but she understood that our son had to be weaned off the benzos.

We found out the next day that he had gotten one quarter of his daily dose. I still fretted. I decided to call the nurse and ask her, "Why is Randy in isolation?" She politely replied, "The medical department has nothing to do with where an inmate is placed. This was a security issue." I asked her, "Has he had done something to cause him to be isolated?" She froze up with the HIPAA law again. I was getting nowhere.

I told her that when we got patients in our detox unit who were withdrawing from alcohol, we gave large doses of benzos and IVs. She assured me that Randy got what he needed to avoid a seizure. I wasn't so convinced. I worried constantly about him, doubting if we should have left him there.

After my phone call with the nurse, Randy was removed from isolation. We never knew why. He was placed in the reception area where there was an open room with about fifty cots. There were inmates waiting to go to federal prison with constant twenty-four activity.

When Randy called, he would fill us in on how bad it was there. I could hear the yelling in the background. He told us that the TV was on twenty-four hours a day and he couldn't sleep. He was cranky and still complaining about his throat. My guilt from not bailing him out was overwhelming. No matter how angry I was with him, I didn't want him to suffer.

The next day he called to tell us that the doctor looked at his throat, telling him if he treated him for an illness, he would have to go in isolation. I guess that cured Randy of his sore throat, yet I worried about mono. He wasn't safe there. He wasn't safe anywhere.

For the next week, Randy continued his request to be bailed out of "here." He told us that he was the only DWI case in there. The other prisoners laughed at him. They filled his head with some "real" crime stories. They were intimidating and tried to take his commissary items. Why did everything have to be so tough?

He continued to whine about his treatment there as I was losing some patience with him. I reminded him that he was in jail, not a hotel, and life was going to "suck." There was nothing I could do to help him. I had tried for years, so many times, but I couldn't prevent this day. He had made a serious mistake. It was going to be tough, not just for him; it was tough for all of us, but he never seemed to think of anyone else but himself.

He was in a jam, and he wanted us to fix it, just like we had done before. Jeff and I realized that bringing him home only made his life spiral farther downward. We were not the answer for him. We were his parents, and we couldn't help him. Randy was behind the glass, and we could only look at him.

It was a painful thought, but I knew that I had to go see him, just to make sure that he was okay, just to let him know that I loved him. No matter what, I loved him.

As soon as I walked in, I felt my skin crawl. I hated this place already. Hadn't I stood outside the barbed wire fenced in this building just a few years ago? I had known that I would have to face this day. It was destined to happen, no matter what I did or how hard I tried to prevent this hell; it had happened just the same.

I walked up to the one-way mirror. There was a black phone on the side of the huge mirror and a metal box. I didn't see any police officers, just people waiting around. I didn't know what to do. I asked the young lady beside me who had four children with her all from a different race. At first, I wasn't sure if she would even talk to me, but she smiled at me, telling me what to do.

I hesitantly walked up to the black phone.

A voice on the other side said, "May I help you?"

I gave him Randy's name then put my license in the metal box. I waited while they got on the computer back there to make sure that I wasn't a criminal. I hated this place. Time moved slowly. I was starting to wonder if I had run a red light or something, or maybe those two traffic warnings I had gotten recently were on my record.

Slam, the metal box clicked back to me. I opened the lid and took out my license. I guess that meant that I could visit Randy.

The waiting area was jammed with a continual flow of people just waiting to talk to someone they loved for twenty precious minutes.

There were only six booths and three of those had phones that didn't work. There were huge signs on the glass windows that said "out of order." As we waited for the visiting time to begin, an officer came from the side door, walking past us like we were ghosts. He walked up to the booths taking down all three signs. Then he walked past us again to return to whatever he did behind the one-way glass. I turned to thank him, but he didn't respond.

We all soon discovered that the three phones were still broken. What was the point of him taking down the signs? No wonder he didn't answer me. His gesture just seemed to be a mean plot to make the visitors suffer for the crimes their loved ones had committed. He had created great conflict as different ones sat in their booth patiently waiting for a visit time with a phone that was broken.

The young men on the other side of the booths were all dressed in orange jump suits. It saddened me to see such young men whose lives were all turned upside down somehow. Babies were crying; visitors were cursing into the phones that actually worked as they had arguments during the short visit. I could see the angry faces on the young men who were locked away from their families. It was so sad.

Finally, I got to talk to Randy. It was enough to break my heart to see him back behind the cyclone fence. I couldn't bear to call it a jail, but he had put himself there. The glass, or bulletproof Plexiglas (whatever it was), separated us as we sat on stools.

Our conversation seemed to center around why he wasn't being bailed out of this "hellhole." He told me every horrible story he could think of, all his efforts for me to feel his pain. But he didn't need to waste his energies on words; I already felt his pain. It crushed my chest like pain I had never had before. He was in a huge mess.

He wanted a "real" lawyer, offering again to work to pay us back. But he never paid us back anything we loaned him because he couldn't keep a job long enough to save any money. As soon as he got a paycheck, he managed to spend it rather quickly. He didn't seem capable of planning his income to include items like gas for his car, and he made very few car payments. If we hadn't paid the payments, the car would have been taken by the bank, but Jeff's name was on the loan, and this was his credit as well. But what did all that matter now? The car was gone forever.

I was glad that the car was gone. Now I didn't have to worry about him driving impaired. Now I didn't have to worry about him killing himself or someone else. Now he was locked away. Yet I found that I was still worrying about him.

He wasn't a tolerant person with bucket loads of anger pent up inside him. I could see it in his eyes. It was going to be a long few months waiting for the hearing.

Within a week after daily calls, Randy finally seemed to accept the fact that he had to stay where he was. Then he totally surprised me by telling me that he signed up for the drug treatment program at the detention center. He was told that as soon as a bed opened, he would be moved to a different area. It sounded like a grand idea to me.

I was impressed that he realized that he needed help. Randy told us that he couldn't control his drinking, that he would never be able to drink alcohol again. His phone calls were more polite. I was praying that a bed would open up soon.

I called the supervisor of the rehab program. She took Randy's name while she assured me that beds opened up at odd times, but he was on the list. I found out that later that day this same lady went to tell our son that he could enter the program. Randy told her that he wanted to think about it. In the name of heaven, what was the matter with him?

When he told me that news, I went right away to the detention center for visiting hours that night. I was distraught with him. Why couldn't he make a good decision for himself? Why did he continue on this path to nowhere? At least the rehab offered some hope. He could get some counseling and find out why he was so angry with his own parents that loved him beyond what he could ever imagine.

I immediately told him to get into that program as soon as possible. What was the point in staying in jail? Then he told me that the program was ninety days long that he would miss Christmas. I assured him that we would save Christmas for him when he came home. I had to work Christmas this year, and Brad was flying out-of-state to spend the holidays with his girlfriend.

There would be no Christmas for us this year. Our home that had been full of surprises and Christmas Eve dinners would be shut down. I couldn't bear not having him home for the holidays. How sad was all this going to get anyway?

The depression was pushing me down into the ground. It was too heavy for me to bear. I was sinking, fast. How was I going to cope with all this?

I spent the next week working in his bedroom. I had to do something with all my nervous energy. I threw the curtains and his bedspread away; they smelled old and dirty. The pillows were full of stains, beyond washing; out they went to the trash. I bought a multi-colored quilt with shams and dark blue curtains. I straightened the closest and every drawer. I threw away old clothes with holes. I organized all his papers, just like I did the year before. What a waste of time that had been.

This time, I was more of a fanatic. I scrubbed the windows, the mattress, and the floors. I shined the furniture. I cleaned the fan, even the little covers over the light bulbs. I was going insane with energy. Then I decided to paint the room.

I looked at the walls. There were stains from beverages all the way to the ceiling. The light switch was black with fingerprints. There were posters of half-naked women, one of which I bought him for his birthday. If I had known what this young woman was displaying, I would never have purchased it. I ripped it off the wall and threw it in trash where trash belonged!

I went into a painting frenzy. I painted the walls in white and the trim as well. I felt as if I was cleansing it by making it white as snow. I ironed the new curtains and put them on the spotless windows. I covered the bed with the beautiful new quilt and shams. I scrubbed the floor one more time to remove the spattered white drops of paint before they dried.

I stood in the doorway looking at the beautiful room. It was a clean room, ready for a clean man to come home, a man that was ready to start his life anew.

I walked over to his radio sound machine that I had bought him last Christmas and searched for the Christian station. If Satan was in his bedroom, I was going to make his stay there most unpleasant. A clean man had to come home to a perfectly clean room. There would be no evil forces to create havoc in Randy's mind. There would be no evil at all!

I paused to ask myself, "Just how many times are you going to cleanse this room?" Wasted energy!

The soft music was playing in the quiet of his room. It was soothing as it drowned the deafening silence that I had heard when I painted and cleaned his room. The music was peaceful, like the story in the Bible about the harp David played for Saul to ease his troubled spirit. The music was good. I liked it.

The room had a smell of strong, fresh paint, which had replaced the musky odor of a neglected room that had been occupied by one who didn't take any pride in its appearance. The room that used to smell like dirty clothes and wet socks was no more.

I took one last look at the room before I turned off the light. Then I reached down in the dark and switched on the nightlight.

There was a soft glow in the room. The only thing missing was Randy!

THE OASIS

Miracles! How few I had seen in my time, but I did see one. It was a miracle of perfect timing, perfect planning, and far surpassed any dream that I ever had in my life. The miracle offered an oasis, a welcome relief from difficulty, but it was so much more. It was a gift from God in a time of trouble. The miracle was a reminder to me that God was in control, with too many angles, and too many tiny elements that fell into place. No human could have planned such an event. It was divine and flawless, bringing the sweetness of a much-needed oasis.

The morning of the hearing brought the first round of miracle work. Our lawyer, Mr. Matt Divine, that had agreed to do the out-of-county violation case, called to tell me he was coming to our county court to be with Randy. I was shocked since I knew that he didn't do those cases. He gave the cases in our county to his assistant, who had already seen Randy to discuss the case. She had been the one I had talked to on the phone. She had all the paperwork of the hearing dates and verification of the psychiatrist's visits with Randy.

As we talked on the phone, Mr. Divine told me, "I feel like I let Randy down in court a few months ago when the doors were slammed shut on the rehab in New Jersey. I wanted to come to court today because the circumstances of the hearing were a direct result of the refusal to let your son cross the state line."

I knew how he felt. I felt guilty that I hadn't just put Randy in the car and taken him anyway. I would have been a contributor to a violation, but it would have been worth it to save us all from this hell.

Jeff and I met Mr. Divine at the courthouse. It was so good to see him, such a relief. He had a genuine concern for his clients. He told us that he needed to see Randy to talk to him about ideas that were only to be discussed with Randy. Randy was being held and guarded in a room with the other offenders who had a case that day. We hadn't seen our son or had the opportunity to tell him that Mr. Divine was going to be in court just for him. I only wish that I could have seen Randy's face when this well-respected man walked up to him and told him he would stand with him before the judge.

After Mr. Divine spoke with Randy, he wanted to talk to us. He saw a change in our child, a different man, a man that had lost everything knowing that alcohol had taken his life away. Whatever Randy said to him made him feel the compelling urge to help us.

We all agreed that Randy was not safe in our house and that we had tried everything we knew except to make him leave our home. He needed long-term counseling and rehab, but how was this going to happen? He was facing more jail time. The secular drug rehab was skating across the surface of Randy's issues with substance abuse.

Our lawyer spoke of the rehab in New Jersey again, stating Randy still wanted to go, but that door was just not penetrable. What was the use to even talk about it? We ended our conversation with total agreement that our son needed help.

We all went back to the courtroom to wait for Randy's case to be called. I was looking in my big pocketbook where I had stashed a good pair of black shoes and a vest for Randy. The inmates could wear street clothes for court without a belt. I was hoping that the lawyer could give them to him so his wrinkled clothes that I left at the detention center months ago could be exchanged, but the opportunity had not arrived. Then I noticed a folder in the bag with the court dates. As I leafed through the papers, I saw the two letters that we had written to the judge a few months ago, begging him to allow our son to go to New Jersey. There was also a letter from Wayne on church letterhead, addressed to the judge in an effort to persuade him to allow Randy to go to Keswick. How odd! Why were they in this bag? I didn't even remember putting them in there. Anyway, Mr. Divine's assistant had a copy, which I had given her a few weeks before. She had this information since she was the one who was assigned to this county, but as I said, there was a last minute change. What was going on?

Mr. Divine took big cases in a big county. We were little potatoes to him, yet he was here in court. He will never know what comfort it was for me to have him there.

For some reason, I leaned over the bench where the Mr. Divine sat, asking him, "Do you have the copies of the letters to the other judge?" He said, "No, but I do need them." He took them from me. I had no idea the piece of dynamite I had just delivered.

I was restless in my seat as we waited for Randy's name to be called. Tom called that morning with his special way of making a person feel that he had all the time in the world for whoever needed him and had joined us in the courtroom. It was such a comfort to have him there. It was as if an angel was sent to calm the troubled spirit, reminding me that God was in control.

At last, we heard Randy's name called. He was ushered in, shackled hands and feet, wearing his orange jumpsuit that was much too big for him. It saddened me to see my child so removed from society and treated like a dangerous criminal who might bolt out of the courtroom unless he was locked in chains. I moaned inside that I had left him beyond the cyclone fence. Why had I left him in jail? Where in the name of heaven were his clothes? I had delivered them to the jail a month ago, clothes just for court.

Even then the clothes had been an ordeal. The belongings were carefully searched. They tossed me the belt and the socks. Huh? I had to be content that they at least took the clothes. With all that aggravation, he was still wearing inmate clothes.

The lawyer presented a moving speech to the judge, talking about the "Garden" rehab and the one in New Jersey that never happened. He told the judge about the hearing two months ago with the state line issue preventing Randy from entering a rehab that would have avoided this day. He was powerful and convincing. He gave the judge a copy of the letters, but I really couldn't tell if he read them. Our lawyer then asked us to come join him before the judge.

I could feel my knees shaking as I stood up. I walked past Randy to stand between him and the lawyer, but not before I sneaked a hug around my son's waist. It felt good to touch him. I missed him, and I had to make myself take my arm away from him. I wanted to hold him, to make everything better, but I couldn't.

Jeff was stopped by the court guard and not allowed to get within ten feet of us, as if he was a threat of some kind. Now what was that all about? The lawyer turned to me and asked me if I had anything to add. I wished I had a speech prepared, but I was shaky and sad. When I started to speak, I didn't even recognize my own voice.

I recall telling the judge that rehabs were just about impossible to get into. I told him about the trip to court a few months ago and that it had all been a waste of time. I told him about the insurance companies that refuse inpatient treatment over and over; even when our son overdosed, the answer was no. The answer was always no.

I told the judge that Randy needed help, and there was none. Then my voice cracked as I almost lost composure. I ended with my last comment, "We are afraid that we will lose him!" My eyes filled with tears as I glanced over to Randy. His head was down. It was all so sad.

Then the lawyer asked Jeff to speak. He said, "Our son is a nonviolent offender, and his drinking is out of control!" There really wasn't anything else to say. He told the judge that we needed help.

I never took my eyes off the judge. He was quiet. He looked at the pitiful sight before him, and I believe that he was moved. I hadn't noticed, but the probation officer had snuck in the courtroom and was sitting with the prosecuting attorney. I was angry with him all over again. Couldn't he have prevented this day? Why should he be sitting on our side of the court? He wasn't interested in helping us; he just wanted to make sure that the laws of the interstate compact were upheld. I knew that he was whispering that very thing to the state's attorney. I refused to see that he was just doing his job.

The judge spoke first, telling Randy he wanted him to finish the drug treatment program at the jail, which ended January 11, just a few months away. The judge then surprised me beyond my wildest dreams. He asked me if I would pick up Randy on January 12 and take him to New Jersey, to Keswick, the Colony of Mercy, the rehab that had been impossible to get into. I thought that my knees were going to buckle and cause me to fall down. Was I dreaming?

Before any sentencing, the judge decided to wait until Randy finished the program at the detention center, wanting to see Randy in court again. He wanted Randy to get more treatment, believing that he needed it.

The probation officer spoke a short time about the law and leaving the state. I stared at that tall, skinny man as he spoke. Wasn't it about time for him to retire? I felt like hitting him. What was the purpose of his comments? Didn't he know how badly our son needed help? Maybe he was still sulking over my tirade in his office.

Whatever comments the probation officer made didn't seem to make an impact on the judge's decision. At least there was hope. Hope was all we had!

I watched as the guard took Randy away from us, from the people that loved him the most in the world, away where we could not touch him. He was back at the cyclone fence to finish the sentence. There was nothing to do but wait.

We walked out of the courtroom with the lawyer who was very optimistic with the judge's decision. Our son had to finish the drug treatment in jail without a hitch, and with the help of God, we could take him to New Jersey.

I was ecstatic and couldn't wait to get home to call Keswick. I got voicemail and left a brief message. She returned my call within an hour, but I was not prepared for what she said.

They still had Randy's application on file. She told me, "Your son has not called since August; therefore, we took him off the waiting list."

I reminded her that this was as a result of the court trip at that time where he was denied crossing the state line to go there. There was no need for him to call.

I told her, "He is in a detention center and could not call as required. Perhaps Keswick will make an exception to the call weekly rule!"

She said, "Keswick could not be a court ordered situation and that it could not be used in lieu of jail time!" I explained that he had been in jail for two months now and was in a drug treatment program that he willingly requested to be in. She was new at Keswick and was hesitant to talk about the situation we had.

I told her that his program ended on January 11. If things went well in the treatment program, he would go back to the judge and be allowed to go to Keswick. She asked me, "What if a bed in not available?" I replied, "We are praying that it will be!"

She told me that in order to get on the waiting list, Randy had to call Keswick weekly. Again, I told her that he couldn't call her weekly as requested since he couldn't make long distance calls from jail. She paused, telling me she had to take the matter to the director. I thanked her, thinking to myself that while she was doing that, I would take it to the almighty one and leave it there for him to fix. We needed more divine intervention.

I wrote a long letter of request to Keswick. I then called Wayne, who knew the man who ran the rehab, and told Wayne that I needed his help. I got his voicemail.

I was starting to panic. We had been so close. I couldn't feel the oasis now. The lawyer called and left a message that the court date to see the judge after the rehab was changed to January 19 since the judge was on vacation the week of January 12. What next? For the love of heaven, what is next?

It was far from over. The court date for the violation of probation was four days away to see the same judge whom we saw in August in another county. The only good news was we had the same lawyer and the same story. At least this judge knew the situation. What would the judge do? Would he punish Randy for the violation, or would he feel a pang of guilt for not helping us a few months ago when we tried desperately to get him in the rehab? Would he remember the letter Randy wrote to him talking about all the drinking he did? He had admitted then to the violation, so there was no surprise in that letter.

Would this judge agree to wait to sentence our son until he returned from New Jersey, or would he sentence him jail time first? It was unbelievable stress. I had to let it go. It was too big for me. Hadn't God already shown me a miracle? Randy needed a break; he needed to see a miracle. We all did!

My oasis was too short a time. I needed so much more. I was still struggling to keep my head above the depression that threatened every day to disable me. I was making myself physically sick. I knew that something had to change.

Randy called us twice a day, once in the morning to talk to me and once in the evening to talk to his father. He was sad that there was little mail. My aunt, my mother, a few of his cousins, my friends, my sister-in-law, Jeff and myself were the only ones that wrote him. But as my mother has always said, "We find time to do what we want to do." If anyone wanted to write him, they would find the time. Mail was all he had to look forward to, and there was so little of it. He hadn't even gotten the money order that I sent four days earlier. What was with the mail?

He seemed encouraged by the first hearing, but was still fretting over the one for the violation of probation. We were all worrying, but it was totally out of our hands. It was a mountain that only God could move. It was big and mighty. We were low on faith. Was God listening?

My friend Deb left me a phone message that her letter to Randy was returned to her because she didn't have his ID number on it. No one knew what that number was, and I never put it on his letters. Why in the name of heaven won't they just let the inmates get mail? Someone went to great lengths to make sure that the correspondence was cut to a minimum, as if to cause more pain. But this kind of nonsense caused me pain. What I had done to deserve it? It made me wonder what real prisons were like, and I started to feel compassion for people that I didn't even know that were locked away.

I left my friend a message to send her letters to me, and I would just switch it to my envelope. What an extreme measure just to get a note, just to hear from the outside world! It was so sweet of her to take the time to write Randy. Randy and her son had been good friends years ago. Their interests had driven them apart, but Deb and I still kept in touch. She was always there for me. She was a good friend.

There was little encouragement to someone living beyond the cyclone fence. Being locked away from everyone you loved was not enough. There had to be little punitive acts to make life even worse, if that was possible. The outsiders like me had to be punished too. I had to watch my child suffer. I was just another invisible parent who managed to raise a child who got into serious trouble with the law. I was surprised that I was even allowed to write or visit and feared every day those privileges would be taken away for no good reason.

The mail issue was not worth discussing to the detention center since even a small sticky stamp would cause the whole letter to be trashed. There were rules.

We were two hours away from court time. My stomach was in knots, and my anxiety was dangerously high. What if the judge sentenced him right then and there to go back to that awful place Randy had been in the year before? But why would he send an incarcerated man to another incarcerated place? What would be the sense in that? And did any of this have to make sense? Whatever happened today was going to make a huge impact on all of us!

I must be dreaming. When would I wake up?

MIRACLE ON CHESAPEAKE AVENUE

Jeff and I decided to ride together to the courthouse on Chesapeake Avenue. The ride was quiet. We were both tense with anticipation of Randy's fate. I thought of Randy riding in the back seat of a police car, handcuffed, with the company of an armed officer to face the hearing. I felt nauseated again.

My stomach was in knots. I didn't feel any consolation that the jail had found his wrinkled clothes since I hadn't known that they were even lost. There was no peace.

We arrived a few moments before the hearing and went in to sit down to wait for our lawyer.

I watched and listened as cases came before this judge. Was it my imagination, or was he unusually irritable today? The judge was annoyed at one young man who stood alone. The judge wanted to know where his lawyer was. The young man said that he couldn't afford one. Then the judge asked him why he hadn't gotten a public defender, and the young man said the same thing. The judge lost his patience with him and asked him why he didn't have ten dollars to secure representation. I couldn't hear the rest, but the young man went to sit in the back of the room.

A young woman who had been driving on a suspended license was next. She also stood alone, admitting her guilt. The judge allowed her to speak and for some reason, he believed her, giving her probation.

Wow, being a judge must be tough. I was not able to predict which way he would decide. It was so unsettling.

Then Mr. Divine came, motioning for us to follow him to the lobby. He told us that he would present the case again about the rehab in Keswick. He wanted me to talk to the judge. At least I was more prepared this time.

Just before we walked back to court, the probation officer showed up, looking solemn and unfriendly. Now why did he have to come? Didn't he have better things to do? I assumed he had an agenda to make sure that Randy stayed in jail and not a rehab.

We sat down with our lawyer as we heard Randy's name being called. He was not in the courtroom. I wasn't even sure if anyone went to get him. Where was he?

Then I heard someone in a uniform say that he was in lockup. Of course, that's where inmates are stashed, but which lockup was he in? Had they brought him from the detention center in our county?

In a few minutes, a guard ushered Randy in, handcuffed, and dressed in his wrinkled clothes. Well, at least he wasn't in that horrible orange jumpsuit. I didn't see him look at us. He was asked to sit down to wait for the judge to call him again.

Was this ever going to end?

His name was finally called, and our lawyer left us to go stand before the judge with Randy. The probation officer went to his favorite spot to sit with the state's attorney where he could object to anything. Why was the very sight of him so annoying to me? But really I knew why, Randy had broken the law and it was mandated for him to be followed by a probation officer. How sad!

My attention went back to Randy. All I could see was his back with his wrists shackled behind him. I saw him motion to the officer to remove them, but the officer shook his head no.

The judge opened the case by stating that he remembered seeing us in court in August and that he felt badly that we were all back again. Did he really mean that?

Our lawyer began his case by telling the judge that this day could have been avoided and that he felt he had let Randy down, but the judge had our letters of four months ago in front of him and was seemingly disinterested in what our lawyer was saying. Mr. Divine asked the judge if the "parents" could speak. The judge granted permission and was very polite by saying that he would like to hear from us.

I walked up bedside Randy, sneaking in another hug, but Jeff kept a few feet away for fear of being told to stay back again.

I spoke first. As soon as I mentioned Keswick in New Jersey, the judge stopped me. He explained that no one under probation could leave the state and no judge would allow anyone to go. He further went on to tell the same story about the man who was allowed to leave our state and while he was away, he killed someone. The judge was stern, saying that New Jersey didn't want our son there, and then paused a moment to ask the probation officer for the answer from New Jersey. The probation officer stood for a second and told the judge that the answer was no.

I wished I had asked to see that answer in writing, but I was in no mental state to think coherently.

I felt despair with tears welling in my eyes. The judge asked me if I had anything else to say.

With a shaky voice, I said, "Your Honor, I can not understand how our state will allow our son to drive where he is a real risk, but will not allow him to go to a rehab in another state. He will not be free in New Jersey to come and go; he will have to stay in the rehab. He won't be a resident in that state." I went on to say how hard it was to get our son in rehabs, and how the insurance company always found a way to say no. It was all so frustrating. I had the same old sad story again!

I felt as if I was losing the war. I had nothing else to say. The judge then asked Jeff to speak. I was shocked by what he said.

At first, I didn't even recognize his voice. He said, "I know people that work everyday with this system and interstate compacts. Couldn't the legal system and the probation officer have done something to help get Randy in the rehab?" He was obviously agitated. I wondered where all that venom had been for the past few months. The lawyer picked up on his attitude right away, turned toward Jeff, and motioned with his hand for Jeff to calm done.

It was at that moment that the judge got really annoyed. He defended the system and the probation officer. Then he said what I already knew as he pointed his finger at Randy, "Sir, it is your fault that you are here today and no one else's." By then, tears were flowing down my face. He then asked Randy if he had anything to say.

I glanced over at him. He looked calm, ready to speak. He admitted to the judge; "Sir, my life has been in shambles. I have lost my education and relationships. I am lucky to be alive. I will never be in this court again. I know the only way for my life to change is to never drink again."

His speech was moving, or was that just because I was his mother? I felt his pain. This was so difficult. I feared that the judge was going to give him a maximum sentence for violating his probation. I watched the judge as he listened, looking directly at Randy. I waited for the blow!

The judge spoke to Randy, telling him that he felt sorry for us and why shouldn't he? We were unfit parents; we were to be pitied. Good parents don't beg before a judge while their son is in handcuffs.

The judge said, "Sir, I believe what you just said to me. I am going to be lenient with you in this court today."

Then the judge gave the sentence. Everything was such a blur by then that neither Randy nor I heard what was said. I recall hearing something about four months in the detention center, but which one? And was this subsequent or concurrent? Why in the name of heaven didn't everyone just speak English?

Randy looked at me. We were both confused. The guard took him away to sit down by the door as we walked back to our seats with the lawyer. I looked at our lawyer, telling him that I was sure Randy didn't understand the sentencing since I didn't either. But the lawyer was smiling at me. He walked over to Randy to talk to him a few minutes. I saw Randy smile. Then I saw the lawyer put an envelope in Randy's shirt pocket since he was still handcuffed. I found out later that it was a personal letter that the lawyer had written just to him. I never got to read it.

I watched in a state of confusion as the guard took our son away to a place where we couldn't touch him or kiss him. I stood staring at Randy's back as he was ushered out of the courtroom.

Jeff and I went back to our pew seat with the lawyer as he collected his brief case. My heart was pounding. The probation officer walked past us without saying a word.

We walked with our lawyer to the lobby as he sat down with us to explain the decision of the judge.

The sentencing was four months in jail to run concurrent with the time he was now serving. The four months would be up on Jan 20. The judge had not extended probation or given him more jail time. In essence, when Randy got out of the detention center, he would be free, meaning he could go out of the state. He could go to the rehab!

The judge had been firm just minutes before by telling us that granting Randy permission to leave the state was out of his jurisdiction, but the sentence he gave our son actually gave him the window to do that very thing.

We had gotten a break, a huge break. The judge saw people every day that were liars and abusers of the system, but he knew a tragedy about to happen. He felt our pain by being merciful to our son.

This was an early Christmas present, a gift from the judge to two parents that were hurting and to a young man that was lost in substance abuse. The judge wanted Randy to get help. He had read the letters.

Our lawyer was at a loss over the judge's decision, who admitted to us that the outcome could not have been better and that the decision shocked even him. We were all elated with the hope that Randy would finally get the help he needed. This was Christmas, for sure, a time for miracles.

I could hardly wait to talk to Randy. When he called us that night, he was convinced that only his talk with the judge made any difference; not the lawyer we had hired or the letters I had sent or the sad speeches of two desperate parents. Randy gave himself the credit. I thought to myself, *What a waste of talent he had!* He should put that talent to good use. He had a gift.

He had managed to convince one of the sternest judges in that county that he was sincere in wanting to start his life over. He had spoken with heart and soul in a speech that flowed off his tongue as if the words had been planted by God to warm the very heart of a judge, a man with the power to seal his very fate.

Since the judge in our county was on vacation the week of January 12, the court date was moved to January 19. This judge wanted Randy to complete the drug program at the detention center first before he would make a decision on Randy's case. I was upset and called our lawyer, leaving him a message about the two dates. The drug treatment program ended January 11; where would my son go until the 19? Would they send him back to the open room with fifty cots and the TV blaring twenty-four hours a day?

Matt, our lawyer, was a busy man, who probably tired of whiny mothers like me, so I got his voicemail. After a few days, when he didn't return my call, I felt like the anxiety was back even more than before. What was going to happen?

Matt was always on top of things. We received a letter with a new court date of January 4 to meet with the same judge we met in November for the DWI. The lawyer had gotten the case to be heard a week early, just before the drug treatment program ended. The court date was just a few days into the New Year. Randy would not be home for Christmas, but at least he was alive. Even though he wouldn't be home with us that morning to open packages, he had already gotten gifts. The lawyer was his Santa Claus, and the judge was his Christmas.

But there was still a sentencing to happen. There was a cloud hanging over all of us. Randy was fretting already with the date a month and a half away. He was growing impatient, and the miracle on Chesapeake Avenue was wearing off. He was worrying about this judge and what he would do. We all were. We were in this together.

All these court dates were so intense. If a person violated probation by drinking, there was a court date. If a person had a DWI, there were two court dates, one with the judge and one with the MVA judge. If a person violated a drinking probation in one county, he had to go to the first county where the initial sentence was given. It was so complicated.

When Randy was upset, so was I. When he was anxious, so was I. When he got depressed over missing the holidays with us, so did we. It was rebounding anxiety. It was difficult for everyone.

I got a surprise package in the mail, a long letter from my friend Mary. She told me that she felt the urge to pray for me. I never even told her about Randy's accident. She sent a book written by a mother whose only son had killed someone and was sent to prison. My friend thought that I would get comfort from the book.

I read only a few pages. When I got to the part where the other prisoners beat her son almost to death, I crumbled like a cookie. The tales of this mother's frustration with the agitated personnel on the phone and her denied efforts to see her son was more than I could bear. When she finally saw him, his teeth were cracked, and he was bruised and beaten. I started to cry.

She wrote about seeing him behind the glass and picking up the black phone. She and her son just cried together. I shut the book and went to bed, but sleep would not come. I was in a worse emotional state that I had ever been.

I had to snap out of this pity party and move on with my life. This was not a dream! I was not going to wake up. This was reality, and I had to face it.

God had heard my prayers in court last week. I had not been abandoned. God would be there on January 4 beside us, all the way.

The month of December was almost impossible to bear. It was a season of blessing, joy, and Christmas spirit, yet I could not begin to function. Putting up the tree was torture, especially after I picked up Randy's little ornament he made when he was in elementary school. I stared at the ornament, thanking God that I didn't know then what was to come.

Brad decided to spend the holidays with his girlfriend's family. I couldn't say no; he was a man now, but oh how I needed him this year. That was just selfish of me; I had to pretend that I was okay with his going. Maybe he preferred to be away from his own home. How sad that thought was for me!

In essence, both boys had made decisions to be away for Christmas Day, one consciously and one unconsciously. This would be the first

Christmas in twenty-four years that my sons would not be in my home to celebrate as a family.

I had to work this Christmas Day for twelve hours. Maybe it was all meant to be; at least I wasn't IN a hospital bed, but I was healthy to take care of those who were sick.

The days went slowly by, with Randy calling twice a day. His main concern was "getting out." He wrote a letter to Brad, sent to our home address, which we kept on the table sealed to be opened only by his brother. I got a letter, but there were no apologies or regrets for anything he had done. We were all hurting, yet he thought only of himself and his miserable time in jail.

Was he sorry? Did he know that he wasn't alone?

FILLING THE VOID

With just a few weeks before Christmas, I felt the hole in my heart expanding. I was full of unjustified sadness; after all, the war in my house did not compare with the war in Iraq where many young men had already died, never to be home for the holidays. At least my sons were safe!

I had taken care of at least three patients in the hospital that week that helped me put my life situation into perspective. One woman was forty years old, dying with cancer, and was being transported to a near by hospice unit. Her stoic children marched solemnly behind the stretcher. Their mother would not be home for the holidays.

Another woman, also in her forties, was admitted for withdrawal of alcohol; she was trembling so badly she couldn't hold a cup in her hand. Her main meal for the past ten years had been Vodka. She had lost her family, her job, and was about to lose her life.

Another woman around the same age was admitted for seizures. Staring me in the eyes, she denied any recreational drug use as I glanced at the critical cocaine levels on her lab report. Her droopy eyes were full of lies, but I had seen that look before. Her small children would not have their mom home with them for the holidays. Why did the holidays have such an impact on substance abusers?

I needed to move on, but something else was missing, causing a sadness that I could not explain.

Every time I spoke to Randy from the detention center, he kept talking about our precious, bad dog Peproni girl that was put down. The sadness of her loss still lingered in all our hearts, but I was determined not to allow my heart to feel such love and pain again.

In the middle of my sadness about Randy not having any gifts for Christmas, it occurred to me that we needed a dog. I didn't want a dog; I just needed a dog. I began to search the ads for puppies, scheming on how I could sneak the little dog into the jail. How hard could it be?

I called several owners, and one dog caught my attention. The dog was red, but I had to travel one hour in unfamiliar territory to get the little dog. I took down the directions, which seemed a little confusing, but I was getting anxious about Christmas being so close and no dog.

The morning arrived for me to go get the dog, but everything went wrong. The checkbook was locked in the safe, which took me thirty minutes to open. I had to call the owner to say that I would be late.

Then I got lost three times and had to call her on my cell phone. By the time she received my third call, she became irritated on the phone, and I was as well since I had been driving around for two hours already. She was rather rude, and I was rather upset. I saw a familiar road, turned around, and went home. No dog, no little Lucy! I had reached a wall. This was not to be our dog.

I came into the house and started to cry. No dog, no children, no surprises, nothing. Then I did the one thing that I should have done first. I got on my knees and asked God to help me find the right dog. I hated to bother God with such a trivial matter since there were people with much greater needs than mine, but I knew that without God's help there would be no dog.

I got up and went back to the newspaper, searching the pet ads. I called another lady. She had two five-month-old black puppies left. Brad agreed to go with me to direct my way.

We found the house right away. As soon as we walked in, the lady was holding a brown dog in her arms. Brad walked over to pet the dog and the dog responded with a growl as he tried to bite him. The owner was shocked at the response, but I knew right away that this was a sign, a very bad sign. This was not the dog for us. That dog reminded me of our Peproni girl, who hated everyone but the immediate family members.

Brad and I sat down on the sofa, while a little four pound black, longhaired, Yorkie puppy leaped off the floor into my son's lap as if the little dog was airborne. The little dog licked Brad repeatedly jumping on and off the sofa, like a hyper Yorkie will do. The dog was friendly, refusing to stop playing with Brad. This was the sign. This was the dog for us!

There were many other dogs in the house barking nonstop. I never noticed that this dog didn't bark, not even once.

We took our little treasure home. He immediately started to hide from us in various places in the kitchen. I had our old cage cleaned and ready. Sometime later that day, he went in and wouldn't come out. He was so cute as he poked his head out watching us with timid curiosity.

Now that we had the dog, we had to keep it a secret from Randy, who was not going to be able to touch or pet the dog. It was a huge task not giving away the Christmas Eve surprise.

For two days, the little dog wouldn't eat or drink. Even stranger, we never heard him bark. I was worried that he may not last to Christmas. I took him to the vet, who was reassuring and wasn't concerned. The little dog needed "some time to adjust."

Ever so slowly, he started to trust us. He ate from my hand and drank some water. I kept giving him little spoonfuls of honey. He loved being held. I was falling head over heels in love with this dog.

The owner named him Little Blackie, but we didn't like that name. We spent a week arguing over the name. I won by naming him Chico Man. But he never barked. How strange was that?

I mentioned to the vet that I planned on sneaking the little dog into the detention center, but he thought it would be best to ask first. Yeah, right. And what would that answer be? No way; it was going to be a carefully thought out plot of sincere trickery.

After a week, the dog was more trusting, doing the cutest things, even though I tried not to notice. I had three different collars for him and a little outfit, all of which were a challenge for a hyper dog, but great amusement for a family that had a void. We played, we laughed, and we loved.

As Christmas Eve was just a few days away, my plans to sneak the dog in to Randy were challenged by everyone. The family thought that I would be handcuffed and taken away. I was willing to take that risk. I started to scheme each day. I was determined.

I went to the pet store where they had carrier things that looked like a large purse. I carefully selected one and took it home to experiment. Anyone that knows anything about Yorkies knows that a pocketbook is a joke, and so it was. Chico Man refused to lay down in it. So I returned it.

Then I thought maybe I would use my big blue beach bag. Once again, the dog went nuts, refusing to stay in the bag. I was in a panic. I didn't want to bother God again, but I was getting upset. My little surprise was going to backfire right in my face. Wasn't it bad enough that Randy was in jail, but no surprise either? I started to cry again. This was all too sad for me.

With one day left before Christmas Eve, I got my next challenge. After months of searching for the right dog, finally getting it, and two weeks of supreme secrecy, Randy phoned to ask us not to visit him Christmas Eve night. I begged him since Christmas Day was on a Monday with no visiting hours and I had to work as well. I told him how much we wanted to see him, but he said that if we came, he would not come out when called. There was no need to argue with him. He was handling being away the only way he could. It was tough on all of us.

But I never let it stop me from the surprise. I said to him, "Okay, we'll visit this afternoon (the day before Christmas Eve). We want to see you." For some reason, he agreed.

How odd, two weeks, and no barking. What was with that? I pushed the thought aside, fearing that the little dog may be saving some shrill attention-getting barking just for the surprise visit.

Now, how to get the dog unnoticed into the jail? I was like a crazed animal with only one thing on my mind, to break a rule without a consequence. I was beginning to sound just like Randy. We definitely had the same genes in that area.

Chico Man had gotten used to a black sweatshirt that belonged to Randy. I put in on the floor at night, in case he got cold, so he could snuggle up in it. The morning that we were to visit, Chico Man was so lost in the sweatshirt, that I didn't even see him. Then it hit me; carry the dog in the sweatshirt. If I couldn't see him, then how would anyone else?

So Jeff and I plotted a situation to sneak Chico Man into the jail. We rehearsed the scene over and over. We had a plan.

We put Chico Man in his cage for the trip to the jail. We left him in the car while we went to check our license into the metal box. I had the empty black sweatshirt in my arms, making it appear to be part of my attire. I went back to the car to check on Chico Man, who was in the far corner of the cage. I decided to have a talk with him, "Listen little dog, this is no time to bark. Got it?" Even though he had not barked once since we brought him home, this was no time to start. So I prayed, bothering God again and asking him to let the dog be quiet for just another hour. What a ridiculous thing to ask of a mighty God, but I needed his help.

Plan B went into effect when Jeff called me on my cell phone just to make sure we had connection as he waited for Randy to come to the booth. I walked back into the waiting area with the empty rolled up sweatshirt, again.

I was a nervous wreck. I went back to the car as planned, waiting for the phone call from Jeff, the one that would mean he was talking to Randy, which was the signal for me to come in.

My heart was pounding. I took the little dog out of the cage, carefully wrapping him in the sweatshirt as I smiled with a devious smile. This was feeling so good. My cell phone rang, "Okay," said Jeff. Chico Man and I rushed out of the car. I paused for a moment, making sure that the little dog was totally concealed.

The waiting area was crammed with people and no one was interested in a lady carrying a loaded sweatshirt, except one woman. She was a visitor, watching me as I hurried up the steps. For some reason, she knew that I had something in my arms other that a sweatshirt.

"What is that you are holding?" she asked with obvious curiosity.

"Don't ask," I quickly replied.

Oh great, I thought, *so this was going to be a problem.* Surely the guards would notice.

I ignored her and kept hurrying in past the onlookers with my little bundle. I went right to the booth where Jeff was talking to Randy. Jeff was sitting in the booth, and I pulled up a chair. Randy saw the look on my face. I could tell that he wondered what was up.

I slowly pulled back the hood of the sweatshirt as Chico Man poked his little head out with his big ears and eyes full of wonder. Randy smiled a look of disbelief. He stared at the little dog and then at me. Since Jeff was on the phone and Randy couldn't hear me, I mouthed the words, "Merry Christmas!"

He had a zillion questions about the dog. I had dressed the dog with the USA handkerchief, just like the bad dog that he loved on the Internet. I had carefully sought out a dog that looked exactly like that one. But I couldn't take any of the credit; this was all God's work.

Jeff, who had serious doubts about the trickery, wanted me to take the dog back to the car, but I refused to move. The dog was quiet, busy staring at Randy. They were looking at each other. I choked back the tears. I knew how much he wanted to hold Chico Man.

I took Chico Man out of the sweatshirt and put him on the little shelf right where my son could see the entire beauty of our little dark dog. Randy looked back to see if the guard saw the dog and asked me to put Chico Man back in the sweatshirt.

I can't remember having such fun and pulling off such a great surprise. My entire family knew of the plan, including my co-workers. Even people that didn't even know our son had tears in their eyes when I told them of the surprise.

The twenty-minute visit zoomed past. We took Chico Man home. He had done his job well! He still hadn't barked, not even once.

Randy called as soon as we got home to ask about the dog. He was so excited, but all too soon the reality of not being able to pet the dog set in to spoil the fun. The sadness was still there.

Christmas Eve morning I walked into the kitchen, hearing a soft sound coming from the dog. He did a weak little bark, the first one in two weeks. If you are familiar with Yorkies, you know that not barking for two weeks was a miracle. He finally barked and had waited until the time was right.

But this dog was not an ordinary dog. He was sent from God to our home to touch our hearts and bring us joy when we had to search for peace.

This dog was sent to heal and touch our lives. He was sent to fill the void in our hurting family. He was a gift from a God who knew what we needed.

Christmas Day came and went as I did my busy twelve-hour shift in the hospital. There was no time to whine about my home situation without either of my boys being home. It was what it was. I didn't have the power to change any of it.

It wasn't until Christmas night that I learned that Tom had visited Randy in jail at 10:00 a.m. on Christmas Day, leaving his small children and his wife at home. He made the appointment in advance with the clergy when he found out that we couldn't visit our son that day. Who does things like that?

I was blessed with three brothers, but Tom was in his own class. Randy was so close to him!

Brad came home from visiting his girlfriend's family the day after Christmas. He was jolly and a pleasure to have around the house. He looked as if he had grown again. He wasn't a boy anymore; he was a man.

We had our little Christmas with him, but it was all strange without Randy. He was the missing piece of the puzzle.

I talked to Brad about his brother for only a short time. I asked him if he wanted to visit his brother, and he readily agreed. I never knew if he did it for me, for his brother, or for himself, but it didn't matter. The end result was the same. He would make an effort to see his brother. I let them talk the whole twenty minutes. Brad never told me what they talked about; the conversation was theirs alone.

On New Year's Eve, Randy called us. I knew immediately that depression had a strong hold on him. He didn't want to hear about our little dog. He complained that we got the dog knowing he wouldn't even get to know the dog or pet him, as if we had planned to hurt him. But weren't his words the actual thoughts that he had about us?

We were his parents, and we loved him; we never wanted to hurt him or see him in pain.

He just didn't seem to understand that he was not in this alone. We all felt the emptiness in the house. We felt his absence.

The phone calls from him were getting farther apart, and his voice was in a monotone at times. He told me that he had "passed over." When I asked him what that meant, he wouldn't explain. He doubted the need to go to Keswick. It was all a bad sign. He was listening to lies from the enemy.

Randy was deeply depressed, and he worried me. Was he safe behind the cyclone fence? Was he safe anywhere?

He had been in jail for over one hundred days. He had missed Halloween, Thanksgiving, Christmas, and New Year's Eve.

When was I going to understand that alcoholics had no control over their deeds once they were under its evil influence? Someday, I would, but it would be a long time coming and only then would I know the peace of forgiveness.

I always hated waiting, or was it the dread of impending doom that I hated? Was it the dark cloud that hovered over my house, capable of sending down torrents of bad weather, or was it the bad feelings that I tried to hide in my troubled mind? I felt as if I was hanging on the edge when the slightest disturbance of my little world could shatter my being like broken glass. Anxiety is a horrible feeling, used by the evil one to weaken a vessel. Each day, my mask was harder to wear. My cover was weak at best. I was barely holding on to my own sanity. When would I let this all go? When would I turn my troubles over to almighty God? Was there any peace to be had?

The court date was sneaking up on us. Randy was calling more often, asking us to talk to his lawyer as if he had hired him. It slightly annoyed me that he referred to Matt as his lawyer. Randy was totally focused on getting out "of this place" on January 4. There was little talk of Keswick, making me wonder if he really felt that he needed rehab at all. His serious denial was a bad sign. He was high risk to self-destruct. Sadly, he was the only one who didn't know that.

I had already planned to touch base with Keswick just to make sure that he was still on the waiting list. I called a few days before court, leaving a message. As always the intake officer returned my call and not only was Randy on the list, but she was holding a bed for him.

I could hardly believe it, but then I started to fret as to how long she would hold the bed. I realized that Randy got all his anxiety from me. I was a wreck. We didn't even know if the judge would let him out on the court date or make him stay longer. Life was in limbo for everyone.

What if the judge gave him supervised probation? He couldn't cross the state line. We would be back at square one. The more I talked to Randy, the more concern he had for simply being free. Was he losing sight of the real issue?

With the court date just days away, I called our lawyer, leaving a message on his machine telling him that I would see him on January 4. I was still worried that the drug program at the jail did not end until January 12. Would the judge make him stay to complete the program? The next day, he left me a message having a conflict in his schedule with a civil court case that same day.

For the love of heaven, when will all this torture end? Now we would have to go to court with another lawyer who didn't even know the whole situation. I listened to his message and cried. Then I decided to call him leaving another message.

"Hi, I got your message. I found it to be rather disturbing for some strange reason. We have decided not to tell Randy since he will only worry. Please tell your associate that I will be sitting outside the courtroom at 1:00 p.m. on the parked bench for unfit mothers if he wants to discuss the case." I quickly put down the phone before I started crying again. I had very little control over my emotions. I didn't want him to doubt my sanity.

Keeping the news from Randy for two whole days was hard to do. My efforts were in vain since he sensed that something was wrong as soon as he heard my voice. He even asked me if I was keeping something from him. I lied to him. I hated lying, and I hated liars even worse, but what was the point in raising his anxiety level to equal mine? At least I could go shopping and get my mind off things for a little while. He could only sit and think of his plight or his fate. He was in the "timeout" chair!

He hated the drug treatment program at the detention center, but that was understandable since he never thought that he needed to be in one. He had some serious group sessions there where he always thought that someone was trying to "push his buttons." Maybe someone was getting too close to the real issue, the issue that he bitterly denied. He was an alcoholic!

On January 4, I left home early, so early that I decided to do a little shopping for distraction purposes. My cell phone rang at 12:30 p.m.; it was our lawyer. He was going to make every effort to get to court for us, but he would be late and asked me if I would I tell the district attorney. You bet. I was elated. I felt like the weight of the world was lifted from my shoulders. It was a comfort to me to know that Matt would be in court. He knew the judge and Randy's case so well. At least Randy's chances for fairness in court would be more favorable now. Maybe we were going to get a break and get Randy some help before he could destroy himself. There was hope.

I sat in court alone, waiting for our lawyer. Jeff was out of town and wasn't sure what time he would return. What irony, that his job was a priority. I was going to have to deal with whatever happened in court alone. I took care of patients with addictions. Wouldn't you think that I could help my own child?

I stood in the long line to talk to the district attorney with all the other people who had last minute issues. When I told the attorney that Matt would be late, he was instantly annoyed saying that he had witnesses that had to wait. I told him that it would only be a half hour; our son had to have a lawyer present. There were tears in my eyes as I was anticipating Randy standing before the judge alone, but I guess the attorney saw a mother about to crack. He relented by saying, "Okay, we'll wait." I rushed to an empty pew to sit down where I could have my silent nervous breakdown.

As bad luck would have it, there was another young man with our last name and believe me there was some confusion, but I was close enough to whisper to the state's attorney that the first name called was not my son. A young man was escorted into the courtroom in an oversized orange jumpsuit with handcuffs. I felt like crying. How sad this all was!

Another young man stood alone when his name was called. I couldn't hear what the charge was, but they handcuffed him, taking him away. He had no lawyer. He was just a kid. In the name of heaven, what kind of a generation were we raising?

Every time the door of the courtroom opened, I turned to see if Matt had arrived. Finally, he came, fifteen minutes sooner than he planned. He walked in, sitting down where I could see him. He smiled at me. He seemed confident and not jittery like me. I was so glad to see him.

After a few more cases, they called Randy's case. He was escorted in with his wrinkled clothes and handcuffs. The guard removed his handcuffs. Matt went to stand by him before the judge.

I had problems hearing anything that was said, but it wasn't like I would have understood any of it anyway. Matt turned and asked me to come join them to talk to the judge about Keswick. I thought that I was going to vomit, but I got up and stood by Randy after sneaking in another little hug. It felt so good to touch him.

I told the judge who I was and that I had spoken with the Keswick intake officer this week. He asked me if a bed was available. I told him that she was saving a bed for Randy. I was glad that he never asked me when because the bed wasn't available until the next week. I hadn't lied; I just didn't give any unnecessary information.

He asked me the date of my son's incarceration, and I told him, "September 20, 2006," 106 days ago. For almost four months, Randy sat in jail with not much to do except think. Surely, he had learned a lesson of some sort in there, but had he?

The judge asked me to go back and sit down. He asked Randy and Matt to sit where they were in front of a desk, which was a few feet from the huge desk of the judge. The silence was unbearable. The judge looked over the Keswick information, keeping his head down so that his face was shielded from me. I couldn't tell what he was thinking as I sat fretting over his verdict. This was absolutely nuts! I kept telling myself to settle down.

The judge finally looked up at Randy and began talking to him. I couldn't hear any of it, but apparently the whole ordeal was over since the guard came and put the handcuffs back on Randy's wrists. I saw the confused look on my son's face, but Matt was smiling and talking to Randy.

The guard took our son away again as I sat in bewilderment. Matt put his papers in his briefcase and turned to leave, motioning for me to follow. As I followed, Jeff was just coming in; he got back in town earlier than expected. He looked at me and asked what the judge said, but I was in some kind of shock and couldn't say anything.

We both followed behind Matt into the lobby as he explained what the judge had said. He had given our son unsupervised probation. That was all I needed to hear. He could go to Keswick now. The judge asked for a report from his progress at Keswick by June 30, 2007, which was six months away. He read the information on Keswick, knowing that the stay was a minimum of 120 days, which could be much longer if the client needed to stay. The judge wanted to see Randy get some help.

"Matt, when will he be released?" I asked.

Matt smiled saying, "Now! Let's go down and wait for him."

Now, today, in a few minutes, unbelievable! I could hardly soak it all in. What a powerful God to make this all fall into place! What small faith I had! Where was my faith? My faith was always a step away from the doom of anxiety. I was a ship with a hole in it on the high seas. I was in jeopardy most of the time.

We walked down to the lower level of the courtroom where the probation officer's office was, and I kept looking at his door. I guess that I expected him to come out and say that I had dreamed all that stuff that had just happened in court.

We chatted with Matt awhile. He shook our hands as he left for his next appointment. He wanted to help Randy, and he had. The verdict today was huge.

Jeff and I sat for one hour, waiting. No one in the courthouse seemed to know where Randy had been taken. I walked over to the detention center, but they didn't know either. Well, surely he was somewhere between the two buildings; eventually they would let him go.

Jeff decided to go on home since it was senseless for both of us to wait in two separate cars. I decided to make a quick trip to the mall to waste some time.

I rushed back to the detention center parking lot. I had just parked the car when I saw the lone figure walking in his wrinkled clothes and carrying a small garbage bag of belongings containing the few letters he had received. I got out of the car, resisting the urge to run and fall on his neck as the father of the prodigal son had done. It was too soon for that, and I knew better. Randy had suffered just like the prodigal son. He had deep pain. I often lost focus of that thought.

I slowly walked toward him. He was so handsome, even in his wrinkled clothes. The closer to him I got, the better he looked to me. His eyes were dark and shiny, all clear and free of any substance abuse. He had a long road ahead of him. I had no idea the battle that was to come. Talk about anxiety; imagine knowing that something horrible was just a few days away. Think of the worry while watching the clock. Oh, it's a good thing that we didn't know what was coming next in our lives.

We met, and I wrapped my arms around his tall frame. In the distance, I could see the steeple of the church. The sun was setting, and the stained glass was reflecting the glow.

We got in my car and went home.

How strange! We got a letter from Randy from the Detention Center while he was right downstairs in our very home. I put it aside not opening it for two days, but it kept staring at me. I couldn't figure out why I didn't read it. Finally, I couldn't resist any longer and I opened it.

Mother,

I just wanted to write you a little letter. It's good ole December 30 right now. I hope you understand my concerns about not wanting to be out of society for another three months. Jail is horrible. I still have an open mind, pray, read my Bible, and ask God for his guidance through all of this. It is a tough one! Mom, my number one goal is never to drink again (any drugs is a given). If I don't drink anymore, all things are possible. I will do anything to not drink anymore, even if that means Keswick. The last thing I want is to come home on probation and be sitting around and doing nothing except eating, watching movies, and calling girls. I'll have meetings and church, but I need more. I'll do what it takes, and I think you know that very well. Alcohol is poison. I have a lot of willpower, and God is on my side. Also,

I have tons of support. I can't wait to get started on life, and I hope you understand my concerns. I love you, Mom. Tell Chico Man I say "Hi."

Love,
Randy

I put the letter aside, thinking to myself that he was trying to bail out of going to Keswick, but what I had really done was to miss the message he was sending. He was crying out for help. I missed it. The letter didn't come clear to me until it was too late. He wanted my help, and I was going to fail him miserably. What kind of a mother could miss that message? But I had blinders on that day, causing me to miss the plea.

The words of the letter came back to haunt me. I sat down to read them again. Unfortunately, it was too late.

The dream of Randy going to Keswick was fast becoming a reality. Surely, only God could have stepped in performing such a miracle. How could two judges in two different counties pass a sentence that would allow our child to get the help he needed? It was all a plan from an almighty God, who knew that our son was in trouble. God had always known. Those times I thought God wasn't listening to me and all those prayers that I thought were not heard had not been in vain. God had heard me and was being merciful.

We had six days to get ready for Keswick. As the days started to creep by, I noticed that I was the only one thinking about the trip. Randy was showing some signs of depression, withdrawing from us, as if he had a little plan of his own. He had mentioned more than once during the long week that he really didn't think that Keswick was the place for him, that he really didn't want to be locked away from "society" for another long time.

As the day grew closer, I wondered if sending him to Keswick was the right thing to do. After all, there were young men on a long waiting list to get in there. If Randy showed this side of himself to the counselors there, they would ask us to come get him. The thought of that was scary! We had come so far. Was this another trick of the enemy? Was it a last effort of Satan to suck the breath out of my child? Would he never relent?

Randy and I took a day to go shopping for some running shoes and clothes that he thought he would need in Keswick. I was getting annoyed with him before we even left the house because the drug rehab was not a little vacation. He shouldn't think that he should have expensive clothes for the trip. Of course he didn't like most of the clothes that I picked out for him for Christmas and wanted to select his own.

The mall he wanted to go to was a maze of four levels that required a map for the zillion stores that went north, east, south, and west and all expensive. I was tired from my two previous late shifts. I hated shopping on a good day. I lectured myself to just go and spend time with Randy; after all, he had been away for months and was leaving again.

We plundered all over that insane mall, but he just couldn't find the right shoes. After a few hours of aimless looking, I was ready to take my splitting headache home. Shopping with a needy child was just not fun. He was hard to please, and I was edgy.

He recognized my attitude when he saw me sit down in the mall, just like I used to do when I was a little girl shopping with my mother. I was tired of looking. It was as simple as that.

He selected a pair of shoes, more expensive than they should have been, but I didn't even care at that point. The bargain hunting was a waste of time in that mall. I didn't see the sense in looking anymore.

We found our car at last, and the ride home was quiet. As always, he listened to his music.

I was relieved to get home. Now we could pack. We had two whole days to get ready for the trip to Keswick. I wanted to make sure that he had all he needed.

Randy thought of a few reasons not to pack that evening, spending a lot of time playing with Chico Man. He would come upstairs and play with the dog, then go back down to seclusion. I noticed that his eyes were "pea-eyed." I asked him if he was sleeping well at night. Surely his eyes just were tired. He told me that he was having trouble sleeping, so I brushed the thought away that maybe he was downstairs drinking.

Thursday morning Jeff told me that Randy went to a movie with an old friend late the evening before. She happened to be a young woman who used to party with him and sneak alcohol into our home when he was not yet twenty-one years old. I have to say that I really didn't have any use for her.

I decided to ask him how his evening went. He must have known what I was thinking since he told me how "she had her life together now." I didn't believe a word of it. She was a sly fox, and so was he. Were they drinking? Couldn't I have a good thought these days?

Later that day, his old friend called, one of his drinking buddies. I was immediately annoyed when I answered the phone, but I was angry with the wrong person. The young man told me that he was just returning Randy's call. I told him not to call back.

I slammed down the phone. I was angry. As usual, I was angry with the wrong people. Randy was making phone calls to get rides with old friends. What were they doing? He didn't even have any money. Why would he want to hang out with them? Two of them had DUI's before. None of them cared about drinking and driving. They were all a bunch of stupid kids, but they weren't even kids; they were young adults. Did any of them have any sense at all? Couldn't at least one of them grow up and tell Randy to do the same thing? What was it going to take to wake them up from their dream world of party time?

But his old friends kept their jobs, and somehow they drove cars. They were back in society and several of them had finished college. The one with the real issues was Randy, who couldn't keep a job and hadn't finished college. He was the one who was in trouble, not them. It was Randy who needed help.

Before I knew it, Thursday was coming to a close and Randy had not packed the first bag. I mentioned it more than a few times, offering to help him, but he had retreated to his little world downstairs with his rented movies. At the last minute, I ran out to the store to get him a few toiletries. I was rushing around before I sort of came to myself, asking myself what in the world was I doing?

I was getting agitated with Randy for his lack of initiative, yet I was making it all so easy for him by doing the work that he should be doing. He didn't even want to go with me to select the few things for his travel case. Obviously, he wasn't interested in packing or worse yet, he wasn't interested in going to Keswick.

When I returned, I called downstairs to him to come up and get ready to pack. There was no response except a grunt from him that told me he heard what I said, but didn't care what I said.

At 10:00 p.m. that night, the night before our trip to Keswick, I realized that Randy just didn't want to go. Jeff and I called for him again before he finally came upstairs, announcing that he wasn't going to Keswick but that he was going to leave our home that night. He told us that he would not be in his bed the next morning.

"So, I see. Well son, it's like this. Either you pack, or I will throw your things in a garbage bag for you. But you are going tomorrow to Keswick. This is what you have asked for in court more than once, and it is going to happen." I was close to yelling by then, but anger had no place in this scene. Anger just made more anxiety for all three of us.

I was edgy with Jeff, snapping at him to turn off the TV to come help me pack. He was equally agitated because I had set the scene before him, a scene of command and a scene of needing him to intervene. One could have cut the tension in our home with a knife. It was brutal.

At 10:30 p.m., Randy joined me in his room, tossing items of clothing on the bed. He wasn't interested in the least, getting distracted by letters from old girlfriends that he felt the need to read. For some reason, this annoyed me even more. Why didn't he just pack? It was late, and I was bone tired. His attitude was just plain out of line.

We didn't talk while I tried to fold his clothes. I was afraid to speak. I glanced at him, and I started to feel sorry for him. He had spent 106 days in jail; he was home for a week and had to leave again. He commented on how long he hadn't drunk alcohol. He was very convincing that week that he didn't need rehab. He had "quit drinking" on his own.

I put all his bags in the kitchen. By 11:30 p.m., I dropped into bed exhausted, not from physical labor but from mental anguish. He didn't want to go to Keswick. After all that begging in court and hiring the lawyer to have the legal system work in his favor, here we were with him trying to walk away. What was he thinking?

I tossed and turned all night. I was so stressed out about Randy leaving our home and not going to a place that I knew God wanted him to go. What if he left in the night? What would become of him?

At 6:00 a.m., Jeff and I got up. Randy's bedroom door was closed. We walked into the kitchen to get our morning coffee, but all I could think about was whether Randy was in his room or not.

Jeff and I just sat at our usual spots, not talking, and thinking the same thing. Was our child in his room? After fifteen minutes, I couldn't stand the suspense any longer. I went down to his room, knocking on the door. No answer. I waited a minute knocking louder. I heard a groan, a familiar groan, the same groan I always heard when I woke up this child. He hated mornings as much as I did, but he was in his room. He hadn't left our home. He had decided to go to Keswick.

We packed the car, and I tossed a pillow in for him. He always hated long drives. He was not a good passenger. We could only hope that he would fall asleep during the four-hour drive. Early into the trip, we got him some breakfast, thinking if his stomach were full, he would be sleepy and easier to deal with.

We had two online Map Quest directions, and they were both wrong. We were well into New Jersey when we got lost, but we were just a few minutes away from Keswick. The drive was becoming much more pleasant just knowing that.

I called the intake officer, telling her where we were, and she gave us directions to get to Whiting. We pulled into the Keswick resort, which was a Christian retreat located on a beautiful lake in the woods. The buildings were lovely with A-framed windows and looked fairly new. I wondered if this was the Colony of Mercy, but I doubted it.

We stopped the car and asked a man who was walking along the path where the Colony was. He directed us on a dirt road through the woods. We passed a small chapel located by the lake, and then we pulled up in front of the Colony of Mercy. We made it; we were here!

There was one large building, an office, and a chapel. As we walked up to the door, two men came out to the car and started to unload Randy's things. No one asked them to help us; they just did.

The intake officer was waiting for us, and the three of us sat down. Randy was intimidated by the whole scene and asked her if we all needed to be in the room. Simultaneously, Jeff and I rose to leave. We were glad to walk away. We were tense.

We were directed into a small room with a huge stone fireplace. One of the men that had unloaded our car told us that they were searching our Randy's bags, and he sat down to talk to us. He had been addicted to cocaine and Xanax. He spoke of his depression of how his life had spun out of control. I looked at his face; he was smiling. He was content. He had gotten the help he needed in this warm place. This must be heaven!

He soon left us to ourselves as we waited while Randy had the intake interview. I was so worried that Randy would tell her he didn't want to be there and that we would have to turn around to take him home. Who could blame her for that? He was acting like a punk, whatever that was.

Soon another man came in giving us a tour. He was the nicest man that I ever met. I felt the warmth of the love of God just pouring off of him. He was full of smiles and good news. He was a changed man. He seemed so happy.

After the short interview, Randy came to join us. It was time for our good-byes. Jeff gave Randy a handshake and a brief hug. I could tell that Randy was uncomfortable. I looked awkwardly at him into his beautiful brown eyes. I walked up to him to hug him whispering to him, "I love you." But I couldn't say another word. I turned to leave with tears in my eyes, but they were not unnoticed. The first young man we met touched my arm, saying to me, "He will be safe here," as he smiled at me with complete reassurance in his eyes.

Quietly, Jeff and I went to the empty car and headed home. For two weeks, we would not be able to talk to Randy as he would have no privileges. The two weeks were a trial time, a test of sorts. Would he pass the test? Would he stay in Keswick? Would he seek God's help there? Was he going to see the light?

That night, I was exhausted, but I went downstairs to put the Christmas boxes away since Randy had left them in a pile. I wandered into the room where I kept the Christmas stuff. I had arranged the room in a neat fashion two weeks ago as I had to make sure there was no alcohol hidden anywhere, no left over bottles.

I aimlessly walked to the back, looking at the shelf behind the boxes where Randy had often hidden his alcohol. The shelf that was empty last week contained the remains of two six packs of beer and an empty bottle of hard liquor. He had been home less than a week, and he had given in. He had been drinking. That's why he was distancing himself away from us. He was watching his movies and drinking just like he had before. He was not safe in our home.

I carried the bottle upstairs for Jeff to see. Out of nowhere, we had the worst argument that we have had in our marriage. We screamed at one another, saying ridiculous stuff that made no sense to either of us. I was close to a mental collapse, and we were both hurting. As always, we didn't know how to comfort one another, so we blamed each other for Randy's choices.

I was trembling inside and fighting for my own sanity and self-control. So this is the way it was to be. Our son was safe from the grasp of Satan, but we weren't. Satan was after us, and he was in his glory. Was I going to let him destroy what was left of my marriage? What were we doing to each other?

I took a shower, and then I walked into Randy's empty room. I got on my knees beside his bed, asking God to watch over him and soften his heart. I pleaded with God to help him and us. I felt such sweet relief on my knees in the dark with only the soft glow of the nightlight. I got up and walked into the living room; Jeff was standing in the middle of the room. We looked at each other and collapsed in one another's arms.

We cried!

There would be two long weeks with no phone calls, no communicating, and no letters. Every time the phone rang, I jumped. I ran to the phone to check the caller ID, dreading that Keswick would call for us to pick up Randy. Time moved so slowly, even the silence was stressful. There was a dread of not knowing and a dread of fearing the worst—that he might just call a friend and leave. I couldn't relax. I certainly didn't have any faith in God. If I did, I would have trusted God to watch over Randy. After all, I had given my child back to God. I had failed as a mother. Maybe God would fix everything in time. Maybe he would fix my broken child for me, before it was too late.

As the days crept by, a ray of sunshine broke through the clouds. We received a letter from him. I recognized his handwriting immediately. I was shaking as I ripped open the envelope. I was still full of anxiety wondering what he had written. What if he hated it there? What if he asks us to come get him?

Mom and Dad,

So I just received the package that you guys just sent me. I am still on the orientation stage here where I can't do certain things like talk on the phone; go to the gym/

pool and everything else. Everything is very good here, but I really don't want to get into the whole sending and receiving mail thing, because it'll make me think of everything outside right now and that's the last thing I want.

Everything here is nothing short of amazing. It truly feels like a Christian school. There are five million things I want to tell you about this place, but I'll tell you after I'm 100% adjusted (after the two-week orientation phase). I just wanted to shoot you guys a letter and let you know that things are well here.

At this delicate stage I really do not want to focus on things that are going on back home whatsoever. I think even calling anyone who may possibly upset me is a terrible idea. It may just be you guys, Uncle Tom, and my good friend, Rebecca. Yes, you heard right, Rebecca.

Even the thought of what exactly I'm going to do when I'm finished is scary. But my progress as a Christian is nothing short of truly amazing, and it's only day eight. But the thought of coming back home to the same stuff, i.e. (no job, no car, no church functions all week) really is the only thing that scares me. And I can't think about that right now. I will make plans with God's guidance when the time comes. I'm not sure when that time is, but I know that it isn't right now.

I am trusting God very deeply with everything in my life as its gets better each day. But like I said, everything is VERY well here and I don't feel like I'm "away" at all. It's just that when this is over, I'm very anxious to start getting on with my life productively in every single aspect.

So I guess, send up the phone card. I'll be able to talk on the telephone in less than a week. I'll give you guys a buzz then and explain everything as best as possible.

I've only spent $2.50 of the $50 and I'm honing my ping-pong skills. I do miss Mr. Chico Man though, I will say that. I need a girlfriend, also.

Okay, I'm out of here for now. I guess tell anyone who asks that I'm doing well.

Love, Randy

Here it was an unbelievable letter. He was making the best of things. It was an answer to prayer, so why didn't I feel like celebrating? I was still on edge, full of doubt. How long would this last? Would he be satisfied to stay? Was this the place for him to meet God?

When Randy was finally allowed to call us, I immediately noticed how unhappy he sounded. Each phone call had a new complaint, either a snoring roommate, annoying people, his shoulder hurt, and lastly, he had been sick for days with a fever. It was all a bad sign. My anxiety level was unbelievable. How hard was it to just trust God?

On the date marking one month at Keswick, I got the phone call from Randy that I had feared was coming. He wanted to leave!

I knew as soon as I saw the pay phone number that it was him. I could tell by his voice that something was up. It was going to be a bad conversation.

"Mom, you might as well come get me. I am going to be kicked out anyway. And I only agreed to come here for a month," he spoke in a monotone. He sounded so sad, yet I had no pity for him.

"We will come get you in May, when you graduate and not before then. You are in a one hundred and twenty day program. You have to stay," I replied with no compassion in my voice, but my heart was ripping apart.

"Don't bother with me, a friend will come pick me up," he said with certainty.

"Really, son, a four-hour drive one way? And what good friend would do that?" I asked.

"Mom, you don't understand. I am going to be told to leave," he persisted, and I was becoming annoyed with the whole conversation.

"That's a stinking shame. What have you done to be asked to leave?" I demanded to know.

He gave me several reasons, like skateboarding once and saying a curse word. Then he said, "Somebody ratted on me. I have lost my gym privileges, which was the highlight of my day."

I was getting agitated with him.

"You know the rules. There are rules for a reason, Randy. Why can't you just do what is expected of you?" I asked.

I could tell that our conversation was going nowhere, but I refused to give in, wishing him good luck in finding a ride.

But he was not so easily put off, presenting another angle.

"So you want me to pack a bag and leave alone to die by the river? Is that what you want, Mom?" he knew he could hit a nerve. What mother would not shudder at the very thought of losing her child? I had to focus on one thing; we were losing him in our home. He was not safe here either. What if he ventured out alone and did die by the river? How could I live with that guilt?

"No, son that is not what I want for you. But death is surely going to knock on your door if you continue this pace for your life. I am already losing you, a little at a time. If you decide to have someone to pick you up, you cannot come back home to live. If you stay there until your graduation in May, you can come home then and not before," I responded, trying frantically not to lose control of myself.

The phone went dead. The conversation was over. He was angry. I was depressed. All I could think about for the next week was that he had packed a bag and was walking along the river where he would freeze to death.

Several days slipped by. I couldn't stand the agony of not knowing if he left the rehab any longer. I called the intake officer at Keswick. It was a great gamble for me to call, thinking they might tell me they were getting ready to call me to come get him. What were we going to do with him?

My excuse for calling was genuine, not altogether true, but he had been sick. I pretended to want to know if he was feeling better. The lady that answered told me exactly what I wanted to know.

"I just saw him, and he looked fine. Is there a message for him?" she kindly asked.

"No message. I'm sure that he will call us soon. Thank you so much and have a great day," I sounded chipper, but I was far from satisfied.

He had stayed after all. He hadn't been asked to leave. It was going to be a day-to-day with this Keswick program. If he got kicked out, it would just be another bad choice on his part. When was he going to make good choices for himself? Would I live to see that day?

As the weeks passed with Randy adjusting to his situation, the tone of his voice seemed different when he called. He sounded like a different man on the phone. He didn't complain and had made a few friends there, but I still couldn't relax trusting God for a miracle. Every day, I knelt beside his bed praying for a miracle, but I didn't trust God enough to believe that I would see one.

Tom preached a sermon once about the importance of intimacy with God, challenging us to pray at least fifteen minutes a day. How hard could that be? I tried at bedtime while I was alone in the dark and after a few minutes the words were aimless, begging phrases. Sometimes I fell asleep before I finished the prayer.

I knew that prayer was my only hope. I got a book with a zillion prayers for various concerns that any parent could have. I went into his room with my cell phone beside the book, knelt down, and checked the time. I would read prayer after prayer, and it would seem like thirty minutes had passed, but when I paused to check the time, it had only been ten minutes. Why was it so hard to pray? Why couldn't I stay focused?

I had been praying the same prayer for Randy for so long. I was starting to believe that God just didn't understand. If he did, then why didn't he answer me? I was tired. It wasn't as if I was asking for the impossible. I just wanted Randy's life to be changed before I lost him.

I heard an incredible amount about miracles in testimonies from people whose lives were changed forever. They always gave God the glory. Without God, life, with its many twists and turns, is near impossible to face as you struggle to keep your head above water.

I was growing tired of praying the same prayers and waiting for the answers. For twelve years now, I had fretted, cried and practically driven myself to a complete breakdown. I had to hide those terrifying feelings I had in the still of the night. My thoughts of despair scared me.

One day, Randy called me in the early afternoon to tell me about a meeting with Chaplain Jay, who was assigned to our son. The chaplain met with him once a week, and apparently this man was right out of heaven.

Randy told me that he talked with Chaplain Jay about his anger with God over the loss of his pitching arm. They talked about the constant pain he had in that shoulder. Chaplain Jay asked our son to pray, but Randy was reluctant because he knew that praying over those things that tormented him would reduce him to tears. He would have to let go!

Chaplain Jay told him it was time to stop blaming God for the shoulder injury that he had to move on with his life. They got on their knees while they poured out in tears to our loving God. Randy told me that he finally let it "all out" after talking to God for a long time. The healing was beginning. This was the first step of many to come where he would learn to talk to God, trusting him for everything.

Don't we all struggle with that at times? Is God really there? Why does he allow such pain?

Randy had a great respect for Chaplain Jay. He mentioned him almost every time we talked. On one conversation, he told me "When I graduate from here, it will be all because of Chaplain Jay. He knows my heart, and I am going to thank him at graduation."

I thought about those words "when I graduate" for weeks to come. So, he had made up his mind to make the right choice. He was making plans in the right direction.

A week before Easter, Randy called. He wanted to see his Uncle Tom and Drew, the pastor of recovery in our church. As part of the continued healing process, Keswick believed in a follow-up plan by requesting a covenant to be written before graduation. Randy would have to sit down and present his covenant to Tom and Drew. Together they would go over the goals, coming to a mutual agreement with reachable goals and outcomes. The covenant was to be followed for a year. Randy would be accountable to Drew. It was going to be tough for Randy since he didn't seem to bond with Drew. Drew knew the drill of substance abuse. There would be no easy road to take as far as Drew was concerned, just one road and only one.

Drew could not be snowed. He knew all the lies and all the tricks. Drew had a testimony about his life before he let God take control. He had DUI's and had been in jail. Besides Tom, Drew was the most humble man I knew. Sometimes in church when he spoke, I was reminded of a God of miracles. Drew and his wife were miracles of changed lives with a powerful testimony.

Tom never knew that way of life. He didn't know about the power of addiction, but he was always ready to help Randy anytime I needed him. The problem was the long trip, two men with heavy schedules, and I didn't want my brother to have to take a whole day, but I knew I had to ask him.

I should have known my own dear brother much better than I did. I was asking the same man who left his family on Christmas morning to visit Randy in jail just a few months ago. I had not asked my brother to go see him; after all, what selfish sister would ask such a thing of someone on Christmas Day? I have never quite gotten over his act of love.

He didn't even hesitate to say yes when I called him. He didn't give me any excuses about being too busy, which I knew would have been the truth. He picked a day that he and Drew could go. I wrote to Randy with the date. Chaplain Jay had to be there as well. It was a serious meeting and a requirement to graduate.

Tom and Drew left early on a Wednesday for their 11:00 a.m. appointment. It was a rainy day, and the commute traffic was slow. The four-hour drive took about five plus hours. They were late for the meeting, so late that Chaplain Jay could only see them for five minutes.

I found out all this from my brother that night, when I called to see if he got home all right. He didn't complain about horrible traffic, about Chaplain Jay having to leave, or the long day. He was excited about their meeting with Randy, telling me that they spent two hours with him.

As far as my brother was concerned, it had been a good day. Most people could not begin to understand Tom. He gave, never expecting anything in return. He took the long trip because Randy needed him; no questions asked, no excuses, he just picked a day and went. What did I ever do to deserve to be blessed with such a little brother who loved me and my child unconditionally?

Tom told me that the meeting went well and that Randy looked good. I never knew what was in the covenant. I never would know. My brother would never disclose the privacy of the meeting, even to me. He was like that, a man you could trust and a man you could depend on. I wondered if his congregation knew what he was all about or knew how they were blessed with such a pastor. His life was a testimony of God's mercy and love. His love had no limits.

When Randy called us a few days later, he was excited about the meeting. He was so happy to see his uncle and Drew. He spoke briefly about their meeting, and I assured him that I knew nothing of the covenant, that his uncle did not discuss it with me. Then I got a huge surprise.

We had not visited Randy since we left him at Keswick in January. We were afraid that he would beg to leave since often his letters asked us not to come for that very reason. It was a few days before Easter when he called me with the unusual request.

"Mom, can you and Dad come up and visit me Easter Sunday? There is going to be a huge dinner that the staff will serve to us. I think it will be a nice dinner," he said as he went silent waiting for my response.

Originally, I had been scheduled to work on Easter Sunday. Holidays are just another day in a hospital. Two days prior to his call, I was told by my manager that she had taken me off the schedule on Easter since there was enough staff that day. Rarely does this sort of thing ever happen. I had worked Christmas, and it was crazy busy all day. I was free to visit!

"Sure, we would love to come. You aren't going to be all packed to leave, are you?" I asked him as I chuckled.

"No, Mom," was his short reply.

Randy was slowly changing. I felt it.

Early Easter Sunday, we got up and left for Keswick.

THE RAINBOW

At 6:00 a.m. on Easter Sunday, the loud music from the alarm caused me to sit upright in bed with sleepy confusion. I never got out of bed early. For a few seconds, I wasn't sure why I had set the alarm in the first place. As I turned off the music, I was fully aware of what this day was all about. I was going to see Randy. It had been three long months. I wanted to hold him.

If I could take all his hurts away, I would. I wasn't even sure what the hurts were, but I knew that I had caused some of them with my angry words to him. I was beating myself up over those hasty words, the same old words that swirled in the air, never really leaving my mind; words that were used by the evil one as they came in and out of my thoughts at free will, words that would torment me as a mother. I had failed this child, and the guilt I was carrying was powerful enough to shut me down. I felt a weight on my shoulders; it was always there.

I had done some nutty stuff in the name of saving my child. I was a mother bear who felt threatened and had to protect her young, even from himself.

Would I ever forgive myself for having boatloads of anger that served no purpose? Would he forgive me? I was a cookie about to crumble. I couldn't shake the depression that threatened every day to lower me to doom. I was in a private war in my own head, and I was losing.

The ride to Keswick could not have been nicer. The sun was shining. The air was warm. It was a day that was meant to be. We took my car, which meant that I drove. I had to constantly check the speedometer because I was in a hurry to see Randy. My foot was heavy on the gas pedal.

Two hours into the drive, I was annoyed at red lights and tollbooths. These were just obstacles in my way. I was trying to smother my agitation at drivers who didn't care if they arrived anywhere alive. I was pretty sure that they didn't care about my life either. I was tense.

My mind drifted at the wheel as I became tormented with thoughts that Randy may be all packed, sitting at the exit door with a sad speech asking us to take him home. How tough would that be? He had one month left at Keswick. As far as I was concerned, the time was flying.

I had housecleaned his room again, changing the comforter to "man" colors. I had a load full of nervous energy that I needed to let out somehow, so I was a clean-a-maniac. I inspected my hours of labor a million times, putting air fresheners in the room. The spices lingered in the air. His room was waiting for him after my insane cleaning once again. I didn't want to count how many times I had done this one thing.

I had the Christian station playing on his radio most of the time, again. Sometimes when I ventured into his room to pray, the station had disappeared. I couldn't help but wonder why it was so difficult to keep the station playing? It was as if some interference kept moving the dial of the clock radio, just a fraction of an inch causing the signal to be interrupted.

I often just stood in his room before I went to bed. I wondered how he was doing, if he was sleeping and eating. I was full of worry. I hadn't really turned him over to God. I thought that I had, yet I was always trying to give God a hand. He wasn't working fast enough for me. He needed some help. I was forever ready to take over the task since God just wasn't stepping in to help me.

I couldn't even relax knowing that Randy was safe, surrounded by Christian men, who were in the same situation. They had something in common. They had all been through hell and so had the families. There was pain left behind in all of their homes. They had not suffered alone.

We were going to meet many of these men today. Randy made a few friends with a group of men who wanted help; men that were at the end of their rope, beaten with no place to live.

The long ride continued as I glanced over at Jeff. He was quiet, and I wondered if he worried about Randy like I did, but I think that I worried enough for both of us. Worrying was insane. How could I convince anyone to trust God if I was always upset about my child? Didn't I have any faith?

Randy could make decisions for himself. God gave all of us a free will, to choose right from wrong, to walk with God or without him. There were no gray areas when it came to God; a person was either with him or against him.

My mind went back to the traffic, and I was beginning to wonder if we would ever get there. Then I saw the sign "Welcome to New Jersey." We were close to our destination.

We arrived at Keswick forty minutes early. We pulled into the parking lot beside the auditorium and decided to wait in the car for Randy, so we could walk in the chapel together. As I sat there, my eyes wandered all over the resort. The scene was calming to my soul.

There was a dirt road that led to the Colony where the men lived. The resort was in the front of the property that overlooked the peaceful lake. There were ducks and geese swimming around. The sun was putting a mirrored glow on the quiet waters. This was such a peaceful place. Was heaven like this?

As we waited, I watched as several groups of young men were walking on the dirt road, headed to the chapel. Each man was dressed in a suit with a tie. Some were young and some were older, but they were all cleaned-up, shaven, and ready to go to church.

I kept straining my eyes to see if Randy was in one of the groups. We weren't sure where we were supposed to meet him, but as time passed with it getting closer to worship time, we decided to walk to the chapel to wait there for him.

The parking lot was blocking the view of the chapel entrance. We walked around the side of the auditorium, and as we turned to step on the white sidewalk, we saw the entrance of the chapel. It was then that I saw him.

There was a handsome, young man in a black suit standing in front of the chapel. He was obviously waiting for someone. He was carrying a small Bible. He looked anxious as he was pacing while he looked around in his anticipation for the arrival of someone.

What a sight to see! As I got closer, I knew that this young man was Randy. He was as beautiful as a rainbow in the sky after a drenching rain. His dark eyes were crystal clear and shining. He was incredibly handsome, or was I just biased because he was my child? No, he was just plain pretty.

Someone had shaved his beautiful dark hair and even though I hated the short hair, it reminded me of his senior pictures, a time in his life that I would never forget. He was happy then.

Our eyes met as he started to walk toward us. I had to restrain myself from running to him. I knew he didn't like "mommy attention" in public, but I had missed him.

He walked faster, coming up to me first. He bent down to hug me. I didn't want to let him go. I wanted to hold him, protecting him from any evil that lurked around. Why couldn't I help my own child?

The hug was brief. Then he looked at his dad, embracing, but only a short time. He was glad to see us. We were elated at how good he looked. In three short months, he had transformed into the same young man that we used to know, the one who cared about his own life, the one who had goals and knew what it took to get where he needed to go. I could tell by a single glance into his brown eyes that he was changing.

We walked together into the chapel to sit down. I was surprised that the pews were only half-filled, but learned that many of the staff had gone to their home churches for Easter Sunday to be with their families.

We sat toward the back where I could see the front audience that consisted of about forty men from all walks of life. In church, they all looked the same, just young men in suits carrying a Bible. They looked refreshed and humble. They were beautiful!

The service was not long. Afterwards, we gathered in the lobby to wait for the dinner to be served. It was then that we got to meet some of his friends. They were smiling and warm to us. They had a special relationship with Randy. There were little jokes, introductions, and wisecracks that were inside jokes of some kind.

Some of the men were alone. I never knew if they had any family left or not. Several of the men had been pastors of churches, one was a nurse, one was a state trooper, some were rich and some were poor. The men were someone's brother, someone's father, someone's husband, someone's son, and they had suffered losses that no one knew. Some of the men were homeless, and most of them had lost many things they once held dear to their hearts. But they had chosen.

I thought this way for a very long time. For sure, they said "yes" to the first drink or the first drug. Then a powerful ugly addiction overcame them, and their lives spun out of control.

They had spent valuable time blaming others for their own misery, the demon that drove them to drink and drug. That demon was powerful enough to tear down a whole house, leaving it in ruins. That same demon was waiting for them to leave this place of safety, so he could attack them again. He was just lurking in the shadows.

We sat in a cozy room with a fireplace as we waited for dinner to be served. We talked to Randy, laughing with him. He seemed relaxed. It was so great to know that he was doing so well. He bore no resemblance to the hollow-eyed young man we had left there a few months ago.

He mentioned graduation being just a month away. I was so proud of him. He was going to finish this program after all. He hadn't packed or begged us to take him home. He was staying. He was making a good choice. He knew that he needed to stay there.

Several times our conversations were interrupted as a different friend would wander over to say "hi." After the friend would walk away, Randy would tell us their story, but even though they all had a different story, the end had been the same. They had suffered, and they had lost. You could see the pain in their eyes.

Finally, the dinner was served, and we had an assigned table. I was amazed at the beautiful dining room. There were small round tables with linen tablecloths, linen napkins, and a small salad with bread at each setting. There was a soft glow from candles and from the long tables that had small flames burning to keep the food warm in silver dishes. There was tons of food.

We sat with four other people. Two of them were on the staff at Keswick who had been doing the same type of ministry for twenty-five years. They were getting old, but they were not even thinking of retiring. I listened as they talked about their experiences and the men they had helped. We learned that 18,000 men had completed the program there. I was amazed at their commitment. What a beautiful ministry they had!

They talked about Keswick and how it was maintained by gifts alone. I wondered if they even got a salary or if they cared about money at all. They were in this mission for a selfless reason. It was not about money. Material things come and go. They were much deeper than that. When they died, they left their earthly possessions behind; money wasn't going with them, not where they were going.

The elderly couple must have been angels! Angels don't care about material things. They are on a mission to please their heavenly Father and him alone.

I glanced around the crowded dining room. I could not possibly tell which men in that room were clients of Keswick. Everyone looked the same. The only thing we did know was that the people waiting on the tables and cooking the food were staff members. It was such a humble act on their part to show such sacrifice on Easter Sunday. They had given that day to their clients, leaving their own families behind. But that was what the whole place was about, sacrifice and showing the love of God. That love was bouncing all over that dining room. I will never forget the feeling I had as I sat there with Randy. I didn't want the day to end.

After dessert, we went back to the large room to sit and say our good-byes. I could tell that Randy was fully aware that we had to leave soon, but I hated to walk away from him.

He walked with us to the area where the dorm rooms were. He gave us a hasty hug then turned abruptly to go inside to the haven of rest for a troubled soul.

Just like that our day with our son had ended, but it would be a day I would never forget.

I had a warm feeling in my soul as we drove away that day. Soon he would be home.

Just when I was about to take a breath of air to relieve my own anxiety, I had to abruptly turn all my attention on Brad. He came home from college for a short visit. There was something about him that

I couldn't put my finger on. When I asked him if everything was all right, he denied any problems, but there was something that he was keeping from me. Mothers just have a way of knowing.

It was weeks later before I learned that his girlfriend of three years, Nicole, had broken up with him. I was shocked and deeply saddened. There had been no warning. He knew that I would be hurt, so he had tried to keep the news from me, but mothers know when their children are hurting. They can tell.

I felt as if someone had died, and my heart ached for Brad. If I felt so horrible, I wondered how he must have felt, but he kept his feelings tight inside him. He was trying to move on and get over the loss. I had to do the same, but I was already in a poor state of mental health. This was the icing on the cake.

My anxiety for him increased when he told me he was having problems sleeping and had lost thirteen pounds. I was so busy fretting over him that I hadn't noticed that I wasn't sleeping and my appetite was totally gone. In just a few days, I lost weight that I couldn't afford to lose. My anxiety was so great that I awakened in the mornings with my heart pounding so fast to the extent that I couldn't even drink one cup of coffee with caffeine. My fingers trembled, and my insides were jumping all over the place again!

My life was spinning out of control. I didn't think that I could deal with one more thing, but one more thing came anyway.

That same week, Brad called us telling us that his pitching arm was hurting so badly he couldn't pitch the upcoming weekend. The team was traveling to Albany, New York. He felt a great sense of responsibility to his team and the coach, but he was injured and the trainer thought he had torn his labrum; another blow, another hurt arm. When would all this agony be over? What if Brad didn't cope with the stress, turning to the quick fix like Randy had done for years now? Our little boy, so strong and confident had to deal with the losses in his own way.

I was in too much pain to offer him support, but he had always learned to cope; that's how he got along in the world. He had coping skills that I never had. Deep down inside, I knew that he would move on. At least that is what I thought. I knew that I had to find a way to do the same thing. I had to leave it all at the cross. My burdens were too great to bear. Why couldn't I pray?

I didn't wonder now why some people turn to alcohol or drugs to get relief from their pain inside. At least they got temporary relief!

The day finally arrived. We were going to bring Randy home. He saw the program to its end and was going to graduate. What anxiety he must have been facing; anxiety that no one could relate to, just him and his new friends, friends that would remain behind to graduate. What was he coming home to—too much time on his hands, old friends, and the lure of the old world? He was in for a huge spiritual war. If he fought the war alone, he would lose, but he knew all that.

A few days before the trip to bring him home, he called to give us a huge surprise. He had been selected to be on the cover of the flyer from Keswick, the fundraiser flyer that was sent all over the country. He had written his personal testimony with his picture on the front. He mailed several flyers to us. I was so proud that I framed one of them. The flyer was a treasure, a reminder of things hoped for. He was a different man now who would pick up his life and start over.

He called us several times in those last few days so excited about his graduation. He wanted everyone in the family to come, but only a few could make the trip. Graduation was on Mother's Day at 7:00 p.m. on a Sunday night. This was a long ride for all of us. Two of my brothers, who were pastors, had a long day on Sunday since they got up early, preaching three services. I didn't expect them to go.

But there was one, and I should have known that Tom was going to take the trip even though he had such a long day. He wanted to go. He was different from the rest of us. We were normal people who expected some kind of tangible reward for our little deeds. He was going because he loved Randy and believed in him. He had hope. He had faith. Where was my faith?

My oldest brother, Dan, lived one hour from Keswick. He called to tell me that he would be there for the graduation. My brother, Wayne, did not go.

My brothers were all different men. I knew that if I really needed either one of them for anything that they would come to my rescue, but I never had to ask my brother Tom. He never would say, "Call if you need anything." He would say, "What can I do?" He was my constant one. He never let me down, ever. I would always be indebted to him. He was a cut above the people that live on this earth. God has his hand on him. When you got near my Tom, you could feel God's presence.

I walked into the empty bedroom room one last time. I felt uneasy, anxious, and worried for some strange reason. What if Randy sunk into that dark world that was waiting to entice him? That world that made him forget his troubles? That world that would drop him to nothing? He had been in that world for such a long time, surely he was ready to say good-bye to that life and begin again. His fight with addictions would last a lifetime.

I wanted to protect him, but how? He had to run the race on his own. He had to speed past the old world, not looking back.

Mother's Day was a day I will never forget. I got to spend my day with both sons as we celebrated the graduation. It was a joyous family time, the best time we had in ages. Our family had taken a beating. We were all affected by the choices of just one member. There were hurts that only time would heal.

No one seemed to mind the long ride to New Jersey, our last trip. Brad got to go with us, which was a last minute surprise. No one ever knew that I called the coach of Brad's baseball team, begging him to let Brad join us on this special day. It caused me pain to have to lay out all the family secrets, but I had to. Of course, I started bawling.

The coach responded with this, "Brad needs to be with his family!" He understood. I'm sure Brad had no idea how badly we wanted him to be there. It was all in the timing.

We arrived hours before the graduation, parking by the lake. Keswick was more beautiful, if possible, than it was on Easter Sunday, just a few weeks ago. Spring was in the air. There were a few geese swimming around, leaving little ripples in the water. The sun was reflected on the lake like a mirror. The trees were the greenest I had ever seen. There was calmness in the air. There were a few men walking along the banks; otherwise, the place seemed deserted. Soon the scene before me would be gone to never return except in my dreams. I loved this place. God had blessed the ministry here.

Maybe this was what heaven was like, no worries, no troubles, a place of safety and peace. Part of me was dreading taking Randy out of this safety net, where no evils could get to him. He was safe here.

The three of us got out of the car to stretch as we strained our eyes across the lake to see if we could see Randy walking along the path anywhere. A young man walked past us. We asked him, "Have you seen Randy? Do you know where he is?"

"Randy will be along soon," he assured us.

The young man with soft brown eyes had a peace about him. He smiled again, saying, "So, this is it, Graduation Day!" And so it was. We would take Randy out of this place of hope and take him home into a place of doubt and worry. I was so anxious about the uncertainty of the weeks to come that I couldn't even respond with a comment to the young man.

We sat on a picnic bench beside the lake, watching the ducks, just waiting for Randy. Then we saw him, so handsome, tall and lanky. He had lost twenty pounds and looked so much like he had years ago, refreshed and clean. We took turns giving him a hug. He was surprised to see his brother there. But there was something troubling in his eyes; he was anxious and nervous. I could see it.

A friend of his had driven alone, a girl from church named Rebecca, to think that she would take her whole day just to come for his graduation. I wondered about her, if she cared for our son in a romantic way, but I knew that he thought of her as a friend. I doubted if he would continue their friendship once he got home. She was a good influence, a good girl, and she was beautiful inside. She was a reminder of things that were good and clean. Did he want that world? He looked on the outside. I wondered if he even recognized her inner beauty. She was the light, the good.

Would he leave the old world behind?

He was all packed, and we helped load the car. We went inside to wait for the service to begin as the sun was lowering in the sky.

Randy took his shower and got dressed for the ceremony. Tom, my mother, and Dan came together in one car. It was so great to have them come. This was a special night. They will never know how much it meant to me to have their support. They had given their time, and their very presence meant unconditional love to a troubled soul.

We huddled outside of the chapel, taking pictures. Everyone was dressed in their Sunday finest: shirts, ties, sport coats, and dresses. We were a handsome bunch. We took pictures of Randy with some of the men that he especially liked. These pictures would be memories that would last a lifetime, memories of a time when our son was out of danger, far away from Satan. Satan had no power here, unable to penetrate this haven.

The service was long and not at all what I had expected. Instead of a graduation speech, we listened to a sermon from one of the chaplains there. This man had been in jail for a very long time, and he had plenty to say. His message was on sex and even though what he said was biblically true, it just seemed out of place for a graduation. We were all tired and restless in our seats. My mind kept drifting during the fifty-minute message as I was starting to wonder if he would speak all night.

Finally, he had the two graduates come up front, one was Randy. The first graduate appeared to be in his thirties. He tried to speak and recite a verse, but he was overcome with emotion. This man had endured some painful times. I didn't doubt for a minute that he was a changed man. He was sincere. He was going to make it.

When Randy got up to speak, I guess he forgot his verse to recite. Instead he appeared to be saying what he thought we wanted to hear. He told the small congregation that he was going to help his uncle in his church. There was no emotion, no humble spirit like the man before him. It made me uneasy.

Then the two graduates were given a reference Bible as a graduation gift. They were asked to stand beside the altar and the other thirty-eight men walked forward, putting their right hands out, while surrounding the two graduates in the most beautiful huddle I had ever seen. It was touching, and there were tears. The congregation was asked to do the same as we recited Deuteronomy 31:8 (KJV) that was on a plague on the wall facing the congregation: "And the Lord, he is that doth go before thee; he will be with thee, he will not fail thee, neither forsake thee; fear not, neither be dismayed." I had heard this verse before, but did I believe it? Did I believe that Randy would seek the help of the Lord? My thoughts were whirling all over the place, and I had to make myself focus on the scene before me—a church full of people that were acknowledging a mighty God.

It was a moment in history, a once in a lifetime event. Brad, who was standing beside me, turned to look at me as he put his arm around me. He knew the gravity of this moment. It was a great Mother's Day!

We lingered only a short while after the service since it was 9:00 p.m. with a long ride ahead of us. I worried about Tom who had been up since 5:00 a.m., but that was wasted worry. My brother looked as fresh as could be. He was up for this day. He wouldn't have missed it for the world. He will never know how much I loved him that night, not just for coming to the graduation, but for always believing in Randy. He would never give up hope. It was a reminder to me that my faith was weak at best. Didn't I know that God loved my child more than I did?

The day was over.

Randy decided to keep Rebecca company on the long ride home. I was glad that he was riding with her since the trip was at night. She would have been alone.

Randy stood by her car, glancing around as if to soak up the serenity of this haven of rest. He knew that he was going into a personal war. He had been in that war for a long time. He knew what he needed to do to fight off the poisonous arrows of Satan.

We were all just lingering outside the chapel, as we, too, looked around one last time. I can't ever remember seeing such a clear night. The stars were shimmering like diamonds and the air was cool. Maybe it was my imagination, but there seemed to be a reluctance to leave. Keswick represented security for Randy. I didn't have to worry about him here, but it was time to leave.

We left Keswick by 9:15 p.m. We trailed one another out of New Jersey, talking on our cell phones, so we didn't get lost.

Keswick was over, 120 days of rehab. Where did the time go? I hadn't wanted it to end. Many of the men in the program stayed for a year, but Randy wanted no part of that. He wanted out. It was painfully obvious. I saw it in his face.

We arrived home a few minutes before Randy and Rebecca arrived. Rebecca drove the few miles to her parent's house for the night. He stood in the kitchen briefly, seeming to be uncomfortable with the whole scene of coming home.

Then he bolted for the downstairs to his computer. I later learned that he was letting all his friends know that he was home, the bad and the ugly, but not the good. Where was the good? He stayed at the computer for some time as if he didn't want to be with the rest of his family. He wanted to be left alone. I had a sickening feeling in the pit of my stomach that this was all a bad sign. We were his support now; why was he pulling away?

The next day he was picked up by his friend who was not his girlfriend, just someone who liked to party. I was agitated as soon as I saw her name on the call ID. It was the same scenario as the time he left jail. It was as if Satan was dialing directly from hell. I was shocked that Randy would even consider spending time with her. Wasn't that like putting a temptation to the worst test ever? It was another bad sign.

The next few days went by slowly, as he tried to get a job. The rejections were starting to mount. I could tell that he was stressing. All the bad feelings that he had tucked away were re-surfacing to torment him; no job, no money, no license, and no car. He was going down. I knew it as I sat by powerless to prevent the fall, again.

On Sunday morning, one week later, I woke him up for church. It was then that I saw the very thing I had been dreading, my worst fear—he was under the influence. His eyes were drooping, and his speech was dull. I didn't smell alcohol, so I had to assume that he was taking pain pills again. The pills made him feel good inside; they pushed out all the bad feelings, making him forget his troubles. I watched him out of the corner of my eye while I drove us to church. I felt sick inside. The hell was back!

He slept through the entire message. This wasn't his first time to sleep in church. Why did I get so worked up about it? He hadn't heard a word the pastor said. I had to admit that I hadn't heard much of the message either. I was consumed by how Randy looked, fearing that others in the congregation may have noticed.

Jeff didn't seem to think that Randy was "too impaired," whatever that means, but he was. I didn't need anyone else to agree with me. I could see!

The covenant Randy made with Tom and Drew were just words on a paper. He was not living up to his part of the bargain. He was pulling away from the good and everything that represented the good.

In the next few weeks, he went to Celebrate Recovery twice with some old friends, who looked like they needed to detox. Why was he even bothering to go in the first place? It was just a show, a half-hearted effort. It was bad enough to let us down, but how could he let Tom down, my dear brother who would do anything for Randy? What in the name of heaven was he thinking? Why was he running away from the people who could help him? It was as if he wanted to self-destruct.

We were back to square one after 106 days in jail and 120 days in Keswick. He had already spent Thanksgiving, Christmas, and New Year's, all alone. Now it was Easter and his birthday, more celebrations when he was locked away somewhere. Wasn't that enough of a consequence to wake him up?

We were allowing Randy to stay in our home no matter what he did or didn't do. Nothing had changed in our home either. I was overcome with pain.

When would this nightmare be over?

THE SUBSTITUTE

Hell had come back, or maybe hell never went away. Hell was always there, waiting to consume our family, ready to retrieve our very souls. Was death going to be our only relief? Would darkness have to come before there could be light?

I had to hang the burden at the cross before the darkness took over my weak soul. I seemed to lack the power I needed to allow the entrance of the light.

I couldn't shake the fear that I was going to lose my child. What was I saying? I had already lost him.

The dread was a sign to me that I had never left Randy at the cross. I meant to, but I hadn't. I had carried him with all his weight while my knees were buckling, yet I was refusing to put him down. I started to doubt that God knew about the hell in our home. What home? There was little left of our home. It was being chiseled away piece by piece. Soon there would be nothing!

We had a vacation planned for that summer of 2007. We hadn't had a vacation together in ten years. Randy blamed the lack of vacations on Brad's summer baseball schedule that ran right into August each year. I could sense his resentment. It seemed that every August, Jeff and Brad got to travel to some state to play in a tournament. It was the same as a vacation: hotels, swimming pools, golf, eating out, and of course tons of baseball. I got to stay home to keep a watchful eye on Randy, the one we dared not leave home alone.

Jeff and I already blamed the lack of vacationing on Randy who wanted to take the same old friends who were over twenty-one years old now. What kind of mischief would they get into? They would have been a major pain in the butt, but no matter who or what we all wanted to blame it on, the truth was, a vacation just hadn't happened.

How strange that a time when we were pulling away from one another emotionally, we would be thrown together in close proximity for four whole days.

Jeff had to pay a year in advance for all four of us to go to visit Cooperstown, New York. The event that year was the Hall of Fame ceremonies and our iron man, Cal Ripken, was being inducted along with Tony Gwynn. My sons were huge Ripken fans. None of us had seen the Hall of Fame.

Jeff and I had numerous discussions about our mutual concern that Randy might become impaired on the trip and what would we do? Could he even have a good time without his self-medicating? We doubted it, but the money had been paid. He was going with us. It was a done deal. We could only hope for the best.

Two weeks before the planned trip, I saw a drastic change in Randy's behavior. The first surprise was his new job. He had actually been hired without a background check. He was so excited! I tried not to think too far down the road with my usual worries about how long he would stay employed. The good news was that the job was close to home, and getting him to and from work would be easy.

The next surprise was his announcement of wanting to see a doctor for his "problems," which was a little word for so many issues. I tried to find out more about the doctor, such as what kind of doctor he was, but as usual Randy shut me out. It was none of "my business." How I wish that was true. I wish I could mind my own business, but since he had no health insurance, I feared that the doctor would surely become my business at some time.

It wasn't until I saw the receipt from the doctor's office that I had my questions answered. The doctor was an expensive addiction MD. Not only were the visits three hundred dollars a month, but he wrote Randy a prescription that would cost one dollar a milligram. This didn't sound like much at the time, but he would be taking twelve milligrams of this medicine a day, which would be close to four hundred dollars a month.

Randy had discovered this MD on his own, got a ride for the appointment, and charged the medicine at the pharmacy. When he brought the medicine home, I was more than curious.

As soon as I saw "addiction counselor" at the top of his receipt, I was ecstatic. Randy had sought help, admitting that he couldn't deal with his addiction alone. God hadn't been enough for him, not enough for him to resist the temptation of narcotics. He was weak. He knew that!

A brochure for the medicine was lying on the table. I sat down to read it to educate myself on a drug that I had never heard mentioned. The name was Suboxone. I took an immediate dislike to the very sounds of this drug.

It was used for patients with a narcotic addiction; it was a substitute. Was it like Methadone for heroin users? Did it give the narcotic euphoria? If so, it was what I thought; it was a substitute. My negativity for the medication continued for days, almost putting blinders over my eyes, causing me to miss the change in Randy.

After a few days on the medicine, he was slowly becoming a different person. He was calmer, less argumentative and seemed more at peace with his present situation. The health costs were more than he could afford on his low wage job.

I was unsold on this new doctor. It seemed that the prescription could be filled at just one pharmacy in the whole county. There were no discounts. The charges for the medicine and the doctor had to be paid up front. How in the name of heaven did poor people manage without health care?

Jeff and I did not need to debate long on how to help him. We paid for his new medication each month. We liked the person he was becoming; at least his addiction was being monitored.

In two weeks, he was a changed man. He was signed up for a class at the community college, he was dealing with the stress of learning a new job, and he was making phone calls to the MVA about his driving license. The MVA was a secretive place that hid a license as long as they could. They wanted to protect the public from drunk drivers. Surely, though, his punishment would end, and they would give him another chance.

He did not return the phone calls of old friends. Even though he did not go to church, I was still encouraged. Maybe now, he was going to turn his life around.

Our worry over our little vacation had started to fade. We would go as a family. It would be the most fun we had together in a long time.

The bus trip was long, but the whole four-day visit to Cooperstown was an experience we would never forget. We had a picture taken of us outside the Hall of Fame, the one I made into our first Christmas greeting card. Now I was the bragging mother that sent my prizes for all my friends to see, two of the most beautiful men in the world, my boys.

But the trip wasn't totally a perfect world. My sons were thrown together for some serious one-on-one. They sat together on the long bus ride to New York and on the numerous bus trips from the hotel to Cooperstown. I watched them from a few seats back, wondering what they found to talk about, if they left the past issues behind in our crumbling house.

Several times while we were waiting together to eat in one of the restaurants, I heard little comments they made to one another. Brad was used to poking fun at fellow teammates, which seemed to be a college athlete delight, but his one-liners were agitating Randy, who didn't find any humor in the attacks of so-called fun. I guess this was just sibling stuff. Maybe I was reading too much into it all, yet when a family is forced to be together for four whole days, a mother sees things that she hasn't seen for a long time. I should have been happy that they were at least congenial. What was the big deal?

I guess in the back of my mind, I worried that they would grow so far apart that they would never want to be together. Some families do that. How sad!

We survived the trip. Randy continued in his job, never missing a day, and our Brad's girlfriend had re-entered our lives. I never knew why she bailed out of their relationship. I would never know. It only mattered that she was back. Forgiveness was part of life. I had to let it go for Brad's sake and for my own peace.

Our family was on the upper swing, just in time for another blow. Brad needed an operation on his pitching shoulder. We had known he was having pain for some time. Now the worry was here, staring in our faces.

Was it going to be another loss? Jeff had lost his opportunity to play for the minor leagues years ago during his college days due to an injury of his pitching arm, but he had survived to move on. He hadn't let the loss drop him to despair as Randy had done. Life could throw some nasty curves at us. Our responses to them define us eventually.

I found myself fretting over Brad, worrying that he may become empowered by negative thinking or that he would fall prey to substance abuse. After all, it did run in the family. What would I do if I started to lose him, too? It was too sad a thought.

I tried to focus on the person this child was, shaking myself to remember that he always found a way to move on with his life. I was the one who got stuck in the anxiety mode. He would rise to the top. Wouldn't he?

The day of his surgery was a time to remember. I saw Nicole for the first time in six months. She drove him to the surgical center. I knew that she would be there and how awkward it would be for her. As soon as I walked in, I searched the waiting room for her. She stood up, walked toward me, and I wrapped my arms around her. She was back. I didn't know where she had been or what she had done. Nothing mattered except she was back.

We sat down and made idle chitchat, avoiding the topic of what pain had occurred over the past few months. There was no point to that anyway.

The surgery was laparoscopic. Even though the doctor didn't find any tears, the shoulder capsule was loose. The doctor would not comment on Brad's future as a pitcher. He had no "crystal ball." All we had was time and rehab. His future would be whatever it would be. Nothing could be done to change the path. We would have to accept the uncertainties, trusting God for direction. It was out of our hands.

My focus went from one child to the other as mother's do. I knew Brad would be all right in time.

Over the next few months, Randy continued his positive upward climb. He became a trusted employee. His employer referred to him as her "rock." Wow! He learned his new job, faced nutty customers, and learned to deal with co-workers. It was just plain beautiful to see the change.

Old girlfriends were coming out of the woodwork, none that wanted to start a new relationship with him, but still they were hovering around. One in particular was rather a sticky case; the girl that he loved so much in high school started to e-mail him.

Allison was married now, and she and her husband were missionaries in a remote area of Pakistan, but they were having marital problems. She confided in Randy via e-e-mail, but I never knew what was really going on with her. I knew she was carrying a lot of guilt around over her failing marriage. I understood that well. But it takes two for a marriage to fail.

How odd that less than a year before I had told Randy that her marriage wasn't going to work. She was the one who had visited Randy numerous times late at night, just weeks before her marriage. It wasn't a good sign. I envisioned the last scene in the movie *The Graduate*. I could see Randy storming into the chapel to disrupt the wedding just before the kiss of the married couple. I could see her bailing out at the last minute. She was having some serious bridal jitters. This girl still had feelings for Randy. He cared for her. Maybe she thought that getting married and moving so far away would be a miracle cure for her feelings. But it hadn't happened.

Their e-mails got testy, with Randy not knowing how to handle the situation. How difficult to try to understand someone who is living across the world married to another man! She was coming home for a short visit in December to see her parents. I wondered if she would still be in touch by then.

She was the force in his life years ago that helped him stay on the right side of the tracks. The loss of their relationship had also sent him over the tracks. Deep inside me, I dreamed that she would be back some day, that she would be the light for him, a source of strength. She understood him better than anyone. Then I thought of her parents. I knew that they would never want her to leave her marriage or see Randy. I understood that. I thought that they would somehow blame our son, like all the times before when parents of his girlfriends tried to reason with their daughters to move on to something better for them.

His other old girlfriend, beautiful Jessica, was ten hours away in college. She still talked to him on the phone daily. Her poor parents, if they only knew! Didn't parents know that they couldn't change the hearts of their children? Love was too strong a force to control. It just couldn't be done.

Children had to learn their lessons in life, as we parents stand idly by and watch. The urge to hold them up is so real. We knew about those lessons. We had already been there and done that!

Jobs, like relationships, were just plain work. We knew how hard it was to work with the public and bosses. We knew how hard it was not to tell them to stick it somewhere. Oh, the times I have felt like doing and saying some insane things. I found out the hard way to tolerate others that the public could be nasty for no reason, that co workers may not do a thorough job, and that bosses were unreasonably demanding at times. It all went with the territory.

People were people, and it didn't matter if they were church people. They were all human beings, capable of being hard to get along with at the drop of a hat, capable of potential road rage, and capable of making someone else's life miserable. Yet we had to learn to move around them to avoid confrontations that would go nowhere.

This was life in the real world. Randy was learning how to cope with situations that he couldn't do one thing to change. It was hard work, but he was starting to grow up.

Wasn't it time for me to stop worrying about him? Had I left him at the cross? Was he at the foot of Jesus? Was I still going to look over my shoulder to make sure that Jesus saw him there?

After seven months into his new job, we started seeing a negative change in him. He doubted his need for Suboxone, no longer feeling the "effects," and decided to quit taking the medication. Besides, it was "too expensive." He had lots of excuses, but all too soon, he was dismissed from his job.

Jeff was not as concerned as I was since Randy managed to get his AA degree. Jeff always looked at the positives. Why couldn't I? I fretted over the negative entirely too much. What good would come from that kind of thinking?

We signed the title of the truck over to Randy, shifting the responsibility to him. Would this make him more responsible? I leaned over to sign the form. Why did I feel like this was a death sentence? Was I signing his life away? The MVA had made the decision for me. Our son could drive at last.

I realized at that moment that I had not left Randy at the feet of Jesus. I had to help God, move him along just a little. I had no intentions of taking my watchful eye off of my child. I couldn't detach myself. I couldn't even walk away from him for too long. What if I lost him? The fear continued to rob me of joy. It was as if deep down inside me, somewhere far, far down. I knew that the war was not over. I knew that another battle was coming. I hadn't even gotten over the last battle. I never bothered to put on the armor. I was never ready.

"I'd love to stay longer to chat with you, but I have an appointment to get an interlock installed on our truck," I explained to my old friend, Pam.

She looked puzzled and asked, "Interlock? What's an interlock?"

Of course, she didn't know what it was! She didn't know anything about probation officers, community service, or what a cyclone fence was. This was an innocent question from a mom whose kids never did anything wrong. Pam's two girls were the same age of my boys. Her girls had grown into responsible women; they always had a "designated driver." Her girls had careers and worked full-time.

Pam was proud of the accomplishments of her girls with every reason to be. I wished that I could be happy for her, but I wasn't.

She and I hadn't seen each other for twenty years, but we always sent Christmas cards. She sent pictures and a newsy letter each year. They were a busy, happy little family, and I envied them. I sent her one picture of us, the one at the Hall of Fame. I often glanced at the picture. We looked like a normal, smiling family. The picture was a huge cover-up with smiles that were not all real. We had all been hurt. There was pain in our eyes!

We agreed to meet for lunch while we talked for hours. There was so much to catch up on and so much I was trying to hide from her. I couldn't bear to tell her how worried I was about Randy. I was afraid that if I started to tell her about the past eleven years, I would go insane. If I started to cry, I wouldn't be able to stop. I was hanging on a cliff with rocks below. I had to keep it all bottled up inside me. I didn't want her to know.

After all, I was not a good mother. If she knew about the turbulence in my family, then she would know that I did a poor job as a parent. Deep inside me, I blamed either myself or Jeff. I never wanted to put the blame where it really belonged. When would I face the truth and stop punishing myself?

I danced around her questions as if they were bullets, aimed to pin me down. She looked me square in the eyes. I wondered if she saw the pain, or was I doing my usual job of acting? I had learned to be an actress. I could act the part for a while, but only for a short time.

We sat in that little restaurant giggling like schoolgirls. It was so good to laugh again. I couldn't remember when I laughed so hard.

We got the attention of everyone that came in and out for those three hours. I am sure that folks thought we were tipsy, but she had two caffeine cokes and I had water with our lunch. Neither of us needed alcohol to have a good time.

It was toward the end of our time together that she told me about her oldest daughter, Jessie, who had seen our family Christmas picture. Jessie had asked Pam, "Who are these hotties, Mom? Where have you been hiding these two?" She was referring to my two sons. Indeed they were handsome, even to someone other than their mother.

Then the questions started to tumble out; were they available or dating or what? It was more like a what? What should I say? Should I tell her the truth? I decided to be as honest as my pride would allow me to be. They were in fact, available.

It seemed odd to me that they didn't have women all over the place. I was accustomed to Randy not having a steady girlfriend since he was expecting the "perfect" woman. But Brad, that was another story. Nicole had just bounced out of our lives again, a few weeks ago. She had become a yo-yo to me. She came; she went. Brad told me, "Mom, it's over this time. It is good-bye. You need to let her go!" I was going to struggle with that idea. It was a cardinal sin for a mom to love her son's girlfriend. I had to learn that lesson the hard way!

Brad seemed to have gotten used to the breakup much faster this time around. He was angry with her, having been betrayed. There was no forgiveness in him. I knew, though, that he would move on. I knew that I had to do the same. He looked great. He was going to be okay. There would be another woman. If only I could think like that.

I was praying that there were two good girls left in this universe who would fall in love with either of them, giving me grandchildren. Was that too much to ask? Was that a miracle kind of prayer? It was beginning to look like it to me. Where were these women? When would they arrive to help me out, to love my sons and live happily ever after?

Randy got a new job and after seventeen months, the MVA made their decision to allow Randy to drive. Finally, my punishment was over too. I was a MODD, Mother of a Drunk Driver. I had to learn a lesson just like the driver who didn't have the senses to know that he was under the influence and shouldn't be driving.

At first, I was elated, but that soon came to a halt. The condition to his driving would be the interlock for two years. Randy still belonged to the MVA. He didn't know how to drive the stick shift in the old truck that we were going to let him drive.

I had hoped that he would have restrictive driving, like to and from work only, but the decision was out of my hands. The interlock had to be installed on the truck. Everyone that drove the truck had to breathe and hum into it for seven seconds. It was a monitoring device.

Why didn't we look into such a contraption before? I thought of the interlock as some kind of an angel. I didn't even know what it was all about, but I watched the video, listening intently.

I heard about the device from somewhere or from someone. I didn't remember how I knew about an interlock, but I knew. I mistakenly thought that if the driver was drinking alcohol while driving and breathed into the interlock, causing the fail light to come on, that the engine would cut off. Now how naïve was that? A vehicle cutting off in traffic would be dangerous, so how was this thing going to be of value?

The interlock had an annoying buzz that reminded the driver to breathe into the apparatus. Every fifteen to thirty minutes, the test was requested. Every month, the truck had to go back to the installer place where a computerized print was sent to the MVA.

As far as I could tell, a driver could drive a whole month with failed tests before the MVA got the proof. It was just a Band-Aid on a big cut. It was a warning, a reminder to the driver.

What would a passenger think? What if the passenger was a woman? There was no lie to cover-up the interlock. It was what it was! The driver was high risk.

I had often wondered why drunk drivers commit that same sin again. Why do they drive while impaired? Don't they know better?

I now know that the drunk driver is too impaired to know that he is impaired. Who with a clear mind would operate a vehicle, risking his own life, and the lives of others? Who would want the deaths of innocent people on their conscience for eternity? I don't think that the impaired driver sits in the car getting a wave of guilt before turning the ignition. If they did, then they wouldn't drive.

If they worried about being caught, having to go to jail, they might think twice about starting the car. If they thought of losing their license for a few years and how that would destroy their social life, then they would not drive.

What are they thinking? They are impaired and don't think. "The priests and the prophets have erred through strong drink, they are swallowed up of wine, they are out of the way through strong drink; they err in vision, they stumble in judgment," (Isaiah 28:7, KJV). The book called *Under the Influence* was a great help for me in understanding how alcohol is processed in the mind and body.

I have to admit that it does annoy me to know that co-workers and friends my own age will have a few drinks and drive. They would not be able to start their car if they had the interlock, which fails for an alcohol level above 0.02. This level could be reached by drinking two beers or by using a mouthwash rinse that contained alcohol. The interlock was sensitive. It had to be. If they drank the night before and had an interlock, they would fail the test in the morning, not being able to start their car.

What if the device had a panic alarm? If the driver decided to drink after he started the ignition, this loud alarm would ring right into the police barracks. What if the license plate popped on a huge screen and the police came right up on the driver?

What if the interlocks were mandatory on all cars? What if teenagers had to have one on their car at all times?

The good news about the interlock is this: parents can have one installed any time they want to. It does not have to be mandated by the MVA. There is no need to wait until you are convinced that your child is drinking and driving. This is the same quandary as with safe sex. The really cool parents believe in passing out the condoms and birth control pills. The only way to insure safety with sex is no sex. So it is with drinking and driving. The only way to insure safety is no drinking.

If all parents used the interlock, it would be standard procedure. If we all had the same standard, the heat would be off our parenting skills. What parent would mind paying a few dollars a month to insure the safety of a young, stupid driver?

I live with the "what ifs," totally being burdened with the blame and the faultfinding. Drinking alcohol is a choice, while drinking and driving is an unconscious choice of an altered mind.

I knew in my heart that Pam's innocent, responsible Jessie would not mesh with my impulsive, irresponsible Randy. She was looking for a man to take care of her. She wanted a man just like her daddy. But the key has been thrown away for those men. Jessie would wait a long time for that man to come along.

Pam was waiting and watching for a son-in-law just like I was waiting and watching for a daughter-in-law. We wanted our children to be happy ever after. Was that a dream world?

Randy learned to drive the stick shift in the truck without killing any of us as we attempted to show him how it was done. It was like teaching him to drive all over again. A stick shift could be complicated, even for drivers that were used to driving with a stick.

One day, in the pouring down rain, Randy wanted to practice. We jumped into the truck. He put the truck in gear bolting down the driveway, hitting the garbage can and scaring me to death. I was starting to wonder if he would ever learn.

Then I thought to myself that he would destroy the transmission in the truck and that would be God's way of taking the truck away, thus easing my fear and constant worrying.

He did learn to drive the truck, liking the shifting. He got a promotion at his new job that included a pay raise and health insurance.

I got him lined up with a counselor, and he found his own psychiatrist. Ever so slowly, it appeared that his life was turning around. I started to see some light. My hell was going to soon end, but more importantly, Randy's own pain would be over. He was going to get help, but he wasn't going to take Suboxone. It worried me! Would something take its place?

All those times that I had been convinced that God just didn't hear my prayers God was with us all the time. He was there through every trial. He had just been waiting for me to trust him, looking to him for strength.

I was in a smoke screen. I was in the middle of the eye of the storm. The turbulence was far from over. Worry and fear were going to team up to destroy me!

PREPARE FOR BATTLE

No deep breath was coming. No sense of relief. The burden was back. I could see it in Randy's eyes. His beautiful, dark eyes were looking shallow and vague. I had seen that look many times before. But this time, he was having his personal party on the weekend, still managing to work. Unless a mother was actually looking for trouble, she might have missed it. Is that what I was, a mother looking for trouble, or was it just obvious to me? And why did I get so angry with Randy?

My sleeping problems had come back with a vengeance. I was recuperating from major surgery. I was a physical mess along with an emotional and spiritual blackout, whatever that was. I know that during a blackout time, praying is impossible, just when a soul needs it the most, it doesn't happen.

I went to see my nurse practitioner, who I had grown to love over the years. Shirley was a great listener. As soon as she walked into the room, I started to cry.

"I'm going over the edge!" These were the only words that I could say. She looked at me with sympathy and asked me to see a professional. At least she didn't send me to yoga. I think that I was way past that point by then. I even consented to a mild tranquilizer to help me rest at night. Any mind starts to mend with some good sleep. That was probably all I really needed, just sleep.

Something had sent me over the edge. I was about to bolt out of my house again.

For two months, Randy and an old friend from Keswick had planned on going to the annual reunion that was going to take place in May. At first, I was elated that he wanted to go, but when the weekend episodes of impairment happened, I couldn't see the point in him going.

Jeff, who amazed me beyond any point of reasoning, volunteered to drive Randy to New Jersey on a Friday and pick him up on Sunday. This was the same four-hour drive one way. The old friend Randy was going to hang around with for that weekend lived in New Jersey.

I was having issues with my chronic back pain, requiring physical therapy, so I couldn't go along. I did suggest to Jeff that he and I plan to go to Atlantic City that weekend to cut down on the driving. We could drop Randy off at Keswick, and then drive fifteen more minutes to a hotel in Atlantic City. Our marriage was in shambles, but Jeff wasn't interested in such a weekend.

Somehow, the whole trip became more ridiculous. Keswick was a place of victory over addictions. What place did Randy have there since he was far from victory?

Jeff thought that maybe a "miracle would happen there," that maybe Randy would see his need to change. For the first time in twelve years, I became aware that Jeff was as desperate as I was. He wanted relief from the worry of Randy just as badly as I did.

As the date grew closer for the reunion, I noticed that Randy seemed increasingly impaired. I started to unravel inside, feeling the need to get out of the house. I needed to get away from all the pain I saw.

The explosions between Jeff and me started again!

After one of the many explosions erupted over absolutely nothing, I retreated by going to bed that night at 8:30 p.m. I lay flat on my back with the light on for four hours. I stared at the ceiling. I was numb. It was too much for me. I needed to go somewhere before I fell to pieces and no one could put me back together.

The next day, I called Tom. He listened to me as I cried in pain. I could talk and complain, but I couldn't pray. He sensed my panic and as usual, he opened his house to me. I packed a few things, leaving my home for the second time in two years. I was hanging onto my sanity by a raveling thread.

I left a quick, impersonal note:

Hi, I need to pull myself together, need some time away!

Love, Me

I feared that I was having a nervous breakdown. I was sinking fast.

Staying at Tom's house was such a blessing. I must have looked horrible as he knew that I was in fragile condition. He spent hours talking to me and listening to me. He wanted me to see a counselor too. Everyone was getting on my nerves about this counseling stuff.

Even their tiny dog knew that I was hurting. The first evening that I was at Tom's I babysat their dog, Janie. She was sleeping on the floor next to me. I started to sob loudly in my pain, wondering when God was going to help me, realizing that I was so alone.

Next I felt something on my thigh. Janie jumped on my lap. Her huge eyes were looking up at me. I stopped sobbing to pat her head. She never took her eyes off of me. Her eyes looked sad. It was as if God had awakened her from her nap, sending her to me to comfort me, a reminder that God was with me all the time.

I had been there for two days before needing to go home and get some more of my things. I arrived at my house at 10:30 a.m. on the Friday morning of the Keswick weekend. I walked into the house to see Randy sound asleep on the couch. He had not gone to work. He had been drinking.

I phoned Jeff to ask him, "Why isn't Randy working?" Jeff replied, "I found Randy in a deep drunken sleep in the recliner this morning. At first I thought that he was dead, and I panicked!" I knew that panic well, but this was Jeff's first panic attack; I had already had many.

In my hurrying around to get my things, Randy woke up. I couldn't bear to look at his sad countenance. He looked a total mess. I just wanted to get out of the house to get away from the sight before me.

After one day at Tom's house, I knew that I was getting more emotionally ill as time went on. What was happening to my family? Weren't they worse without me? I decided to go back home. Didn't they need me? What was to become of my mental health?

Tom had convinced me that seeing a counselor would help me, my marriage, and my family. All I knew was it couldn't possibly make it worse.

That same afternoon I called Jeff's cell phone to tell him that I was coming home. But before I could relay this to him, he had a story for me. He and Randy were on the way to Keswick for the great reunion.

My immediate response was that taking an impaired person to Keswick, a place of recovery for alcoholics, was the most ridiculous thing I had ever heard. I was about to say all sorts of crazy things when suddenly something I heard in Jeff's voice stopped me.

I heard him say, "Maybe something good will come of this trip. Maybe it will do Randy good, and he will turn his life around!"

Jeff had reached my level of desperation. He had seen our drunken son passed out in a chair. He had faced the fear that Randy might have died in his sleep. He had become terrified. He was a father who wanted to help his son.

I soon got over that nice gesture by telling Jeff that Keswick would just kick him out, but nothing I said was going to change the fact that they were on the way to New Jersey in the rain during rush hour traffic.

I found out later that Randy had tried to start his truck three times that same morning. These were fails that would be sent to the MVA. Was he still in such a fog that he didn't realize that he was impaired and couldn't drive? Thank God for the interlock.

The next day I was on edge, waiting for the phone call from Keswick, the call that we should come get Randy. It was quiet around the house. The stillness was like a huge smoke screen, concealing what was about to happen.

We went to Saturday night church, which we loved, since Sunday became a free day to relax. We were on our way home when Jeff's cell phone rang. Then the poop hit the fan.

Randy was on the phone. They were kicking him out since they found him drinking. They wanted him picked up immediately. I guess they didn't realize that it was 7:30 p.m. and with a four-hour ride, a pick up would not be immediate.

One of the chaplains got on the phone. I had Jeff ask him if he could just keep him overnight. We would come get him first thing in the morning, but he refused. I asked if someone would take him to the nearest bus station and again he refused. They had been violated in the worst kind of way. Randy's drinking was a slap in the face to them and to us as well.

I was not surprised at the call. Randy was impaired when he left home. For some reason though, even I didn't think that he would take alcohol into Keswick. Keswick was like heaven; there was no alcohol in heaven.

Jeff looked so distressed that I couldn't even say, "I told you not to take him." What purpose did being right serve? It was pointless.

At 8:00 p.m., Jeff took off for Keswick. In the meantime, without telling us, one of the chaplains at Keswick took Randy to the bus station. When Jeff arrived at Keswick at 1:00 a.m., he was told that Randy was not there and was given directions to the bus station. I couldn't figure out why they decided to take Randy to a bus station in the middle of nowhere without telling us, but it was a sure sign that they wanted his influence away from the other recovering addicts. Apparently, the friend that Randy had planned the reunion with was kicked out as well, but at least he had a short ride home.

When Jeff finally found the bus station, Randy was not there. He called Randy's cell phone; the voice on the other end had slurred speech. Randy was just not thinking clearly at all. He was in a nearby bar where he decided to wait for his father. He could not give his father the directions to the bar, so a stranger got on the line, directing Jeff on how to get there.

Randy, totally oblivious to the chaos he had just caused, the embarrassment to his father who had to go to Keswick to face the dedicated people who had just kicked Randy out, or the hardship of all that driving on his father traveling to unknown places so far from home, decided not to waste a golden opportunity to get even more impaired. He sat on a bar stool and drank.

Randy slept the whole ride home.

I made an appointment with the counselor that next week. As soon as I met her, I liked her. She gave me a different perspective on how all my tactics had not worked. Yelling, begging, snooping, getting angry, worrying, and fearing were all just not working. Something had to change. I had to do the changing. If I was going to survive the stress and my failing health, things had to change. I had to develop new strategies. She asked me to read two books, *The Gift of the Blessing* by Gary Smalley and Josh Trent, PhD and *Under the Influence* by Dr. Jim Milam and Katherine Ketcham.

I didn't really want to change. It was hard work to change, but I knew that she was right. After seeing her for seven visits, I was starting to see some light. I went to sleep at night with the ocean sounds. I practiced relaxation techniques. I was sleeping better, but I was far from feeling well. It was going to take months. Emotional problems were so much harder to fix. I had not wanted to face the fact that I could no longer keep the family intact. It was too much for anyone to try to do. I had to let it all go. I couldn't fix all the hurts.

I spent long hours reading the books, and I learned so much. I had not given my child the blessing; instead, I cursed him with anger. I had a lot to make up for.

Under the Influence taught me how the mind of an alcoholic gets so confused and why they continue to mess up their lives and the lives of those they love. I learned to shift my anger to alcohol and mind altering drugs.

All these years I had spent so much time trying to fix something that was totally out of my control. I was unable to let go of not being able to fix the hurts in my house. I couldn't even fix myself.

I was carrying my child to the cross when I dropped to my knees. The burden was too much for me to bear alone, but I could see the feet of Jesus. He was waiting for me to leave my burden at the cross. The cross was the only place for me and Randy to go. The cross was the light.

I kissed my child. I could no longer be his protector. I had almost destroyed myself trying. Now I had to walk away, leaving him at the feet of Jesus.

Cindy, a dear friend of mine, allowed me to print the following letter from her to her daughter, Katie, who was serving time in prison. Katie was an only child, but somehow she lost her way. Katie and Cindy's relationship had taken a terrible beating, taking a rough course when Katie was just twelve years old. Katie was asked to leave the house at age eighteen, due to drug abuse. She went to live with her father, where her life continued a downhill course. For the next six years, Cindy and Katie had no communication.

Cindy was screaming inside with pain, worry, and fear, and apparently so was Katie. Cindy prayed to God to take Katie if that's what he needed to do. She was prepared for the loss. This letter has been a blessing to me as you will see two hearts start to mend. This letter contains Cindy's exact words!

November 25, 2007

Dearest Katie,

We just got off the phone. It's Thanksgiving Eve, and I'm free, writing again. I'm making a pitcher of tea and am about to carve the turkey. I wish you were here, sober, drug-free, and no desire to ever use.

I'm so afraid, I wrote it, afraid, scared, that I'm going to mess this up, screw it up, say something that will make you shut down, turn away, run away. This is so brand new, I feel like running, running. (I put your two baby bulbs on the tree today!)

I'm opening myself up to feel again. For so long, I've shut down my heart. No more pain. I want to trust you, believe you when you say something, you will follow through.

I really want to be a part of your life. Please don't change again. I like you. I really like you. I want to know everything about you, trust you, like real friends can trust each other. You help me. I help you. You're giving me so much this holiday. I know where you are. You have food. You're clean. You have a pillow to lay your sweet head on, and I am here for you. You call me. You hear me, and I hear you.

I praise God, and I love him like a husband and my best friend. Wow! He answers my prayers, always answers. So I know he will answer yours. It's a done deal. He will answer your prayers about not wanting to wake up from your sleep, but not until you are an old woman.

Its 6:00 a.m., turkey day! Coffee is brewing. It smells almost done. The smell of it hangs heavy through the house. Why do some things never taste as good as they smell? But that's okay. I have to go for now.

I went back and read—don't change again! Me—please, don't change again. There I go again, yak, yak, harp, harp, ding-dong. It's a mom thing. You see, I'm becoming one again (a physical mom, an emotional mom). A mom is a lion who fights and protects her young. It's instinctive like born in the wild.

Woke this morning, praying for your friend's family and her. I'm hurting for her, hurting, hurting. My God, oh my God. She needs to know that God's angels are all around her. The peace will over saturate the pain, and you are there to pray with her. What a warrior you are! My God, you are something, and you are part of me. Just think about it. You will be a woman for God. This is true. He is what this life is all about. Through our pains and sufferings, there is sweetness. Stronger than any drug high.

God will overcome your pain, my pain, and her pain because he is the reason for our very existence, to draw us to him through our suffering and pain, because God is all there is and that's why we are here—to love. No one suffered like Jesus, and he screamed out to God. Oh God, have you forsaken me? And Mary, the epitome of mothers. She worried about her son (ain't that some something?)

Monday, November 26, 2007

We just finished a wonderful conversation on the phone, remembering about my dad, your Pop-Pop.

My dream:

Travel with me as I tell you about this dream that I will not forget. I stood in front of a huge building like that of the Smithsonian Institute, huge steps, very wide, long steps, but not steep, white steps. I walked these steps up on an incline. As I stood at the top of these steps, there sat a man on my left. It was Nannie's husband, my grandfather, Pop. He spoke, "How are you, darling?"

I was speechless. It was great to see him. I smiled a big grin. My eyes felt bright with amazement. I said nothing. He was such a good Christian man. He loved the Lord.

I looked back in front of me. There I stood in front of these cathedral-like doors, huge, white doors. (Intervention is on now.)

I opened the doors, or they opened for me. They were not heavy. There I felt the presence of something that I can hardly explain. The room was white, glowing, soft, sweet, warm, but not cool, like bath water. There all around me were people throughout my life that I had known only I cannot tell you who they were. They were opaque, floating; I could see right through them. There were so many of them, bodies not like ours, but as if they were wearing gowns with no form.

I only know that I felt love as I had never known it before, warm, sweet love, like the smell of lilacs, and I did not want to leave. I wanted to stay. As I walked through all those people, there before me was a huge window, long, from floor to ceiling. In front of the window was a big, long table. The table was dark wood, but beautiful. I sat alone at the table in front of the window. A few seconds went by and to my right walked my father, both legs, young and handsome like he was when I was a little girl.

I stood up, and we began to dance. He told me several times that everything would be okay. We kept dancing, dancing around the room in a wide circle.

When I woke up, I was on the couch in the house in Hebron. I was sobbing, tears flowed down like my face was being washed. I was crying out loud, crying for a long time. I wanted to stay there. I didn't want to come back.

I am about to close now. I'm including this letter. Please, consider this will be time spent healing yourself inside from all the emotional pain you have felt through the years, and this will help heal your addiction.

I love you so much,
Mom
xoxo

Katie and her mom prayed the same kind of prayer while Katie was in prison. Katie asked God to show her mom how to be her mom again, while her mom prayed for God to change her into the mom she needed to be for Katie to be pleasing to God. Katie is now living back at home with her mom, where they are getting reacquainted. Katie is clean. She is free.

"But now abide faith, hope, love, these three; but the greatest of these is love" (1 Corinthians 13:13, NAS).

There is hope! You are never alone.

EPILOGUE

It had been three days, and we could not reach Brad. He didn't answer his cell phone or any of our e-mails. It wasn't as if this was the first time Brad ignored our text messages. Why was I so desperate that he didn't reply? It was a sickening feeling. Something was wrong!

I called his job and was told he was out sick. Huh?

I managed to get his roommate's cell phone number. When I reached Bob, he sounded as if he was hiding a huge secret, being hesitant to even talk to me.

A few moments into our conversation, I told him how I was so worried, asking him if he knew where Brad was. Then the poop hit the fan.

"You do know about his lifestyle. Right?" he asked quietly.

"What are you talking about?" I asked in confusion.

"You know, his drinking problem," he explained.

The pit of my stomach felt as if someone had just hit me hard. The reality that my "invisible son," who had never given me a moment of worry in twenty-three years, was an alcoholic became too unbearable to even begin to process. All those times that Randy made "insane comments" about his brother; he had been trying to warn me. How could I have missed it? I didn't want to hear the truth. I knew I had to act and quickly.

I got desperate and called Nicole to see if she knew where Brad was staying. I got an earful. She told me that Brad had already been hospitalized two months ago for active bleeding in his vomit and stool. The ER doctor told him that his stomach was bruised and that alcohol was causing the problem. I listened to her in a state of unbelief. How come no one told us? Were his friends just going to let him drink until he died? What kind of friends were they?

All those times in Brad's life when I felt he was dealing with issues, he really wasn't. He was binge drinking and had been for at least five years. He lived away from home and hid it from us. There had not been any warning signs. What was I doing, sleeping all that time?

I cried on the phone to Nicole. She was sympathetic, but I got the feeling that Brad's drinking had impacted their relationship.

Then I called all his friends with threats of all kinds. My brother Dan kept trying to call Brad too. Dan kept leaving messages on Brad's phone that he would be calling him every hour. He even left a message that he would come pick him up, which was a two-hour drive for my brother. Brad never replied. The only one Brad would speak to was his brother, Randy. Randy was obsessed with us finding him and bringing him home. Randy was the only one in our house who was not in shock. He had known.

After four days, Brad called Randy at 10:00 p.m. to say he was on his way to our home. We sat in painful silence awaiting his arrival. When he entered our home, I looked into his tear filled eyes, running up to him to hold him. Randy walked in the living room to check on his brother. Brad sat down, handed us his car keys, and said to us, "I can't live like this anymore. I need help!" He bowed his head and cried as he told us his unbelievable story that he had kept a secret from us for five years.

He told, "I came back because Randy and Uncle Dan showed me how much they cared!" He looked at Randy with tears in his eyes, pointed at him, and said, "I am here tonight because of him." Brad's body shook with sobs. Randy had actually saved his brother's life. So the brotherly relationship was still intact. What a force to bring them together! I sat beside Brad, rubbing his back. Once again, I was in a bad dream for sure. Someone needed to awaken me before something else bad happened.

"My drinking is out of control. Sometimes, I drink for days. I took my first drink in college and now my life has spun out of control," he told us as he cried. We all cried.

He was deeply depressed. What happened to my happy-go-lucky little boy? We were in for another long road. I would have to pull myself together to help him now. I didn't know if I had any sanity left to do what I needed to do.

The next morning Brad was shaking and his blood pressure was high. He was nauseated and kept having dry heaves. I took him to the ER to be evaluated. They treated him with medication for tremors and placed him in an intensive outpatient alcohol detox program. They discharged him on an antidepressant. Brad was willing to do whatever it took to get better. He was tired of his secret lifestyle. He knew that he could never drink even one drink again as long as he lived. Could I believe what Brad had just said to us? Would I be able to let God take care of him for me? Would I be able to let him go?

The next day, I went to Brad's apartment to get his belongings. The room reminded me of Randy's room all these years. It was a room of disarray. There were eight piles of laundry. I sat on the floor in the balls of dust and cried.

Follow me in my next journey as I carry my second child to the cross.

As of August 2009, Brad has been sober for four months. As soon as he started his rehab, he began to change his diet and work out on a daily basis. He became fit and looked like the son I used to know. He is taking courses to become a physical therapist.

Both boys have had to further their education due to the tough job market. Randy has committed himself to complete his college degree and wants to be an addiction's counselor.

Substance abuse is powerful; a parent has to take one day at a time. It would be futile and tormenting to look down the road.

My boys are in for a long battle. These battles are here to stay. But God is so good! There is hope!